# Because You Are Mine
# BETH KERY

headline
review

First published in 2012 as an ebook serialisation

First published in 2013 in paperback by Headline Publishing Group

Published by arrangement with InterMix Books,
a division of Penguin Group (USA), Inc.

8

Cataloguing in Publication Data is available from the British Library

ISBN 978 1 4722 0066 2

Typeset in Caslon by Avon DataSet Ltd, Bidford-on-Avon, Warwickshire

Printed and bound by CPI Group (UK) Ltd, Croydon, CR0 4YY

Headline's policy is to use papers that are natural, renewable and recyclable
products and made from wood grown in sustainable forests. The logging and
manufacturing processes are expected to conform to the environmental
regulations of the country of origin.

HEADLINE PUBLISHING GROUP
An Hachette UK Company
338 Euston Road
London NW1 3BH

www.headline.co.uk
www.hachette.co.uk

My deepest gratitude to Leis Pederson, Laura Bradford, Mahlet, Amelia and my husband. I couldn't have made this project happen without you. Also, thank you to all the readers who have supported my books over the years. I most definitely couldn't have made this career happen without you.

# Part One

## Because You Tempt Me

# One

Francesca glanced around when Ian Noble entered the room, mostly because everyone else in the luxurious restaurant bar did the same thing. Her heart jumped. Through the crowd she saw a tall man dressed in an impeccably tailored suit remove his overcoat, revealing a long, lean body. She immediately recognized Ian Noble. Her gaze lingered on the elegant black overcoat draped over his arm. The random thought hit her brain that while the black coat was right, the suit was all wrong. He belonged in jeans, didn't he? Her observation made no sense whatsoever. He looked fantastic in the suit, for one, and for another, according to a recent article she'd read in *GQ*, he was reputed to almost single-handedly keep London's Savile Row thriving. What else would a businessman who was the scion of a minor branch of the British monarchy wear? One of the men who had entered with him reached to take his coat, but he shook his head once.

Apparently, the enigmatic Mr. Noble wasn't planning on

doing more than making a cursory appearance at the cocktail party he was hosting in Francesca's honor.

"There's Mr. Noble now. He'll be so pleased to meet you. He loves your work," Lin Soong said. Francesca heard the subtle note of pride in the woman's voice, as if Ian Noble was her lover instead of her employer.

"He looks like he has far more important things to do than meet me," Francesca said, smiling. She took a sip of club soda and watched as Noble spoke tersely on a cell phone while two men stood nearby, his overcoat remaining slung in the crook of his arm in readiness for a quick getaway. The subtle slant of his mouth told her he was irritated. For some reason, this all-too-human display of emotion relaxed her a little. She hadn't revealed it to her roommates—she was known for possessing a *whatever, bring it on attitude*—but she'd been strangely anxious about meeting Ian Noble.

The crowd returned to their conversation, but the energy level of the room had somehow amplified with Noble's arrival. Odd that such a distinctive, sophisticated man would become an icon for a tech-savvy, T-shirt-wearing generation. He looked to be thirtyish. She'd read Noble had earned his first billion with his breakthrough social-media company years ago, before he'd put it up for a public offering, made thirteen billion more, then promptly started another hugely successful Internet retail business.

Everything he touched turned to gold, apparently. Why? Because he was Ian Noble. He could do anything he damn well pleased. Francesca's mouth curved in amusement at the thought. It somehow helped to think he was arrogant and unlikeable. Yes, he was her benefactor, but like artists throughout history, Francesca had a healthy dose of distrust for the patron shelling out the money. Sadly, all starving artists needed their Ian Nobles.

"I'll just go and tell him you're here. As I've mentioned, he was quite taken with your painting. He chose it hands down over the two other finalists," Lin said, referring to the competition Francesca had won. The winner would be granted the prestigious commission to create the centerpiece painting for the grand lobby of Noble's new Chicago skyscraper, which they were in. The cocktail reception in Francesca's honor was being held in a restaurant called Fusion, a trendy, pricey restaurant located inside Noble's high-rise. Most importantly to Francesca, she would be awarded a hundred thousand dollars, something she could sorely use as a struggling master of fine arts graduate student.

Lin magically materialized a young African-American woman named Zoe Charon to converse with Francesca in her absence.

"It's a pleasure to meet you," Zoe said, flashing an orthodontist's dream smile as she shook Francesca's hand. "And congratulations on your commission. Just think: I'll be looking at your painting every time I walk into work."

Francesca suffered an increasingly familiar pang of discomfort over her clothing in comparison to Zoe's suit. Lin, Zoe, and just about every person at the reception in her honor were appareled in the height of sophisticated, sleek fashion. How was she to know that boho chic wouldn't work at a Noble cocktail party? How was she to know that her brand of boho chic wasn't *really* chic at all?

She learned Zoe was an assistant manager for Noble Enterprises, in a department called Imagetronics. *What the hell was that?* Francesca wondered distractedly as she nodded in polite interest, her gaze flickering again toward the front of the restaurant.

Noble's mouth softened slightly when Lin reached him and spoke. A few seconds later, a detached, bored expression settled on his features. He shook his head once and glanced at his watch. Clearly Noble didn't want to go through the ritual of meeting one of the many recipients of his philanthropic efforts any more than Francesca wanted to meet him. This cocktail party in her honor had been one of the onerous activities that accompanied the winning of the commission.

She turned to Zoe and grinned broadly, determined to enjoy herself now that she'd confirmed her anxiety about meeting Noble had been a waste of time.

"So what's the deal with Ian Noble?"

Zoe started at her bald question and glanced toward the front of the bar where Noble stood.

"The deal? He's a god, in a word."

Francesca smirked. "Not much for understatement, are you?"

Zoe broke into laughter. Francesca joined her. For a moment they were just two young women giggling over the most handsome man at the party. Which Ian Noble was, Francesca conceded. Forget the party. He was the most arresting man she'd ever seen in her life.

Her laughter ceased when she noticed Zoe's expression. She turned. Noble's gaze was directly on her. A hot, heavy sensation expanded in her belly. She didn't have time to draw breath before he was stalking across the room toward her, leaving a surprised-looking Lin in his wake.

Francesca experienced a ridiculous urge to run.

"Oh . . . he's headed this way . . . Lin must have told him who you were," Zoe said, sounding as bewildered and caught off guard as Francesca felt. Zoe was more practiced in the art of social elegance than Francesca, however. By the time Noble reached them, all traces of the giggling girl were gone and in its place stood a contained, beautiful woman.

"Mr. Noble, good evening."

His eyes were a piercing cobalt blue. They flicked off Francesca for a split second. She managed to suck some air into her lungs during the reprieve.

"Zoe, isn't it?" he asked.

Zoe couldn't hide her pleasure at the fact that Noble had known her name. "Yes, sir. I work in Imagetronics. May I introduce Francesca Arno, the artist you chose as the winner in the Far Sight Competition."

He took her hand. "It's a pleasure, Ms. Arno."

Francesca just nodded. She couldn't speak. Her brain was temporarily overloaded by the image of him, the warmth of his encompassing hand, the sound of his low, British-accented voice. His skin was pale next to his dark, stylishly coiffed, short hair and gray suit. *Dark Angel.* The words flew into her brain, unbidden.

"I can't tell you how impressed I am with your work," he said. No smile. No softness in his tone, even if there was a sharp curiosity in his stare.

She swallowed uneasily. "Thank you." He released her hand slowly, causing his skin to slide against hers. A horrible moment of silence passed as he just looked at her. She gathered herself and straightened her spine.

"I'm glad to have this opportunity to thank you in person for awarding me the commission. It means more to me than

I can convey." She said the rehearsed words in a pressured fashion.

He gave an almost imperceptible shrug and waved his hand negligently. "You earned it." He held her stare. "Or at least you will."

She felt her pulse leap at her throat and hoped he didn't notice.

"I earned it, yes. But you gave me the opportunity. It's *that* I'm trying to express my thanks for. I probably wouldn't have been able to afford the second year of my master's program if you hadn't given me this chance."

He blinked. From the corner of her vision, Francesca noticed Zoe stiffen. Francesca glanced away in embarrassment. Had she sounded sharp?

"My grandmother often says I'm ungracious in the face of gratitude," he said, his voice quieter . . . warmer. "You're right to scold me. And you're also very welcome for the opportunity, Ms. Arno," he said, giving a nod of acknowledgement. "Zoe, would you mind taking a message to Lin for me? I've decided to cancel dinner with Xander LaGrange after all. Please have her reschedule."

"Of course, Mr. Noble," Zoe said before she walked away.

"Would you like to sit down?" he asked, nodding at an unoccupied circular leather booth.

"Sure."

He waited behind her while she scooted into the booth. She wished he wouldn't. She felt awkward and ungainly. After she'd settled, he slid beside her in one graceful, swooping motion. Francesca smoothed the gauzy skirt of the vintage beaded baby-doll dress she'd bought at a secondhand store in Wicker Park. The early September evening had been cooler than she'd expected when planning for the cocktail party. The casual denim jacket she wore had been her only choice, given the thin straps of her dress. It struck her how ridiculous she must appear, seated next to this immaculately dressed, thoroughly masculine male.

She fussed anxiously with her collar, and then sensed his stare on her. She met his eyes. Her chin went up defiantly. A small smile flickered across his mouth, and something clenched in her lower belly.

"So you're in the second year of your master's program?"

"Yes. I'm at the Art Institute."

"A very good school," he murmured. He rested his hands on the table and leaned back in the booth, looking thoroughly comfortable. His body was long, relaxed, and taut, reminding Francesca of a predatory animal whose seeming calmness could leap into full-out action in a split second. Even though his hips were slim, his shoulders were broad, suggesting some serious muscles beneath that starched white shirt. "If I'm remembering your application correctly, you studied both art and architecture at Northwestern University?"

"Yes," Francesca said breathlessly, pulling her gaze off his hands. They were elegant hands, but also large, blunt-tipped, and very capable-looking. The vision of them disturbed her for some reason. She couldn't help but imagine what they would look like against her skin . . . wrapped around her waist . . .

"Why?"

She started from her totally inappropriate thoughts and met his steady stare. "Why did I study both architecture and art?"

He nodded once.

"Architecture for my parents and art for me," she replied, surprising herself by the honesty of her answer. She usually made a show of being coolly disdainful when anyone asked the same question. Why should she have to choose between her talents? "My parents are both architects, and it was their lifetime dream that I become one as well."

"So you granted them half a dream. You earned the qualifications of an architect but don't plan to make it your career."

"I'll always be an architect."

"And I'm glad of it," he said, looking up when a handsome man with dreadlocks and pale gray eyes that contrasted with darker skin approached the table. Noble shook his hand. "Lucien, how is business?"

"Booming," Lucien replied, his gaze shifting to Francesca with interest.

"Ms. Arno, this is Lucien Lenault. He's the manager of Fusion, and the most illustrious restaurateur in Europe. I handpicked him from the finest restaurant in Paris."

Lucien rolled his eyes amusedly at Ian's introduction and grinned. "Hopefully, the same can be said of Fusion very soon. Ms. Arno, it's a pleasure to meet you," Lucien added in a delicious, French-accented voice. "What may I get you?"

Noble looked at her expectantly. His lips were unusually full for such a rugged-featured, masculine man, striking her as sensual yet firm.

*Stern.*

From where had that strange thought leapt?

"I'm fine," Francesca replied, although her heart started to beat erratically.

"What is that?" he asked, nodding at her half-empty drink.

"Just my usual drink, club soda with lime."

"You should be celebrating, Ms. Arno." Was it his accent that made her ears and neck prickle when he said her name? There was something unique about it, she realized. It was British, but some other influence seemed to slide into his syllables occasionally, something she couldn't quite identify. "Bring us a bottle of the Roederer Brut," Noble told Lucien, who smiled, gave a slight bow and walked away.

Her confusion mounted. Why was he bothering to spend so much time with her? Surely he didn't drink champagne with all of the recipients of his philanthropy. "As I was saying before Lucien arrived, I'm glad about your architecture background. Your skill and knowledge in that field is undoubtedly what gives your artwork so much precision, depth, and style. The painting you submitted for the contest was spectacular. You exactly caught the spirit of what I wanted for my lobby."

Her gaze skimmed across his immaculate suit. Somehow, his apparent love of a perfectly straight line didn't surprise her. True, her artwork was often inspired by her love of form and structure, but precision wasn't what her work was about. Far from it. "I'm glad you were pleased," she said with what she hoped was a neutral tone.

A smile ghosted his lips. "There's something behind your statement. Aren't you happy that you've pleased me?"

Her mouth dropped open at that. She stifled the words that flew to her throat. *I do my art to please no one but myself.* She stopped herself just in time. What was wrong with her? This man was responsible for changing her life.

"I told you earlier, I couldn't be happier about winning the contest. I'm thrilled."

"Ah," he murmured as Lucien arrived with the champagne and ice bucket. Noble didn't glance in Lucien's direction as the other man busied himself opening the bottle, but continued to study her as though she was a particularly interesting science project. "But being glad of your commission isn't the same as being glad you pleased me."

"No, I didn't mean that," she sputtered, looking at Lucien when he uncorked the champagne with a muffled popping sound. Her bewildered gaze returned to Noble. His eyes glinted in an otherwise impassive face. What in the world was he talking about? And why, despite the fact that she didn't have the answer to that, had his question made her so flustered? "I am glad that you liked the painting. Very much so."

Noble didn't reply, just watched detachedly as Lucien poured the sparkling fluid into flutes. He nodded and murmured his thanks before Lucien walked away. Francesca picked up her glass when he reached for his.

"Congratulations."

She managed a smile as their flutes touched ever so fleetingly. She'd never tasted anything like it; the champagne was dry and icy and felt delicious sliding across her tongue and down her throat. She gave Noble a sideways glance. How could he seem so oblivious to the thick tension in the air when she felt as if she'd suffocate from it?

"I guess since you're royalty, a cocktail waitress won't do for serving you," she said, wishing her voice hadn't quavered.

"I beg your pardon?"

"Oh, I just meant—" She cursed silently to herself. "I'm a

cocktail waitress—I do it to help pay the bills while I'm in grad school," she added, slightly panicked at how cool, and a little intimidating, he suddenly appeared. She lifted her flute and took a too-large gulp of the icy fluid. Wait until she told Davie how she botched this whole thing. Her good friend would be exasperated with her, even if her other roommates—Caden and Justin—would roll with laughter at her latest incident of apparent social idiocy.

If only Ian Noble wasn't so handsome. Disturbingly so.

"I'm sorry," she mumbled. "I shouldn't have said that. It's just—I'd read that your grandparents belonged to a minor branch of the British royal family—an earl and a countess, no less."

"And you were wondering if I despise being waited on by a mere serving girl, is that it?" he asked. Amusement didn't soften his features, just made them more compelling. She sighed and relaxed a little. She hadn't *completely* offended him.

"I did most of my schooling in the states," he said. "I consider myself to be an American, first and foremost. And I assure you, the only reason Lucien came to wait on us himself is that he chose to. We're fencing partners in addition to being friends. The custom of the English aristocracy preferring the status of a manservant over a maid exists only in Regency English novels in the present day, Ms. Arno. Even if they did still exist, I doubt they'd apply to a bastard. I'm sorry to disappoint you."

Her cheeks felt like they were boiling. When would she learn to keep her big mouth shut? Was he telling her *he* was illegitimate? She'd never read anything regarding that before.

"Where do you waitress?" he asked, seeming color blind to her scarlet cheeks.

"At High Jinks in Bucktown."

"I've never heard of it."

"Somehow that doesn't surprise me," she muttered under her breath before she took another sip of champagne. She blinked in surprise at the sound of his low, rough laughter. Her eyes widened when she looked at his face. He looked so *pleased*. Her heart dipped. Ian Noble was spectacular to behold at any given moment, but when he smiled, he was nothing short of a menace to a female's composure.

"Would you mind coming with me . . . walking a few blocks? There's something crucial I'd like to show you," he said.

Her hand paused in the action of lifting the flute to her lips. What was going on here?

"It directly relates to your commission," he said, suddenly crisp. Authoritative. "I'd like to show you the view I want for the painting."

Anger sliced through her shock. Her chin went up. "I'm expected to paint whatever you want me to?"

"Yes," he said without pause.

She set down the flute with a loud clicking sound, jarring the contents. He'd sounded completely unyielding. He was every bit as arrogant as she'd imagined. Just as she'd expected, winning this prize was going to end up being a nightmare. His nostrils flared as he stared at her unblinkingly, and she glared back.

"I suggest you see the view in question before you take undue offense, Ms. Arno."

"Francesca."

Something flashed in his blue eyes like heat lightning.

For a split second, she regretted the edge to her tone. But then he nodded once.

"Francesca it is," he said softly. "If you make it Ian."

She willed herself to ignore the flutter in her belly. *Don't be beguiled*, she warned herself. He was the exact type of domineering patron that would try to dictate, and crush her creative instincts in the process. It was worse than she'd feared.

Without another word, she slid out of the booth and walked toward the entrance of the restaurant, sensing, with every cell of her being, him moving behind her.


He hardly spoke at all when they left Fusion. He led her to a sidewalk that ran along the Chicago River and Lower Wacker Drive.

"Where are we going?" she broke the silence after a minute or two.

"To my residence."

Her high-heeled sandals faltered clumsily on the sidewalk, coming to a halt. "We're going to your place?"

He paused and looked back, his black coat fluttering around his long, strong-looking thighs from the brisk Lake Michigan wind. "Yes, we're going to *my place*," he said with a subtle, mock-sinister tone.

She frowned. He was clearly silently laughing at her. *I'm so glad I can be here to entertain you, Mr. Noble.* He inhaled and stared in the direction of Lake Michigan, obviously exasperated with her and trying to gather his thoughts.

"I can see that makes you uncomfortable, but you have my word: This is completely professional. It's about the painting. The view I want you to paint is from the condominium where I live. Surely you can't believe I'm going to harm you in any way. A room full of people just saw us walk out of that restaurant together."

He didn't need to remind her. It felt as if every eye in Fusion had been trained on them as they left.

She gave him a wary sideways glance as they began to walk again. His dark hair ruffling in the wind seemed familiar to her somehow. She blinked and the sense of déjà vu vanished.

"Are you telling me that I'm supposed to work from your apartment?"

"It's very large," he said dryly. "You won't have to see me at all, if you prefer."

Francesca stared at her painted toenails, hiding her expression from him. She didn't want him to suspect that unwelcome images had popped into her mind's eye at his statement; visions of Ian walking from the shower, his naked body still gleaming with moisture, a thin towel draped on his lean hips the only thing separating herself from a vision of total male glory.

"It's a little unorthodox," she said.

"I'm a lot unorthodox," he said briskly. "You'll understand when you see the view."

He lived at 340 East Archer, a classic 1920s Italian Renaissance building that she'd admired since studying it in one of her classes. It suited him, somehow, the elegant, brooding, dark brick tower. She wasn't entirely surprised when he told her his residence encompassed the entire top two floors.

The door of his private elevator slid open without a sound,

and he extended his hand in an invitation to walk before him.

She entered a magical place.

The luxury of the fabrics and furniture were obvious, but despite the richness, the entryway managed to convey a welcome—an austere welcome, perhaps, but a welcome nonetheless. She caught a quick glimpse of herself in an antique mirror. Her long reddish blonde hair was hopelessly windblown, and her cheeks were stained pink. She'd like to think the color was from the wind but worried the effect came from being with Ian Noble.

Then she noticed the artwork, and she forgot everything else. She wandered down a wide hallway that was also a gallery, her mouth hanging open as she stared at painting after painting, some of them new to her, some of them masterworks that sent a jolt of exhilaration through her to see firsthand.

She paused next to a miniature sculpture set on a column, a very fine replica of a renowned piece of ancient Greek art. "I've always loved Aphrodite of Argos," she murmured, her gaze detailing the exquisite facial features and the graceful twist of the naked torso miraculously carved into hard alabaster.

"Have you?" he asked, sounding intent.

She nodded, overwhelmed by wonder, and continued walking.

"I just acquired that one several months ago. It wasn't easy to get," he said, starting her out of her ecstatic amazement.

"I adore Sorenburg," she said, referring to the artist who had created the painting before which they stood. She turned to look at him, suddenly realizing that several minutes had passed and that she'd wandered like a sleepwalker deeper into the hushed depths of his condominium without invitation, and that he'd allowed her intrusion without comment. She now stood in a parlor of sorts decorated with decadently rich fabrics of yellow, pale blue, and dark brown.

"I know. You mentioned it in your personal statement in the application for the contest."

"I can't believe you like expressionism."

"Why can't you believe it?" he asked, his low voice making her ears prickle and goose bumps rise along her neck. She glanced up at him. The painting she referred to was hung above a deep cushioned velvet couch. He stood closer than she'd realized, so lost had she become in wonderment and pleasure.

"Because . . . you picked my painting," she said weakly. Her gaze skimmed over his body. She swallowed thickly. He'd unbuttoned his overcoat. A clean, spicy smell of soap filtered into her nose. A heavy, hot pressure settled in her sex. "You seem to like . . . *order* so much," she tried to explain, her voice just above a whisper.

"You're right," he said. A shadow seemed to come over his bold features. "I do abhor sloppiness and disorder. But Sorenburg isn't about that." He glanced at the painting. "It's about making meaning from chaos. Wouldn't you agree?"

Her mouth hung open as she stared at his profile. She'd never heard Sorenburg's work described so succinctly.

"Yes, I would," she said slowly.

He gave her a small smile. His full lips had to be his most compelling feature, aside from his eyes. And his firm chin. And his incredible body—

"Do my ears deceive me," he murmured, "Or is that a note of respect I hear in your tone, Francesca?"

She turned to stare sightlessly at the Sorenburg. Her breath burned in her lungs. "You deserve respect in this. You have impeccable taste in art."

"Thank you. I happen to agree."

She risked a sideways glance. He was staring at her with those dark-angel eyes.

"Let me take your jacket," he said, extending his hands.

"No." Her cheeks heated when she heard how abrupt she'd sounded. Self-consciousness slammed into her haze of enthrallment. His hands remained extended.

"I will take it."

She opened her mouth to rebuke him but paused when she noticed his hooded gaze and slightly raised eyebrows.

"The woman wears the clothes, Francesca. Not the other way around. That's the first lesson I'll teach you."

She gave him a fake glance of exasperation and shrugged out of her jean jacket. The air felt cool next to her bare shoulders. Ian's gaze felt warm. She straightened her spine.

"You say that like you plan on teaching me more lessons," she muttered, handing him the jacket.

"Perhaps I do. Follow me."

He hung up her coat, then led her down the gallerylike hallway before turning down a narrower one that was dimly lit with brass sconces. He opened one of many tall doorways, and Francesca stepped into the room. She expected to see yet another room filled with wonders, but instead entered a large, narrow space that ran the length of a row of floor-to-ceiling windows. He didn't turn on the light. He didn't need to. The room was illuminated by the skyscrapers and the reflective lights of them in the black river. She walked to the windows without speaking. He came to stand next to her.

"They're alive, the buildings . . . some more than others," she said in a hushed voice after a moment. She gave him a rueful glance and was awarded with a smile. Embarrassment flooded her. "I mean, they *seem* like it. I've always thought so. Each one of them has a soul. At night, especially . . . I can feel it."

"I know you can. That's why I chose your painting."

"Not because of perfectly straight lines and precise reproductions?" she asked shakily.

"No. Not because of that."

His expression went flat when she smiled. Unexpected pleasure filled her. He *did* understand her art after all. And . . . she'd given him what he wanted.

She stared at the magnificent view. "I understand what you meant," she said, her voice vibrating with excitement. "I haven't taken any architecture classes now for a year and a half, and I've been so busy with my art classes I haven't kept up with journals, or I would have known. Still . . . shame on me for not seeing it until now," she said, referring to the two most prominent buildings that lined the black-and-gold-speckled shimmering river. She shook her head in wonderment. "You made Noble Enterprises a modern, streamlined version of a Chicago architecture classic. It's like a contemporary version of the Sandusky. Brilliant," she said, referring to the echo that the Noble Enterprises building made of the Sandusky Building, a Gothic masterpiece. Noble Enterprises was just like Ian—a bold, strong-lined, elegant, and modern version of some Gothic ancestor. She smiled at the thought.

"Most people don't see the effect until I show them this view," he said.

"It's genius, Ian," she said feelingly. She gave him a questioning glance, noticing the glints in his eyes caused by the lights from the skyscrapers. "Why didn't you brag about it to the press?"

"Because I didn't do it for the press. I did it for my own pleasure, just like I do most things."

She felt trapped by his gaze and couldn't respond. Wasn't that a particularly selfish thing to say? Why, then, did his words cause that heavy sensation to grow at the juncture of her thighs?

"But I am pleased that you're pleased," he said. "I have something else to show you."

"Really?" she asked breathlessly.

He merely nodded once. She followed him, glad he couldn't see the color in her cheeks. He led her to a room almost completely surrounded by filled, dark walnut book-cases. He paused inside the door, watching her reaction as she glanced around curiously, her gaze finally landing and latching onto the painting above the fireplace. She froze. She walked to it as if in a trance and studied one of her own pieces.

"You bought this from Feinstein?" she whispered, refer-ring to one of her roommates—Davie Feinstein, who owned a gallery in Wicker Park. The piece she was staring at was the first painting of hers he'd sold. She'd insisted upon giving it to Davie as a deposit on her share of the rent a year and a half ago, when she'd been broke before they'd moved into the city.

"Yes," Ian said, his voice telling her he stood just behind her right shoulder.

"Davie never mentioned—"

"I asked Lin to procure it for me. The gallery probably never knew who actually bought it."

She swallowed the lump in her throat as her gaze ran over the depiction of the solitary man walking down the middle of a Lincoln Park street in the dark early morning hours, his back to her. The surrounding high-rises seemed to gaze down at him with a detached aloofness, as immune to human pain as he appeared to be to his own suffering. His opened overcoat streamed out behind him. His shoulders hunched against the wind, and his hands were jammed deep in his jean pockets. Every line of his body exuded power, grace, and the resigned sort of loneliness that hardens into strength and resolve.

She loved this piece. It'd killed her to give it up, but rent must be paid.

"*The Cat That Walks By Himself*," Ian said from behind her, his voice sounding gruff.

She smiled and laughed softly at hearing him say the title she'd given the painting. "'I am the Cat who walks by himself, and all places are alike to me.' I painted this in my sophomore year of undergrad. I was taking an English literature class at the time, and we were studying Kipling. The phrase seemed to fit somehow . . ."

Her voice trailed off as she stared at the solitary figure in the painting, her entire awareness sharply focused on the man who stood behind her. She glanced back at Ian and smiled. It embarrassed her to realize tears burned in her eyes. His nostrils flared slightly, and she turned abruptly, wiping her cheeks. It had touched something deep inside her, seeing her painting in the depths of his home.

"I think I'd better get going," she said.

Her heart started to do a drumroll in her ears in the heavy silence that followed.

"Perhaps it's best," he said eventually. She turned and gave a sigh of relief—or was it regret—when she saw his tall form exiting the room. She followed him, murmuring a thanks when he held up her jean jacket once they reached the entryway. He resisted when she tried to take it from him. She swallowed and turned her back to him, letting him put it on her. His knuckles brushed against the skin of her shoulders. She repressed a shudder when he slid his hand beneath her long hair, skimming her nape in the process. He gently drew her hair out of the jacket and smoothed it over her back. She couldn't repress a shiver and suspected he felt it beneath his hand.

"Such a rare color," he murmured, still stroking her hair, sending the alert status of her nerves up another notch.

"I can have my driver Jacob take you home," he said after a moment.

"No," she said, feeling foolish for not turning around to speak. She couldn't move. She was paralyzed. Every cell in her body prickled with awareness. "My friend is going to pick me up in a little while."

"Will you come here to paint?" he asked, his deep voice echoing just inches from her right ear. She stared in front of her, unseeing.

"Yes."

"I'd like you to start on Monday. I'll have Lin provide you with an entry card and password to the elevator. Your supplies will be ready for you when you come."

"I can't come every day. I have class—mostly in the

morning—and I waitress from seven to close several days a week."

"Come whenever you can. The point is, you'll come."

"Yes, all right," she managed through a constricted throat. He hadn't removed his hand from her back. Could he feel her heart throbbing?

She had to get out of there. *Now*. She was way out of her depth.

She lurched toward the elevator, pushing a button on the control panel hastily. If she'd thought he'd try to touch her again, she'd thought wrong. The sleek elevator door slid open.

"Francesca?" he said as she hurried inside.

"Yes?" she asked, turning.

He stood with his hands behind his back, the posture causing his suit jacket to open, revealing a shirt-draped lean abdomen, narrow hips, a silver belt buckle, and . . . everything beneath it.

"Now that you have some financial security, I would prefer you didn't wander the streets of Chicago in the early morning hours in order to find your inspiration. You never know what you might encounter. It's dangerous."

Her mouth dropped open in stunned amazement. He stepped forward and pushed a button on the panel, causing the doors to slide closed. The last glimpse she had of him was his gleaming blue-eyed stare in an otherwise impassive face. Her heartbeat escalated to a roar in her ears.

She'd painted *him* four years ago. That's what he was telling her—that he knew she'd observed him walking the dark, lonely streets in the dead of the night while the rest of the world slumbered, warm and content in their beds.

Francesca hadn't realized the identity of her inspiration at the time, nor had he probably known he was being observed until he saw the painting, but there could be no doubt of it.

*Ian Noble* was the cat who walked by himself.

And he'd wanted her to know it.

# Two

He managed to put her out of his mind for a full ten days. He traveled to New York for a two-night stay and finalized the acquisition of a computer program that would enable him to begin a new network that combined social aspects and a unique gaming application. He made his regular monthly visit to his condominium in London. While he'd been in Chicago, meetings and work had kept him at the office until far past midnight. By the time he'd reached the penthouse, the interior was dim and silent.

It wasn't *entirely* accurate to say that he'd kept Francesca Arno fully out of his mind, though. *Or honest,* Ian conceded sternly to himself as he rode the elevator to his penthouse Wednesday afternoon. His awareness of her would come to him in quick, powerful flashes, penetrating his focus on the details of the everyday world. Mrs. Hanson, his housekeeper, innocently gave him updates during her typical banter about how her weekly projects were going in the house. He'd been pleased to learn that the elderly

Englishwoman had befriended Francesca, inviting her to the kitchen occasionally to join her for tea. He'd been glad to hear Francesca was becoming comfortable in his home, and then asked himself why it mattered one way or another. The painting was the only thing he wanted, and surely the working conditions were adequate for that.

Once, he'd told himself that he was being rude by ignoring her. Surely his avoidance was putting too much emphasis on her, making more of the situation than was warranted. Last Thursday evening, he'd gone to her studio with the intent of asking her if she'd like to take some refreshment with him in the kitchen. The door was ajar, and he'd entered without knocking. For several seconds, he'd stood and watched her work, unnoticed.

She'd been standing on a short ladder, working on the upper-right-hand corner of the canvas, completely absorbed. Although he had been quite sure he hadn't made a noise, she'd suddenly turned and froze, regarding him with startled brown eyes, her pencil still on the canvas. A heavy swath of gleaming hair had fallen out of the clip at the back of her head. There had been a charcoal smear on her smooth cheek, and her dark pink lips had been parted in surprise at the sight of him.

He'd asked her politely about her progress and tried not to notice the throb of her pulse at her throat or the roundness of her breasts. She'd taken off her sweat jacket as she worked and wore a tight tank top. Her breasts were fuller than he'd realized before, their size an erotic contrast between her narrow waist and hips, and long coltish legs.

After thirty seconds of stilted conversation, he'd fled like the coward he was.

He told himself that his hyperawareness of her was completely natural. She was an incredible beauty, after all. The fact that she seemed completely oblivious to her sexuality fascinated him. Had she grown up in some kind of hole? Surely she was used to having males perk up whenever she walked into a room, salivating at the vision of her silky rose-gold hair, velvety brown eyes, and tall, willowy figure. How could she not have learned by age twenty-three that her flawless pale skin, lush, dark pink lips, and slender, lithe body had the power to fell a strong man?

He didn't know the answer to that question, but after close study, he could say with confidence her lack of awareness wasn't an act. She walked with the long-legged, lanky stride of a teenage boy and said the most incredibly gauche things.

It was only when she'd been bewitched as she gazed at his artwork, or when she'd stared out the window at the skyline, or when he'd secretly spied on her while she sketched that night, utterly lost in her art, that her beauty was fully revealed.

And a more compelling, addictive sight he couldn't recall viewing.

He paused presently in the foyer of the penthouse. She was there. No sound emanated from the depths of his residence, but somehow he knew Francesca worked in her ad hoc studio. Was she still sketching on the massive canvas? He suddenly pictured her perfectly, her beautiful face tense with concentration, her dark eyes flickering back and forth between her quickly moving pencil and the view. She became somber and formidable as a judge when she worked, all of her self-consciousness burned to mist by her brilliant talent and an uncommon grace that she didn't appear to know she possessed.

She also was ignorant of her potent sexual appeal. He, on the other hand, was acutely aware of its promise and power. Unfortunately, he was equally conscious of her naïveté. He could practically smell it surrounding her; her innocence intermingled with an untested sexuality, creating a heady perfume that had set him off balance.

Sweat gathered on his upper lip. His cock swelled to full readiness in a matter of seconds.

Frowning, he glanced at his watch and pulled his cell phone out of his pocket. He tapped a few buttons and walked down the hallway, veering off toward his bedroom. Thankfully, his private quarters were on the opposite end of the condominium from where Francesca worked. He needed to get her out of his mind. Purge her.

A voice answered his call.

"Lucien. Something important has come up, and I'm running behind. Can we meet at five thirty versus five?"

"Certainly. I'll see you there in forty-five minutes. Hope you're feeling thick-skinned, because I'm in a real mood."

Ian smiled wryly as he closed his bedroom door behind him and locked it. "I have a feeling my sword is hungry for blood today as well, my friend, so we'll see who requires the thick skin and who doesn't."

Lucien was still laughing when Ian hung up. He stowed his briefcase and withdrew a fencing uniform from his dressing room, laying out a plastron, breeches, and a jacket. He stripped quickly and efficiently. From his briefcase, he withdrew a key. Two large dressing rooms adjoined his private quarters. Mrs. Hanson—anyone save Ian—was prohibited from entering one of them.

It was Ian's private territory.

He unlocked the mahogany door and walked naked into the high-ceilinged room. It was lined with drawers and cabinets on either side and was always kept meticulously neat. He opened a drawer on his right and withdrew the items he wanted before padding back out to his bed.

It was his fault for not realizing this useless desire was mounting to dangerous levels. Perhaps he would arrange to bring a woman here this weekend, but in the meantime, he needed to diminish the sharp edge of his sexual hunger.

He squirted some lubricant onto his hand. His erection hadn't abated. Shivers of pleasure rippled through him when he rubbed the cool lubricant over his cock. He considered lying on the bed, but no . . . standing was better. He picked up the transparent silicone sleeve and grasped his heavy cock. He'd had the masturbator custom made for his dimensions, specifying he wanted the silicone to be clear. He enjoyed watching himself ejaculate. The manufacturer had followed his directions to perfection, the only exception being the addition of adding a dark pink circle around the top ring of the implement. Ian had thought the addition harmless enough at the time, so he hadn't complained. The masturbator wasn't a substitute. He could have any number of skilled, willing women give him head at a moment's notice. Over the years, he'd learned the crucial lesson of discretion. He'd pared down his once considerable list to include two women who knew precisely what he wanted sexually and understood the parameters of what he would give in return.

The masturbator's use was purely practical. He owed the sex toy nothing after it'd served its purpose.

But today, a shudder of excitement went through him at

the sight of the thick head of his cock penetrating the tight pink ring. He flexed his arm, pushing the snug silicone sheath along the swollen staff of his cock within an inch of the root. He moved his hand like a piston, appreciating how quickly the heat from his flesh mounted within the thick, cushy silicone.

Oh, yes. This is what he needed—a good balls-emptying orgasm. His abdomen, ass, and thigh muscles tightened as his fist pumped. The suction chambers squeezed and sucked at him as he moved, mimicking oral sex. He withdrew the sleeve all the way to the head of his cock and plunged into the warm, slippery depths again and again.

Usually, he closed his eyes and engaged in a sexual fantasy while he masturbated. Today, for some reason, his gaze remained fixed on the sight of his cock penetrating the pink ring. He thought of pink puffy lips in the place of the silicone ring. He saw huge dark eyes looking up at him.

Francesca's lips. Francesca's eyes.

*You have no time or business seducing an innocent. Didn't you once get burned doing that?*

He was a reluctant dom, perhaps, but a full-blown sexual dominant nonetheless. He'd long ago grown to accept his nature, knowing it matched his solitary fate in life. It wasn't that he wanted to be alone. He was just wise enough to realize it was inevitable. He was consumed by his work. A control freak. Everyone said it of him—the media, members of the business community . . . his ex-wife. He'd resigned himself to the fact that they were all correct. Fortunately, he'd grown used to his solitude.

*No right at all subjecting a woman like Francesca to his demanding nature.*

The warning voice in his head was drowned out by the sound of his pounding heart and low grunts of arousal as he pumped his cock.

*He would use her for his pleasure, ravish her sweet mouth. Would she be a little alarmed by his forceful possession? Aroused? Both?*

He groaned at the thought and jerked his arm, stroking more rapidly, every muscle in his body growing hard and rigid.

His cock looked enormous when he shoved the shaft fully into the thick silicone sleeve. He didn't want to come by his own hand. He wanted something he shouldn't, however, so his hand would have to suffice.

Even if what he *really* wanted was to restrain a long-limbed, golden-haired beauty, order her to kneel before him, and pound his cock into her wet, tight mouth . . . even if what he *really* wanted was to witness the flash of excitement in her eyes when he erupted in climax and gave himself to her.

Orgasm slammed into him, sharp and delicious. He gasped as he watched himself ejaculate into the transparent sleeve, his semen shooting against the sides of the inner suction chamber. After a moment, he clenched his eyes shut and moaned harshly, continuing to come.

Christ, he'd been a fool not to do this earlier in the week. He couldn't stop climaxing. He'd clearly needed a release. It wasn't typical for him to ignore his sexual needs, and he couldn't imagine why he'd remained abstinent this week. It'd been foolish.

It might have led to a loss of control, a prospect he couldn't abide. People who didn't attend to their needs ended up making mistakes, growing sloppy and haphazard.

His muscles went slack as the final weakened shudders of orgasm rippled through him. He slid the sheath off his sensitive penis. He wrapped a hand around the naked, slippery staff and stood there, breathing rapidly.

She was a woman like any other.

But perhaps she wasn't? She'd caught him unawares with her painting. It made him uncomfortable, that knowledge, like a burr under his skin. It made him want to capture her, in return . . . make her pay for looking into his mind somehow, seeing things she shouldn't see with her unique talent of soulful precision.

He *would* master this slicing, powerful desire. He turned and stalked to his bathroom to clean up and prepare for his fencing exercise.

Later, as he dressed, he noticed that his cock was still overly sensitive and that his erection hadn't completely dissipated. Damn.

He'd inform both Francesca and Mrs. Hanson that he wanted privacy this weekend. He'd make a phone call. Clearly, he required an experienced female who knew precisely how to please him in order to vanquish this strange need.


Lucien hadn't lied. He *was* in a feisty mood. Ian retreated under his friend's aggressive advance with effort, parrying his rapid thrusts, calmly waiting for the extension that would make him vulnerable. He'd fenced regularly with the other man for two years now, and he'd come to understand his style and how his emotions affected his combat. Lucien was an extremely skilled, smart fighter, but he had yet to learn how Ian's moods could influence his actions with the blade.

Perhaps that was because Ian made a point of mastering his emotions and reacting out of pure logic.

This evening, Lucien was surging with volatile energy, stronger than usual, but unusually incautious as well. Ian waited until he saw triumph in every line of Lucien's attacking form. He recognized his opponent's second intention, accurately parrying against the second stroke intended to finish Ian once and for all. Lucien grunted in frustration when Ian riposted and landed a hit.

"You're a mind reader, damn you," Lucien muttered, whipping off his mask, his long dreadlocks whisking around his shoulders. Ian, too, removed his mask.

"That is always your excuse. In fact, it's all quite logical, and you know it."

"Again," Lucien challenged, lifting his sword, his gray eyes fierce.

Ian smiled. "Who is she?"

"Who is *who*?"

Ian gave him a dry glance as he removed his glove. "The woman who has your blood pumping like a randy goat." It puzzled him, this frustrated quality in Lucien, who was usually so popular with women.

Lucien's expression tightened, and he looked away. Ian paused in the action of removing his other glove. His brow furrowed in consternation. "What's wrong?" he asked.

"There's something I've been meaning to ask you," Lucien said in a quiet, pressured voice.

"Well then?"

Lucien glared at him. "Are Noble employees allowed to see one another?"

"It depends on their positions. It's very clear-cut in the

employment contract. Managers and supervisors are prohibited from seeing inferiors, and will be terminated if it's discovered they have. It's highly discouraged for managers to date each other, although not prohibited. It's made clear in the contract that if any adverse situations arise at work from a relationship outside the office, the grounds for termination are met. I think you know it's bad form, Lucien. Does she work at Fusion?"

"No."

"Does she work in a supervisory capacity for Noble?" Ian asked as he stripped off his other glove, plastron, and jacket, leaving only the fitted breeches and undershirt.

"I'm not sure. What if the employment with Noble is . . . unorthodox?"

Ian gave him a sharp glance as he set down his sword and picked up a towel. "Unorthodox . . . as in the manager of a restaurant versus a manager of a department of business?" he asked wryly.

Lucien's mouth twisted into a bitter grin. "Perhaps it's best that I just buy Fusion from you as soon as possible so that neither of us have to worry about it."

They both started when a knock was heard on the door to the fencing room.

"Yes?" Ian called, his brows slanted in puzzlement. Mrs. Hanson usually didn't bother him during his workout. The knowledge that he wouldn't be interrupted helped him to find a zone of total concentration on both his fencing and exercise routines.

He went still in amazement when Francesca entered the room. Her long hair was loosely restrained at the back of her head. A few strands of it brushed her neck and cheeks. She wore not a smudge of makeup, a pair of formfitting jeans, a shapeless hooded sweatshirt, and a pair of gray-and-white running shoes. The shoes weren't the highest quality, but Ian quickly appraised that they were the most expensive item she wore. At the opening of her jacket, he saw the thin strap of another tank top. The image of her supple body outlined in the tight garment zoomed into his brain.

"Francesca. What are you doing here?" he asked, his voice unintentionally sharp in annoyance at the vivid, uncontrollable memory. She paused several feet from the fencing mat. The lushness of her pink lips made even her frowns sexy as hell.

"Lin needs to speak with you about something urgent. You weren't answering your cell phone, so she called the house line. Mrs. Hanson was on the way out to the store to get a few missing ingredients for your supper, so I said I'd come give the message."

Ian nodded once, using the towel he'd draped around his neck to wipe some perspiration off his face. "I'll call her as soon as I shower."

"I'll tell her," Francesca said, starting to back out of the room.

"What? She's still on the line?"

Francesca nodded.

"There's an extension in the hall just outside the exercise facility. Tell her I'll call her back soon."

"All right," Francesca said. She glanced quickly at Lucien and gave him a fleeting smile before she turned.

Irritation spiked through him. *Well, in all fairness, Lucien didn't bark at her like you did.*

"Francesca."

She spun around.

"Would you come back once you've passed the message to Lin, please? We haven't had the opportunity to speak much all week. I'd like to hear about your progress."

She hesitated for a split second. Her gaze dropped over his chest, making him go still in sudden awareness.

"Sure. I'll be right back," she said before she strode out of the room. The door to the fencing room clicked shut behind her.

Lucien was grinning when he glanced over at him. "When I visited the American south, they had a saying . . . 'A long, tall drink of cool water.' "

Ian did a double take. "Hands off," he said succinctly.

Lucien looked taken aback. Ian blinked, a mixture of primitive aggression and shame at the harshness warring in his blood. Something occurred to him, and he narrowed his eyes.

"Wait a second . . . the woman you were talking about just now that works for Noble—"

"*Not* Francesca," Lucien said, his eyes gleaming as he gave Ian a sideways glance and opened the refrigerator for a bottle of water. "Seems to me you ought to take your own advice about intercompany romantic interests."

"Don't be ridiculous."

"So you're not interested in that gorgeous creature?" Lucien asked.

Ian whipped the towel off his neck.

"I meant that *I* don't have an employment contract," he said, his brisk tone making it clear the conversation was over.

"I guess that's my cue to leave," Lucien said wryly. "I'll see you on Monday."

"Lucien."

He turned.

"I'm sorry for snapping at you," Ian said.

Lucien shrugged. "I know what it means to be on a tight leash. Tends to make a man a bit . . . tetchy."

Ian didn't respond, just watched as his friend walked away. He thought of what Lucien had said about Francesca being a long, tall drink of cold water. Lucien had been right.

And Ian was clearly thirsting in the desert.

He glanced toward the entry door warily and saw Francesca walk back into the room.


She was sorry to see Lucien give her a friendly wave and walk out of the room when she entered. The atmosphere of the large, well-equipped exercise room grew heavier when the door closed behind him and she was left alone with Ian. She paused at the edge of the mat.

"Come closer. It's all right. You can walk across the piste in your running shoes," he said.

She approached him cautiously. It made her uncomfortable to look at him. His handsome face was impassive, as usual. He looked ungodly sexy wearing a pair of formfitting breeches and a simple white T-shirt. She supposed it was necessary for the shirt to be so tight because he wore other fitted garments over it. It left little to the imagination, revealing every ridge and slanting line of his lean, muscular torso.

Obviously, working out was a high priority to him. His body was a beautiful, honed machine.

"Piste?" she repeated as she crossed the mat and neared him.

"The fencing mat."

"Oh." She eyed the sword on the table curiously, trying to ignore the subtle scent emanating from his body—clean, spicy soap mingling with male sweat.

"How are you?" he asked, his polite, cool tone not quite matching the gleam in his blue eyes. He confused her to no end. Like that time last Thursday night, for instance, when she'd turned to find him studying her while she sketched. His manner had been almost formal, but she'd grown breathless with expectation when she saw the way his gaze lowered and lingered on her breasts, making her nipples tighten. She couldn't help but recall how they'd parted on the first night he'd asked her to the penthouse, how he'd touched her as he put on her coat . . . his reference to her painting.

Had he been pleased or angry that she'd painted him? And was it her imagination, or had he been warning her that her title for the painting hadn't been as whimsical as she'd once thought, that the subject of her painting truly did walk through life alone?

*Nonsense*, she chastised herself as she forced herself to meet his piercing stare. Ian Noble didn't think twice about her beyond her use as an artist.

"Busy but good, thanks," she answered him. She gave him a quick recap of her progress. "The canvas is prepped. I've sketched. I think I'll be able to actually start painting next week."

"And do you have everything you require?" he asked as he stepped past her and opened a refrigerator. He moved with masculine grace. She'd love to see him fence—leashed aggression in graceful action.

"Yes. Lin did a very thorough job in getting my supplies. I needed one or two things, but she immediately procured them for me last Monday. She's a miracle of efficiency."

"I couldn't agree more. Don't hesitate to speak up if you need the smallest thing." He cracked the cap on the water bottle with a brisk twist of his wrist. His biceps bulged beneath the sleeves of the shirt, looking hard as stone. A few veins popped on his strong-looking forearms. "And is your schedule manageable? School, your waitressing duties, painting . . . your social life?"

Her pulse began to throb at her throat. She lowered her head so he wouldn't notice and pretended to be studying one of the swords on a storage rack.

"I don't have much of a social life."

"No boyfriend?" he asked quietly.

She shook her head as she ran her fingers over an etched pommel.

"But surely you have friends that you like to spend spare time with?"

"Yes," she said, glancing up at him. "I'm very close with all three of my roommates."

"And what do the four of you like to do in your free time?"

She shrugged and touched a different sword grip. "Free time is a bit of a rarity these days, but when I have some, the usual—play video games, go out to the bars, hang out, play poker."

"That's *usual* for a group of girls?"

"My roommates are all men." She glanced up in time to see the shadow of displeasure that crossed his stoic features. Her heartbeat leapt. His short, glossy, near-black hair was damp at his neck from perspiration. She suddenly imagined herself slicking her tongue along his hairline, tasting his sweat. She blinked and glanced away.

"You live with three men?"

She nodded.

"What do your parents think of that?"

She gave him a sharp glance over her shoulder. "They hate it. Much good it does them. It's their loss. Caden, Justin, and Davie are awesome people."

He opened his mouth but paused. "It's unconventional," he said after a few seconds, his clipped tone telling her that he'd edited what he'd been about to say.

"Unorthodox, perhaps. But that shouldn't seem unusual to you, should it? Didn't you tell me the other night you were a lot of that?" she asked, returning her attention to the swords. This time she wrapped her hand around the grip and squeezed, liking the sensation of hard, cold steel in her fist. She ran her hand up and down along the column.

"Stop that."

She started at his tone, dropping her hand as if the steel had suddenly burned her. She looked up at him in amazement. His nostrils were slightly flared. His eyes blazed. He jerked his chin and took a rapid swing of water.

"Do you fence?" he asked her briskly as he set the bottle of water on a table.

"No. Well . . . not really."

"What do you mean?" he asked, stepping toward her, his brow furrowed.

"I do a fencing program with Justin and Caden, but . . . I've never touched a sword before," she said sheepishly.

His puzzlement faded abruptly. He smiled. It was like seeing the sunrise over a dark, brooding landscape. "Are you talking about playing on a Game Station?"

"Yes," she admitted a little defensively.

He nodded toward the rack. "Take that end one there."

"Excuse me?"

"Take the last sword. Noble Enterprises designed the original program for that fencing game you play. We sold it to Shinatze a few years back. What level do you play at?"

"Advanced."

"You should understand the basics then." He held her stare. "Pick up the sword, Francesca."

There was a hint of a dare to his tone. His smile still lingered around his full lips. He was laughing at her again. She lifted the sword and glared at him. His grin widened. He grabbed another sword and handed her a mask. He tilted his head toward the mat. When they faced each other, Francesca's breathing becoming rapid and choppy, he tapped his blade against hers.

"En garde," he said softly.

Her eyes went wide in panic. "Wait . . . we're going to . . . *right now?*"

"Why not?" he asked, taking his stance. She glanced nervously at her sword, then his unprotected chest. "It's a practice sword. You couldn't hurt me with it if you tried."

He thrust. She parried instinctively. He advanced, and she retreated clumsily, still blocking his blade. Even through her haze of alarm and bewilderment, she couldn't help but admire the flex of his honed muscles, the coiled strength in his long body.

"Don't be afraid," she heard him say as she defended desperately. He hardly seemed to be exerting himself at all. He might have been taking an evening stroll, with as much effort as he exhibited. "If you know the gaming program, your brain knows adequate movements to engage with me."

"How do you know?" she squeaked as she leapt out of the way of his blade.

"Because *I* designed the program. Defend yourself, Francesca," he said sharply at the same moment he lunged. She yelped and blocked his blade just inches from her shoulder. He continued to attack without withdrawing, pressing her backward on the mat, the metallic clangs and hisses of their swords filling the air around them.

He advanced quicker now—she felt the amplification of his strength along the shaft of her blade—but his expression remained completely calm.

"You're leaving your octave unguarded," he murmured. She gasped when he struck her right hip with the side of his blade with casual precision. He'd barely tapped her, but her hip and buttock burned.

"Again," he said tensely.

She followed him to the center of the mat, his cool, effortless besting of her making her blood boil in her veins. They tapped swords and she attacked, lunging toward him.

"Don't let your anger at being beaten make you foolish," he said as they engaged.

"I'm not angry," she lied through clenched teeth.

"You could be a good fencer. You're very strong. Do you work out?" he asked almost conversationally as they thrust and parried.

"Run long distance," she said, and then squawked in alarm when he landed a particularly strong blow.

"Concentrate," he ordered.

"I would if you'd be quiet!"

She grimaced when he chuckled. A drop of sweat skittered down her neck as she used all of her energy to parry his thrusts. He feinted, and she fell for it. Again, he tapped her right hip.

"If you don't protect that octave, you're going to get a bruised bottom."

Her cheeks flamed. She resisted an urge to touch the side of the buttock that still stung from his blade. She straightened and forced her breathing to even. His stare was fixed on her shoulder. She realized the opening of her hoodie had fallen down during their swordplay, and she tugged the jacket back into place.

"Again," she said as calmly as possible. He nodded once in polite acquiescence.

She gathered herself and faced him at the center of the mat. She knew she was being foolish, knew it perfectly well. In addition to being an expert fencer, he was a male in prime physical condition. She'd never best him. Still, her competitive spirit would not be silenced. She tried to recall some of the fencing moves from the game.

"En garde," he said. They tapped swords.

This time, she let him advance, carefully guarding all her quadrants. He was too strong and quick, however. As he drew closer, he choked off her ability to attack offensively. She parried wildly, straining to hold him. Her excitement mounted as he closed in on her. She fought desperately, but they both knew he would triumph.

"Stop," she cried out in frustration when he pushed her to the edge of the piste.

"You submit," he said, his sword striking hers so hard she almost lost her grip. She barely blocked his next strike.

"*No.*"

"Then *think*," he snapped.

She desperately tried to follow his instructions. Things were too tight to lunge, so she extended her arm, forcing him to leap backward.

"Very nice," he murmured.

His blade flicked so rapidly it was a blur. She never felt the metal on her skin. She stopped parrying and glanced down in shock. He'd sliced clean through the strap of her tank top.

"I thought you said the swords weren't sharp," she cried out in a choked voice.

"I said that yours wasn't." He flipped his wrist, and her sword flew through the air, landing with a useless thud on the mat. He whipped off his mask. She stared at him, aghast. She resisted an urge to run, he looked so fearsome in that moment.

"Never leave yourself undefended, Francesca. *Never*. The next time you do, I will punish you."

He tossed his sword aside and lunged toward her, reaching. He jerked off her mask and tossed it on the mat. One hand cradled the back of her skull, the other bracketed her neck and jaw. He swept down and took her mouth with his own.

At first, his surprise attack on her senses made her go rigid in shock. Then his scent penetrated her awareness, his taste. He tilted her head back and slid his tongue between her lips, clearly intent on consumption. He thrust, exploring her. Owning her.

Liquid heat rushed between her thighs, the total response to his kiss unprecedented in her experience. He brought her closer, pressing her against his body. He was so hot. So hard. *Lord have mercy.* How could she have thought he was indifferent? His arousal raged against her. It was like being suddenly shoved into a male inferno of lust and left to helplessly burn.

She moaned into his mouth. His lips shaped and caressed hers skillfully, leaving her open for his tongue's possession. She slid her tongue against his, engaging in the kiss just as she had the swordplay. He groaned and stepped closer yet, making her eyes roll behind her shut lids when she felt the full extent of his erection. He was huge and hard. Her sex clenched tight. Her thoughts splintered in a million directions. He urged her backward, and she submitted, hardly knowing what she was doing. He never stopped kissing her as she staggered several feet.

The air whooshed out of her lungs and into his marauding mouth when he backed her against the wall. He pressed, sandwiching her body between two rock-hard surfaces. She rubbed against him instinctively, feeling his defined muscles, stroking his enormous erection.

He hissed and tore his mouth from hers. Before she ever guessed his intention, he shoved down her tank top on the side where the strap was sliced. His long fingers skimmed over the upper curve of her breast as he peeled back the cup of her bra, reaching inside. Her nipple popped out of the fabric, the cup now beneath her breast, plumping the flesh above it, lifting it . . . displaying it. His gaze was hot and greedy as he stared at her bared flesh. She felt his cock lurch against her lower belly and moaned. His nostrils flared and his head dipped.

She made a choking sound when his wet, hot mouth slipped over her nipple. He sucked hard, making her nipple stiffen and ache, causing a tug between her thighs and another rush of warmth. She cried out. Ah, God, what was happening to her? Her vagina squeezed unbearably tight, aching, needing to be filled. Perhaps he heard her cry, because he ceased pulling on her nipple and soothed with a warm, laving tongue. Then he sucked again.

His obvious hunger thrilled her. He was hurting her a little, pleasuring her a lot. What excited her most was his scorching hunger. She longed to feed it . . . make it grow. She arched against him and whimpered helplessly. Never had a man dared to kiss her so roughly or touch her body with such a potent combination of hot greed and consummate skill.

So how was she to know how much she would love it?

He plumped her breast in his hand and molded it to his palm as he continued to suckle her. A harsh moan tore from her throat. He lifted his head, and she gasped at the abrupt cessation of his warmth . . . of her pleasure. He studied her face, his expression rigid, his eyes ablaze. She sensed the rising tension in him, the war. *Was he going to pull away?* she wondered suddenly. *Did he want her or didn't he?*

He suddenly moved his free hand, cupping her entire sex through her jeans. He pressed. Francesca whimpered helplessly.

"No," he rasped, as if arguing with himself. His dark head dipped again to her breast. "I'll take what's mine."

# Part Two

## Because I Could Not Resist

# Three

Francesca had intuited that it would be a bad idea to associate with the likes of Ian Noble. She'd known she was way out of her depth every time he looked at her with that enigmatic gleam in his cobalt-blue eyes. Hadn't he even warned her in his subtle manner that he was dangerous?

Now here was proof of it: nearly two hundred pounds of prime, aroused male flesh pressing her against the wall. He was consuming her like she was his last meal.

He plumped her breast farther into his hand, serving her flesh to his marauding mouth. He tugged on her nipple again, causing a sweet, sharp suction. Francesca gasped, her head banging against the wall as arousal stabbed at her sex, the strength of her reaction unprecedented. His hand at the juncture of her thighs pressed, alleviating her ache . . . mounting it.

"Ian," she said shakily.

He lifted his dark head a few inches and stared at her

breast. The glistening nipple was reddened, the center nubbin elongated and stiff from his ravening mouth and laving tongue. His body tautened; his cock lurched against her belly. He gave a rough growl of male satisfaction at the sight.

"I'd have to be a fucking robot not to want that," he said in a low, savage tone. She whimpered in raw lust and bewilderment. The slightly lost expression mingling with his scoring stare caused something to stir deep inside her spirit. Who *was* this man? She hated the war she sensed in him. She put her hand on the back of his head, furrowing her fingers through his hair. It was every bit as silky and thick as it looked. His gaze flashed up at her. She pushed his head toward her breast.

"It's all right, Ian."

His nostrils flared. "It's *not* all right. You don't know what you're saying."

"I know what I'm feeling," she whispered. "Who better?"

He shut his eyes briefly. Suddenly, she felt the tension break and he was kissing her mouth again, flexing his hips, pressing his erection into her soft, harboring flesh. Francesca clutched at his head, feeling herself drowning in the essence of him. Through an intoxicating haze of rising lust, she heard distant footsteps.

"Oh. There you are . . . excuse me." The footsteps began to retreat.

Ian lifted his head, and she was pinned by his stare. He shifted his body, making sure her bare breast was blocked from view before pulling her loosened hoodie over her exposed flesh.

"*Qu'est-ce que c'est?*" Ian uttered sharply. She glanced

around, confused by the question uttered in French, which she didn't speak.

The footsteps paused. "*Je suis desolé*. Your cell phone won't stop ringing in the locker room. Whatever Lin wants to talk to you about seems really important."

She recognized Lucien's French-accented voice. It sounded muffled, as if he spoke with his back to them. Ian's stare bored down on her. She sensed the moment when he withdrew. His body still pressed against her, hard and aroused, but a door in his eyes seemed to slam shut.

"I should have called her earlier. It was rude of me. Remiss," Ian said, his gaze never leaving Francesca's face.

The footsteps resumed, and she heard a door slam. He pushed himself off her.

"Ian?" she asked weakly. She felt strange, like her muscles no longer knew their purpose, as if the weight and strength of Ian's body had been the only thing keeping her upright. Her hand slapped against the wall in an abrupt attempt to right her world. His arm thrust forward. He grabbed her elbow, steadying her. His gaze ran over her face.

"Francesca? Are you all right?" he asked sharply.

She blinked and nodded. He'd sounded almost angry.

"I'm sorry. That shouldn't have happened. I didn't mean for it to," he said in a stark tone.

"Oh," she said stupidly, her mind reeling. "Does that mean it's not going to happen again?"

His expression flattened. *What in the world was he thinking?* she wondered, mentally flailing.

"You never told me before. The men that you live with— do you sleep with one of them? All of them?"

Her brain stalled.

"*What?* Why would you ask me something like that? Of course I don't sleep with them. They're my roommates. My friends."

His narrowed gaze lowered over her face and chest. "You expect me to believe that? Three males live in the same house with you, and the whole thing is completely platonic?"

Anger streamed into her lust-dazed consciousness. Then it began to roar like a tidal wave. Was he purposefully trying to insult her? It was working. What an infuriating bastard. How dare he say something like that to her so coolly after what he'd just done?

(After what she'd *allowed* him to do?)

She stepped away from the wall, pausing several feet away from him. "You asked, and I told you the truth. I don't care what you believe. My sex life is none of your business."

She began to walk away.

"Francesca."

She paused but refused to turn around. Humiliation had started to brew with her anger. If she looked at his gorgeous, smug face, she might explode.

"I only asked because I was trying to understand how . . . experienced you are."

She whipped around and stared at him in amazement. "Is that important for you? *Experience?*" she asked, wishing the stab of hurt she'd felt at his words hadn't rung in her voice.

"Yes," he said. No softness. No concession. Just *yes. You're not in my league, Francesca. You're an awkward, stupid, onetime fat girl.*

His expression hardened, and he looked away from her face.

"I'm not what you might think. I'm not a nice man," he said, as if that explained everything.

"No," she said with more calmness than she felt. "You're not. Maybe none of the bootlickers you surround yourself with have ever told you this, but that's not something to be proud of, Ian."

This time, he didn't try to stop her as she rushed out of the room.

Francesca sat at the kitchen table and moodily watched Davie butter toast.

"What's got you in such a bad mood? Not that your mood has been stellar since yesterday. Are you still feeling under the weather?" Davie asked, referring to the fact that she'd come home after her classes yesterday instead of going to the Noble penthouse to paint.

"No, I'm fine," Francesca replied with a reassuring smile that Davie didn't seem to buy.

Initially, she'd been bewildered and angered by what Ian had said—and done—in the workout facility two days ago, but then she'd grown worried. Had what occurred threatened her valuable commission? Had her lack of "experience" made her less valuable to Ian, and thus disposable? What if he terminated their agreement and she had no way to pay her tuition? She wasn't a typical Noble employee, after all. She had no contract, just his patronage. And Ian was reputed to be a tyrant, wasn't he?

She'd been so anxious and confused about how that kiss had altered her position with Ian that she couldn't make herself return to paint yesterday.

Davie whisked toast onto her plate and shoved a jar of jam across the surface of the table.

"Thanks," Francesca mumbled, lifting her knife listlessly.

"Eat," Davie ordered. "It'll make you feel better."

Davie was like a combination of older brother, friend, and mother hen to Francesca, Caden, and Justin. He was five years older than all of them, having met them all after he'd returned to Northwestern to get his M.B.A. There, he'd met Justin and Caden, who were in the same program, and fallen in with their circle of friends, of which Francesca was a member. The fact that Davie was also an art historian, returning to school in order to gain the tools necessary to expand his single gallery into a chain, immediately drew him and Francesca together.

After Justin, Caden, and Davie had received their graduate degrees, and Francesca her baccalaureate, Davie had offered to have them room with him in the city. The five-bedroom, four-bath row house he'd inherited from his parents in the Wicker Park neighborhood was too large just for him. Besides, Francesca knew that Davie wanted the companionship. Her friend was vulnerable to the blues, and Francesca knew that having the three of them around helped assuage them. Davie's parents had rejected him when he'd confessed that he was gay as a teenager. The three of them had tenuously reconciled by the time his mother and father died in a freak boating accident off the coast of Mexico three years ago, a fact that made Davie both grateful and sad.

Davie longed for a relationship, but he'd been about as unlucky in the romance arena as Francesca. They served as confidantes to each other, the balm following their many bitter, lackluster, and disappointing dating experiences.

All four roommates were good friends, but Francesca and Davie were closest in their tastes and temperaments, while Justin and Caden often were paired up by the common obsessions of many straight males in their midtwenties—a lucrative career, a good time, and frequent sex with hot women.

"Was it Noble on the phone?" Davie asked, glancing meaningfully at her cell phone on the table. *Damn.* He'd noticed the call she'd just received on her cell phone had upset her.

"No."

Davie gave her a wry spill-it glance after her monosyllabic response, and she sighed.

She hadn't revealed what had happened in Ian Noble's exercise room to Caden and Justin, who as brilliant young men working in high-profile investment-banking firms, were constantly badgering her with questions about Ian Noble. There was no way she'd tell him that the elusive idol they worshipped had held her against a wall and kissed and touched her until her legs no longer supported her. She hadn't told Davie, either, which was a sure sign of how overwhelmed she'd been by the whole experience.

"It was Lin Soong calling, Noble's girl Friday," Francesca admitted before she took a bite of toast.

"And?"

She chewed and swallowed. "She called to tell me that Ian Noble has decided to put me under contract for the painting. He's paying me the total amount up front. She assured me that the terms of the contract were quite generous, and that under no circumstances would Noble be able to back out of awarding me the commission. Even if I don't finish it, he won't request a return of the money."

Davie's mouth fell open. His toast drooped in his slackened fingers. With his dark brown hair falling onto his forehead and early morning pallor, he looked about eighteen years old at that moment instead of his actual twenty-eight.

"Why are you acting like she called about a funeral then? Isn't that good news, that Noble wants to assure you that you'll get paid no matter what?"

Francesca tossed down her toast. Her appetite had evaporated when she'd fully absorbed what Lin was telling her in that professional, warm tone of hers. "He has to have everyone under his thumb," she said bitterly.

"What are you talking about, 'Cesca? If that contract is everything his assistant says, Noble's giving you carte blanche. You don't even have to show up and you get paid."

She carried her plate over to the sink.

"Exactly," she muttered, turning on the tap. "And Ian Noble knows perfectly well that making that offer is the one thing that will *assure* I show up and finish the project."

Davie shoved his chair back to regard her. "You're confusing me. Are you saying you were actually thinking about *not* finishing the painting?"

As she considered how to reply, Justin Maker staggered into the kitchen wearing a pair of sweatpants, his bare, golden torso gleaming in the sunlight, his green eyes puffy from lack of sleep.

"Coffee, stat," he muttered in a roughened voice, whipping the cabinet open for a cup. Francesca gave Davie a pleading, apologetic glance, hoping he'd understand she didn't want to continue the topic right now.

"Did you and Caden shut down McGill's again last

night?" she asked Justin wryly, referring to their favorite neighborhood bar. She handed the cream to her friend.

"No. We were home by one. But guess who's playing at McGill's Saturday night?" he asked Francesca, taking the cream she handed him. "The Run Around Band. Let's all go. Poker night afterward."

"I don't think so. I've got a big project due Monday, and I'm not as proficient at the late-to-bed, early-to-rise routine as you and Caden are," Francesca said as she started to walk out of the room.

"Come on, 'Cesca. It'll be fun. All four of us haven't gone out in a while," Davie said, surprising her. Like Francesca, Davie's proclivity for a wild night out had decreased considerably since they'd left Northwestern. The challenging arch of Davie's eyebrows informed her that he thought a night out would encourage her to spill the beans about what was bothering her.

"I'll think about it," Francesca said before she left the kitchen.

But she didn't. Her mind was already consumed with what she was going to say when she confronted Ian Noble.

Unfortunately, he wasn't there when she arrived at the penthouse that afternoon. Not that she really expected him to be. He usually wasn't. Undecided about what she should do in regard to that kiss, her commission—not to mention her entire future—she wandered into the room she was using as the studio.

Within five minutes, she was painting feverishly. Ian Noble hadn't decided her. Even Francesca herself hadn't.

The painting had. It'd gotten into her blood. She *must* finish it now.

She was lost in her work for hours, finally rising from her creative trance as the sun began to dip behind the high-rises.

Mrs. Hanson was whisking something in a bowl when Francesca staggered into the kitchen for some water. Ian's kitchen reminded her of something one might find in an English country manor—huge, with every conceivable cooking implement ever created, but somehow still comfortable. She liked to sit in there and chat with Mrs. Hanson.

"You were so quiet, I didn't realize you were here!" the friendly, elderly housekeeper exclaimed.

"I was working hard," Francesca said, reaching for the handle of the enormous stainless-steel refrigerator. Mrs. Hanson had insisted since day one that Francesca make herself completely at home. The first time she'd opened the refrigerator, Francesca had exclaimed in surprise to see a whole shelf of bottled club sodas chilling, along with a china plate with sliced limes covered in plastic wrap. "Ian told me club soda with lime was your favorite drink. I hope this brand is all right," Mrs. Hanson had replied anxiously to her exclamation.

Now every time she opened the refrigerator, Francesca felt that same rush of warmth she experienced that first time when she realized Ian had remembered her beverage preference and then made sure it was available to her while she worked.

*Pitiful,* she scolded herself as she withdrew a bottle.

"Would you like supper?" Mrs. Hanson asked. "Ian won't want his for a while yet, but I could bang out something for you."

"No, I'm not really hungry. Thank you, though." She

hesitated, but then blurted, "So Ian is in town? He'll be home later?"

"Yes, he mentioned it this morning. He usually eats at eight thirty sharp, whether I'm cooking for him or he eats at the office. Ian likes his routine. He has ever since I knew him as a boy."

Mrs. Hanson glanced up at her. "Why don't you sit down there and keep me company for a bit. You look pale. You've been working too hard. I have some water on the boil. We'll have a cup of tea."

"Okay," Francesca agreed, sinking into one of the stools next to the island. She suddenly felt weak with exhaustion now that her creative-inspired adrenaline rush was fading. Besides, she hadn't slept well the past two nights.

"What was Ian like as a child?" Francesca couldn't stop herself from asking.

"Oh, an older soul I've never seen in such a wee one's eyes," Mrs. Hanson replied with a sad smile. "Serious. Eerily smart. A little shy. Once he warmed up to you, as sweet and loyal as they come."

Francesca tried to picture the somber, dark-haired, shy boy-Ian, her heart squeezing a little at the image her brain wrought.

"You seem a bit out of sorts," the housekeeper consoled as she bustled about, pouring hot water into two cups and then arranging some items onto a silver platter: two scones, an exquisite silver spoon and knife, two crisp white cloth napkins, Devonshire cream, and jam dolloped into gorgeous china finger bowls. Nothing was ever done small in Ian Noble's household, not even for a casual chat in the kitchen. "Isn't your painting going well?"

"It's going quite well, actually. Thank you," she murmured when Mrs. Hanson set down a cup and saucer before her. "Things are moving along. You should come and have a look later."

"I'd like that. Have a scone? They're especially good today. Nothing like a scone with cream and jam to jump you out of a bad mood."

Francesca laughed and shook her head. "My mother would die if she heard you say that."

"Whatever for?" Mrs. Hanson asked, her pale blue eyes going wide as she paused in the process of ladling sweet cream on her scone.

"Because you're encouraging me to manage my moods with food, that's why. My parents, along with half a dozen child psychologists, have drilled the evils of emotional eating into my brain since I was seven years old." She noticed Mrs. Hanson's bewildered expression. "I used to be quite overweight as a child."

"I'll never believe it! You're as slim as a wand."

Francesca shrugged. "Once I went away to school, the weight sort of fell off after a year or two. I started long-distance running, so I suppose that helped. Personally, I think being out from beneath my parents' critical eye was the real clincher, though."

Mrs. Hanson made a knowing sound. "Once the weight wasn't a power struggle anymore, the fat didn't have any use?"

She grinned. "Mrs. Hanson, you could be a psychologist."

The housekeeper laughed. "What would Lord Stratham or Ian have done with me then?"

Francesca paused in the process of sipping her tea. "Lord Stratham?"

"Ian's grandfather, James Noble, the Earl of Stratham. I worked for Lord and Lady Stratham for thirty-three years before I came to America to serve Ian eight years ago."

"Ian's grandfather," Francesca murmured thoughtfully. "Who will inherit his title?"

"Oh, a fellow by the name of Gerard Sinoit, Lord Stratham's nephew."

"Not Ian?"

Mrs. Hanson sighed and set down her scone. "Ian is heir to Lord Stratham's fortune but not to his title."

Francesca's forehead crinkled in confusion. English customs were so odd. "Was Ian's mother or father the Nobles' child?"

A shadow fell over Mrs. Hanson's features. "Ian's mother. Helen was the earl and countess's only child."

"Is she . . ." Francesca faded off delicately, and Mrs. Hanson nodded sadly.

"Dead, yes. She died very young. Tragic life."

"And Ian's father?"

Mrs. Hanson didn't immediately reply. She looked torn. "I'm not sure I should speak of such things," the housekeeper said.

Francesca blushed. "Oh, of course. I'm sorry. I didn't mean to pry, I just—"

"I don't think you were being impertinent," Mrs. Hanson assured, patting her hand where it rested on the counter. "It's just that I'm afraid Ian has a rather sad family history, despite all his blazing fame and fortune as a grown man. His mother was quite rebellious as a young woman . . . wild. The Nobles couldn't control her," Mrs. Hanson said with a significant glance. "She ran away in her late teens and was missing for more than a decade. The Nobles feared she was dead but never had any proof of it. They kept searching. It was a black time in the Stratham household." Pain flickered across Mrs. Hanson's countenance at the memory. "The lord and lady were frantic to find her."

"I can only imagine."

Mrs. Hanson nodded. "It was a terrible, terrible time. And it didn't get much better when they finally did locate Helen living in some kind of hovel in northern France, almost eleven years after she'd first disappeared. She was quite mad. Sick. Delusional. No one could understand what had happened to her. To this day, no one seems to know. And there was Ian with her—ten years old going on ninety."

Mrs. Hanson made a choking sound of distress. Francesca hastened off her stool.

"I'm so sorry. I didn't mean to upset you," she said, her mind swirling with a combination of curiosity for more information about Ian and stark concern for the kind housekeeper. She located a box of tissues and brought it to Mrs. Hanson.

"It's all right. I'm just an old fool," Mrs. Hanson mumbled, taking a tissue. "Most would say that the Nobles are nothing but my employers, but to me, they're my only family." She sniffed and blotted her cheeks.

"Mrs. Hanson. What's wrong?"

Francesca jumped at the sound of the stern male voice and spun around. Ian stood in the entryway to the kitchen.

Mrs. Hanson looked around guiltily. "Ian, you're home early."

"Are you all right?" he asked, his face tight with concern. Francesca realized that Mrs. Hanson's comment about considering the Nobles her family went both directions.

"I'm fine. Please pay me no mind," she said, laughing airily and throwing away her tissue. "You know how old women can get maudlin."

"I've never known you to be maudlin," Ian said. His gaze flicked off Mrs. Hanson and landed on Francesca.

"May I speak to you a moment, in the library?" he asked her.

"Of course," she said, lifting her chin and forcing herself not to cringe in the face of his blazing stare.

A minute later, she turned anxiously at the sound of Ian shutting the heavy walnut door of the library behind him. He stalked toward her with the smooth, graceful stride of a predatory animal. Why was it she was always comparing such a sophisticated, contained male to a wild thing?

"What did you say to Mrs. Hanson?" he demanded. She suspected it was coming, but she still bristled at the subtle inflection of accusation in his tone.

"I didn't say anything! We were just . . . talking."

His gaze bore into her. "Talking about my family."

She resisted heaving a sigh of relief. Apparently, he'd only heard their last comments and hadn't realized what Mrs. Hanson had revealed about his mother. And him. Somehow, she knew for a fact he'd be far less contained than he was if he knew Mrs. Hanson had been loose-lipped about those particular details.

"Yes," she admitted, straightening and meeting his stare, though it cost her a great deal of effort. Sometimes those angel eyes became the avenging-angel variety. She crossed her arms beneath her breasts. "*I* asked her about your grandparents."

"And that made her cry?" he asked, his tone thick with sarcasm.

"I don't really know the details of what made her cry," she snapped. "I wasn't prying, Ian. We were just talking, having polite conversation. You should try it sometime."

"If you want to know about my family, I would prefer if you asked me."

"Oh, and you'll dish out all the details, no doubt," she countered, her tone just as sarcastic as his had been earlier.

A muscle jumped in his cheek. Abruptly, he walked toward the large, gleaming desk and picked up a small bronze statue of a horse, toying with it. Francesca wondered in mixed irritation and nervousness if he wanted something to do with his hands besides strangle her. With his back to her, she had the opportunity to study him for the first time. He wore an impeccably cut pair of trousers, a white dress shirt, and a blue tie that matched his eyes. Since he always wore suits to the office, she assumed he'd removed the jacket. The starched shirt perfectly fit his wide shoulders. The pants draped his narrow hips and long legs: elegant, raw masculinity defined. *He really was a beautiful male animal,* she thought resentfully.

"Lin said she contacted you this morning," he said, the change in topic taking her off guard.

"She did. I'd like to speak to you about what she said," Francesca replied, anxiety now trumping her anger.

"You painted today," he said rather than asked.

She blinked in surprise. "Yes. How . . . how did you know?" She'd had the impression he'd come directly to the kitchen upon entering the penthouse.

"There's paint on your right forefinger."

She glanced down at her right hand. She'd never seen him even glance in that direction. Did he have eyes in the back of his head?

"Yes, I painted."

"I thought perhaps you weren't going to return, after what happened on Wednesday."

"Well, I did return. And not because you told Lin to call and buy me off. That wasn't necessary."

He turned. "*I* think it was necessary. I won't have you worrying about whether or not you can afford to finish your degree."

"*Plus*—you *knew* that I would finish the painting if I knew you were going to pay me the commission no matter what," she said irritably, edging toward him.

He blinked and had the decency to look slightly abashed.

"I don't like being manipulated," she said.

"I wasn't trying to manipulate you. I just didn't want you to lose an opportunity you deserved because I lost control. You weren't to blame for what happened in the workout facility."

"We made out," she muttered, blushing. "I hardly think it constitutes the faux pas of the century."

"I wanted to do a hell of a lot more than make out with you, Francesca."

"Ian, do you *like* me?" she asked impulsively. Her eyelids sprang wide. She couldn't *believe* she'd just blurted out the question that had been festering in her brain for days now.

"*Like* you? I want to fuck you. Badly. Does that answer your question?"

The ensuing silence seemed to crush her lungs it had so

much weight. The echo of his low, rough growl seemed to hover in the air between them.

"Why are you worried about losing control? I'm not a twelve-year-old," she managed after a moment. Her face grew hotter when his gaze dropped over her.

"No. But you might as well be," he said, his tone suddenly sounding dismissive. Humiliation flooded through her. *How could he go from hot to cold so effortlessly?* she wondered, infuriated. He strolled around his desk and sat in the supple leather chair. "You may go now—if there's nothing else?" he asked, his glance polite. Indifferent.

"I'd like you to pay me when the painting is done. Not before," she said, her voice quaking with barely contained anger.

He nodded thoughtfully, as if considering her request. "You don't have to spend the money until then, if you prefer. But the full commission has already been transferred to your bank account."

Her mouth dropped open. "How did you know my account number?"

He didn't reply, just raised his eyebrows slightly, his expression bland.

She barely stopped the scorching curse from springing out of her throat. Since she couldn't cuss out her benefactor for his arrogance—or his generosity—there was nothing else she could think to say to him. Fury had short-circuited her brain. She turned and started to walk out of the room.

"Oh, and Francesca?" he called calmly from behind her.

"Yes?" she asked, looking back.

"Don't expect to work here Saturday night. I'm entertaining. I'd like privacy."

Something seemed to drop in her gut like a lead ball. He was telling her he was having a woman there this weekend. Somehow, she just knew it.

"Not a problem. I was planning on going out on Saturday night and letting off some steam with the guys. Things have gotten a bit stifling around here."

Something flashed in his eyes before she turned around, but his expression remained unreadable.

As usual.

Davie drove Justin's car surely through the bustling Saturday-night Wicker Park traffic. Justin was a little tipsy after listening to the Run Around Band at McGill's for two hours. So were Caden and Francesca, for that matter.

Thus their insane errand.

"Come on, 'Cesca," Caden Joyner goaded from the backseat. "We're all going to get one."

"Even you, Davie?" Francesca asked from where she sat in the passenger seat.

Davie shrugged. "I've always wanted a tattoo on my biceps—one of those old-fashioned ones, like an anchor or something," he said, flashing her a grin as he turned down North Avenue.

"He thinks it'll get him a pirate," Justin joked.

"Well, I'm not going to get one until I have time to draw the design myself," she said resolutely.

"Spoilsport," Justin accused loudly. "Where's the fun in *planning* for a tattoo? You're supposed to wake up with a truly atrocious, super-sleazy one in the morning and not have a clue how you got it the night before."

"Are you talking about a tattoo or the women you bring home?" Caden asked.

Francesca broke into laughter. She barely heard her cell phone ringing in her purse, thanks to her friends' boisterous teasing and bickering. She peered at her cell phone, not recognizing the number.

"Hello?" she answered, forcing herself to cease laughing.

"Francesca?"

The mirth melted off her mouth.

"*Ian?*" she asked incredulously.

"Yes."

Justin said something loudly from the backseat, and Caden roared with laughter. "Am I interrupting something?" Ian asked, his stiff, British-accented voice a stark contrast to her friends' rowdy banter.

"No. I'm just out with my friends. Why are you calling?" she asked, amazement making her tone more blunt than she'd intended.

Caden cracked up, and Davie joined him. "You guys . . . hold it down," Francesca hissed and was summarily ignored.

"I've been thinking about something—" Ian began.

"No! Turn left," Justin shouted loudly. "Bart's Dragon Signs is on North Paulina."

She gasped when Davie slammed on the breaks and she heaved against the seat belt.

"What were you saying?" Francesca asked into the phone, more disoriented by the fact that Ian had called her than the fact that her brain had just been jostled around her skull by Davie's abrupt change of direction. There was a long pause on the other end of the line.

"Francesca, are you drunk?"

"No," she said coolly. Who was he to take that judgmental tone?

"You're not driving, are you?"

"No, I'm not. Davie is. And he's not drunk, either."

"Who is that, 'Ces?" Justin called from the backseat. "Your father?"

Laughter burst out of her throat. She couldn't help it. Justin's question had been right on target, given Ian's holier-than-thou tone.

"Don't tell him you're about to get a tattoo on that gorgeous ass of yours!" Caden bellowed.

She winced. Her chuckle was a good deal weaker this time. Embarrassment flooded her at the thought of Ian overhearing her friends' joking. She was proving that she was just as immature and gauche as he thought.

"You're not getting a tattoo," Ian said.

Her grin faded. It'd sounded like a decree more than a clarification.

"Yes, I *am* getting a tattoo as a matter of fact," she replied fiercely. "And by the way, I wasn't aware that you had the right to dictate my life. I agreed to do a painting for you, not become your slave."

Caden, Davie, and Justin suddenly went dead silent.

"You've been drinking. You'll regret doing something so impulsive tomorrow," Ian said, a hint of anger ringing in his otherwise calm voice.

"How do you know?" she demanded.

"I know."

She blinked at his taut, quiet response. For a split second, she'd been convinced he was absolutely right. Irritation spiked through her. She'd been trying to forget about him all evening—trying to make the memory of him saying he wanted to fuck her vanish from her brain—and now he had to go and ruin everything by calling her and acting so infuriating.

"Did you call for a reason? Because if you didn't, I'm going to get a tattoo of a *pirate* on my ass," she said, randomly grabbing a detail from her friends' earlier banter.

"Francesca, don't—"

She tapped her finger on the screen.

"'Cesca, you didn't just—"

"She *did*," Caden interrupted, sounding stunned and a little impressed. "She just told off Ian Noble and hung up on him."

"Are you *sure* you want to do this, 'Cesca?" Davie asked, after she'd chosen a tattoo of a paintbrush.

"I . . . I think so," she mumbled, her bright burst of defiance in the face of Ian's arrogance flickering weakly.

"Of course she wants to do it. Here, have another drink for courage," Justin suggested wisely, handing her his etched silver flask.

"'Ces—" Davie said worriedly, but she took the flask. She winced at the feeling of the whiskey sliding down her throat. She hated hard liquor.

"I don't like my clients to drink alcohol before they go under the needle. Increases the bleeding," the bearded, shaggy-haired tattoo artist said gruffly as he entered the parlor where she stood with her three friends.

"Oh, well in that case—" Francesca hedged, seeing a possible out.

"Don't be a wuss," Justin insisted. "Bart isn't going to send you away because you've had a drink or two, are you Bart? He has serious ethics, but he forgets about them pretty quick when cash is on the line."

The tattoo artist glared at Justin, but Justin glared back.

"Lower your pants and get up on the table then," Bart snapped.

Francesca began to unbutton her jeans. Davie, Justin, Caden, and Bart watched as she laid, belly down, on the table.

"Here, let me help with that!" Caden volunteered eagerly as she began to work her jeans and panties down over her right buttock. Davie grabbed his arm, halting him with a forbidding scowl. Caden just shrugged, grinning sheepishly.

"Right here?" Bart asked roughly a few seconds later, stepping forward. His touch on Francesca's skin sent a shudder of revulsion through her.

"Yeah, you could make one of those gorgeous dimples above her ass a sort of paint pot for the dipping brush."

Francesca started at the sound of Justin's subdued tone. She peered sideways. Justin was regarding her partially bared ass with frank male interest.

"Maybe we should have a look at the other cheek just to get a clear picture of things," Caden suggested.

"Shut up, you two," she grated out. It made her uncomfortable to have Justin and Caden look at her that way. Maybe this was a stupid idea after all. Her thoughts scattered when Bart approached, a tube in his hand with a needle protruding out of it. She noticed that his fingernails were dirty. She feared needles. The whiskey seemed to boil in her stomach.

"Wait, you guys, I don't know about this," she mumbled, her eyes clamped shut as she tried to fight off a wave of dizziness.

"Come on, 'Cesca. Hey . . . *what the fuck*—"

Her head sprang up at the sound of Caden's surprised exclamation, the abrupt gesture sending her hair flying in her face and temporarily blinding her. She felt Bart's grip on her jerk as if someone had grabbed his arm.

"Let go of her this instant, or I swear I'll make it so you never live or work in this town again." Bart's grip on her jeans slackened. "Francesca, get up."

She followed Ian's concise instructions without thinking twice. She clambered off the table and pulled up her jeans, gaping at Ian's furious, rigid countenance in stark disbelief.

"What are you *doing* here?"

He didn't reply, just continued to pin Bart with a lancing stare. After she'd fastened her button fly, he put out his hand and grabbed her forearm. She stumbled after him when he began to stalk out of the parlor. He paused in front of the dazed trio of Davie, Caden, and Justin. He seemed to loom over them like a dark, forbidding tower.

"You three are her friends?" Ian asked.

Davie nodded, his face looking pale.

"You ought to be ashamed of yourselves."

Justin seemed to come to himself. He stepped forward as if to argue, but Davie cut him off.

"No, Justin. He's right," Davie said soberly.

Justin's face turned brick red, and he seemed prepared to argue, but Francesca stopped him this time. "It's okay, you guys. *Really*," she assured Justin tensely before she followed Ian out of the tattoo parlor, her hand firmly gripped in his.

She had trouble keeping up with his long-legged stride once they were walking along the dark, tree-lined street. She really didn't think she was that drunk, so why had the world taken on the sheen of unreality ever since she'd heard Ian's authoritative voice ordering Bart to let her go?

"Do you mind telling me what the hell you think you're doing?" she asked breathlessly as she trotted next to him.

"You dropped your guard again, Francesca," he said with tight-lipped fury.

"What are you talking about?" she demanded.

He came to an abrupt halt on the sidewalk, pulled her into his arms and swooped down, kissing her roughly. Sweetly. Why couldn't she tell the difference when it came to Ian's kisses?

She moaned into his mouth, her body going rigid before it molded against his long length. His taste and scent hit her like a tsunami of lust. Her nipples pinched tight, as if that sensitive flesh had learned to associate his taste with pleasure. He tore his mouth from hers way sooner than she'd expected—or wanted—given how hot and hard he felt.

*God, how she wanted him.* The blazing, obvious truth hadn't fully hit her until that moment. She'd never considered that a man like Ian would be interested in her sexually, so she hadn't allowed herself to fully acknowledge her desire for him.

The distant streetlight made his eyes gleam in his otherwise shadowed face as he looked down at her. She felt anger and lust resonating off his body in equal measure.

"How *dare* you even consider letting that unlicensed scumbag put a needle to your skin? And what kind of a little fool bares her ass to a roomful of slavering men?" he bit out.

She gasped. "*Slavering men* . . . those are my friends." She blinked, absorbing the rest of what he'd said. "Bart doesn't have a license? Wait . . . how did you even *know* where I was?"

"Your friend shouted the name of the tattoo parlor loud and clear while we were on the phone," he said scathingly, stepping away from her and leaving her flesh vibrating in protest at his absence.

"Oh," she said slowly. She watched as he lunged across the grass to the curb and whipped open the door to a dark, sleek, very expensive-looking sedan.

She looked at him warily. "Where are we going?" she asked.

"If you choose to get in, the penthouse," he said succinctly.

Her heart started to play a drum solo in her ears. "Why?"

"Like I said, you let your guard down, Francesca. I told you what I was going to do to you the next time you did. Do you recall?"

Her world narrowed to the glint of his eyes in his darkened face and her heartbeat crashing against her eardrums.

*Never leave yourself undefended, Francesca. Never. The next time you do, I will punish you.*

Warm liquid rushed between her thighs. No . . . he *couldn't* be serious. She experienced a wild thought that she should run back and participate in the silly, drunken antics of her friends.

"Get in the car or don't," he said, his voice less harsh than before. "I just want you to know what will happen if you do."

"You'll punish me?" she clarified shakily. "What . . . like *spank* me?" She couldn't believe she'd just uttered those words. She couldn't believe it when he nodded once.

"That's right. Your transgression has earned you a paddling, too. I'd give you more if you weren't a novice at this. And it will hurt. But I'll only give you what you can take. And I would never, *ever* harm or mark you, Francesca. You're far too precious. You have my word on that."

Francesca glanced at the lights of the distant tattoo parlor and back at Ian's face.

This was a madness she couldn't resist.

He said nothing—just closed the door after her when she got into the passenger seat of his car.

# Four

❧

The elevator door slid silently open, and she followed him into the penthouse, experiencing equal parts trepidation and excitement.

"Follow me to my bedroom," Ian said.

*My bedroom.* The words seemed to echo around her skull. She'd never been in this wing of the enormous condominium, she realized distractedly. She trailed behind him, feeling like a schoolgirl that had been caught red-handed. The undeniable anticipation she felt seemed to hint at something she couldn't quite fathom; somehow, she knew that if she crossed the threshold into Ian's private quarters, her life would change forever. As if Ian understood this, he paused in front of an ornately carved wood doorway.

"You've never done anything like this before, have you?" he said.

"No," she admitted, wishing her cheeks didn't flame. They both spoke in hushed tones. "Is that all right with you?"

"It wasn't at first. I want you so much, I've had to come to terms with your innocence, however," he said. She lowered her lashes. "Are you *certain* you want to do this, Francesca?"

"Just tell me one thing first."

"Anything."

"When you called earlier tonight . . . while I was in the car? You never said why you were calling."

"And you'd like to know?"

She nodded.

"I was here alone in the penthouse. I couldn't work or concentrate."

"I thought you said you were going to be entertaining."

"I did say that. But when it came down to it, I couldn't stop thinking about you. No one else would do."

She inhaled raggedly. It did something to her, to hear him be so honest.

"That's when I went into the studio and saw what you'd painted yesterday. It's brilliant, Francesca. All of a sudden, I knew I had to see you."

She dipped her head farther to hide how much pleasure she felt at his words. "All right. I'm sure."

It was he who hesitated, but then he reached and twisted the knob. The door opened. He waved his hand and she entered the room cautiously. Ian touched a control panel and several lamps glowed with golden ambient light.

It was a beautiful room—sedate, tasteful, luxurious. A couch and several chairs were arranged in a seating area before a fireplace immediately before her. A stunning flower arrangement of red calla lilies and orchids in an enormous Ming vase had been placed on a table behind the couch. Over the fireplace was an impressionist painting of a field of poppies; if she didn't miss her guess, it was an original Monet. *Incredible*. Her gaze caught on the huge four-poster carved bed to the right decorated, like the rest of the room, in a rich brown, ivory, and dark red color scheme.

"The lord of the manor's private quarters," she murmured, giving him a shaky smile.

He waved at another paneled door. She followed him into a bathroom that was larger than her bedroom. He reached into a drawer and withdrew a folded garment wrapped in clear plastic. He set it on the counter.

"Go ahead and shower and put on this robe. Only the robe. Leave all your other clothes. You'll find everything you require in these two drawers. You smell like stale smoke and whiskey."

"I'm sorry you disapprove."

"I accept your apology."

Her temper flared again at his quick reply. A small smile tilted his mouth when he saw the return of her defiance. He'd obviously expected it.

"You please me, Francesca. Beyond measure."

Her mouth fell open in surprise at the compliment. Would she ever learn to read him?

"But you must learn to please me in the bedroom," he said.

"I do want to," she said quietly, surprising herself by her candor.

"Good. Then to start, I'd like you to shower and put on this robe. When you've finished, come out to the bedroom, and I'll administer your punishment."

He started to walk out of the bathroom but paused. "Oh, and wash your hair, please. It ought to be a crime for all that glory to smell like an ashtray," he muttered under his breath before he exited, closing the door behind him with a brisk click.

She just stood there for a moment on the pristine marble tile floor. He thought her hair was glorious? She pleased him? How could he possibly be having thoughts like that about her? How could he kiss her until she thought she'd spontaneously combust and yet look at her at times like she was about as interesting as the paint on the wall?

She showered thoroughly, enjoying the experience more than she'd thought she would. The glass-enclosed stall steamed up quickly, the tendrils of warm mist seeming to caress and kiss her naked skin. It was nice to lather up with Ian's hand-milled English soap, cover herself in his clean, spicy scent. Fortunately, she'd shaved before she went out to McGill's, so she didn't have to worry about hairy legs.

*Would he spank her while she was naked?*

*Of course he would*, she answered herself as she slid open the glass door to the shower and exited. He'd told her point blank he wanted her naked beneath the robe. She extricated the garment now from the plastic wrapping. Was it brand new? Did he keep a supply of robes on stock for the women that he "entertained"? The thought made her a little sick, so she shoved it out of her brain, focusing instead on finding a comb for her wet hair, deodorant, a new toothbrush, and a bottle of mouthwash. Everything was arranged so neatly in the cabinet that she took special care returning the items to their proper places.

She folded her clothes and set them on an upholstered stool. Her reflection in the mirror caught her attention. Her image stared back at her, her eyes looking huge in her pale face, her long hair hanging damp. She looked a little scared.

*So what if I am scared?* she thought to herself. He'd said he was going to spank her and that it would hurt. She'd agreed to his apparent warped sexual practices because she wanted Ian so much.

It came down to which was greater: her fear or her desire to please Ian.

She walked toward the door and opened it. He sat on the couch, a tablet in his lap. He set the device on the coffee table when she walked into the room.

"I lit a fire for you," he said, his gaze running over her from head to foot. He was still dressed in the same clothing he'd been wearing when he'd barged into the tattoo parlor—dark gray tailored pants and a blue-and-white button-down shirt. His long legs were crossed negligently. He looked utterly at ease. The light from the fire flickered in his eyes. "It's cool tonight. I didn't want you to catch a chill."

"Thank you," she murmured, feeling awkward and uncertain.

"Take off the robe, Francesca," he said quietly.

Her heart skipped a beat. She fumbled with the sash and drew the robe off her shoulders.

"Set it down there," he instructed, pointing to the chair next to her, his gaze never leaving her. She draped the garment over the back of the chair and stood there, wishing the floor would open up and swallow her, studying the intricate pattern of the Oriental carpet beneath her like it held the secrets of the universe.

"Look at me," he said.

She lifted her chin. There was something in his gaze she'd never seen before.

"You're exquisite. Stunning. Why do you look down, as if you're ashamed?"

She swallowed thickly. The embarrassing truth came unstuck from her throat. "I . . . I used to be overweight. Until I was nineteen or so. I . . . guess I still have the confidence of my former self," she explained, her voice barely above a whisper.

A subtle of-course expression flickered over his bold features. "Ah . . . yes. But you seem so sure of yourself at times."

"That's not confidence. It's defiance."

"Yes," he mused. "I understand now. Better than you might think. It's your way of telling the world to go fuck itself for ever having the gall to look down its nose at you." He smiled. "Bravo, Francesca. It's time you learned how beautiful you are, though. You should always control the strengths you have available to you; never let them languish or, worse, allow others to be the ones to control them for you. Come stand before me, please."

She went to him on shaking legs. Her eyes went wide in confusion when he picked up a jar sitting on the cushion next to him. It was so small, and Ian had filled her senses so completely, she hadn't noticed it before. He unscrewed the cap and put a small dollop of the thick white substance on his forefinger. Glancing up, he noticed her bewilderment.

"It's a clitoral stimulant. It increases the sensitivity of the nerves," he said.

"Oh, I see," she muttered, even though she didn't.

His gaze dropped between her thighs. Her clit pinched with arousal, his stare stimulant enough. "I'm very selfish when it comes to you."

"What do you mean?" she asked.

"I always give a submissive pleasure if she pleases me. I'm not usually concerned if she feels it while she's being punished, however. She might have to endure it to get her reward. I find I've . . . changed my tune a bit with you, however."

"Submissive?" she asked weakly, her brain sticking on that part of his reply.

"Yes. I'm a dominant when it comes to sex, although I don't require elements of bondage or dominance to get me turned on. It's a preference for me, not a necessity." He sat forward on the couch so that his dark head was inches from her belly, his nose near her sex. She watched as he inhaled and then briefly closed his eyes.

"So sweet," he said, sounding a little undone.

She had no time to prepare for what he did next. He boldly plunged his thick finger between her sex lips and rubbed the cream thoroughly on her clit, his touch sure . . . electric. She bit her bottom lip to keep from crying out as concentrated pleasure shuddered through her. "Tonight, I'll punish you, and I won't lie. I'm going to enjoy it. Very much. But I want you to feel pleasure as well. Your nature will determine most of that, but this cream will help to swing things in the right direction," he said as he continued to massage the emollient onto her clit. He glanced up and saw her bewilderment. "I won't have you trained to fear this. I don't want you to loathe your punishments. In a word, I don't want you to fear me, Francesca."

He dropped his hand into his lap. His gaze returned to the juncture of her thighs. His nostrils flared, and his face went rigid before he stood abruptly.

"Over here, please," he said. She followed him to where he stood in front of the fireplace. Her feet stalled when she saw what he picked up off the mantel—a long black paddle. "Come closer. You may look at it," he said when he took in her wariness.

He held up the paddle for her inspection. "I have them made by hand. I just received this one last week. Despite my insistence that I would never really use it to the purpose, I had it made with you in mind, Francesca."

Her eyes widened at that.

"I'll make you burn with the leather side," he said quietly. Warm fluid gushed between her thighs at his matter-of-fact tone. He flipped his wrist, sending the paddle several inches in the air, catching it as it fell. She stared in amazement. The other side was covered with rich-looking dark brown fur. "And soothe the sting with the mink side," he finished.

Her mouth went dry, her mind blank.

"We'll begin now. Bend over and place your hands on your knees," he instructed.

She did as he demanded, her breath coming in erratic puffs. He came and stood beside her. She gave him an anxious sideways glance. The firelight gleamed in his eyes as his gaze ran over her body.

"God, you're beautiful. It frustrates me that you don't see it, Francesca. Not in the mirror. Not in other men's eyes. Not in your spirit." Her eyes fluttered closed when he reached out and stroked along her spine, then her left hip and buttock. A ripple of pleasure went through her. "You really do deserve to be punished for even considering marring this skin. So flawless. White. Soft," he said, his long fingers trailing along the crack of her ass. Her eyelids squeezed tight. Emotion surged in her throat, confusing her. He'd sounded genuinely awed.

She didn't unclench her eyelids until he stopped caressing her.

"Spread your thighs some and arch your back. It will give me pleasure to see your lovely breasts while I paddle you," he said. She adjusted her position, arching her spine. She gasped when he reached forward, cupping one of her breasts. He lightly pinched the nipple, and she quivered in pleasure.

"Now bend your knees ever so slightly. It will help you to absorb the blow. There. That's perfect. This is the position I expect you to take every time I paddle you." She missed his plucking fingers and warm palm when he transferred his hand to her shoulder. "You're skin is very delicate. I'll give you fifteen strokes."

The leather side of the paddle struck her ass. Her eyes sprang wide, and she cried out. The quick flash of pain faded quickly to a burn. "All right?" Ian asked.

"Yes," she replied honestly, biting her lower lip.

He swung again, this time smacking the tender curve of her lower buttocks. He caught her at the shoulder when she spilled forward slightly from the blow.

"You have a gorgeous ass," he said, his voice sounding low and husky. He smacked her again. "I approve of your running. Your ass is sleek and taut and plump. Ideal bottom for spanking."

She exhaled sharply as the paddle landed again. How was it that the burning sensation on her paddled ass was transferring to her clit? The nubbin of flesh felt hot and tingly. Ian landed another smack, and she couldn't repress her cry.

"Hurt?" he asked, pausing.

She just nodded.

"If it's too much, you can say so. I will soften the blows."

"No . . . I can take it," she said shakily.

He abruptly reached across her and cupped her hip, then pressed his crotch against her. She gasped at the feeling of his large cock throbbing against the side of her buttock. "There," he said. "That's how much you please me."

Her cheeks flushed with heat. The burn at her clit amplified. He backed up and landed the paddle again and again with sharp cracking sounds. By the time he was ready to administer the final stroke, her ass felt like it was on fire. Perhaps he noticed the tremble in her thighs, because he murmured, "Hold steady" and his grip on her shoulder tightened. He pressed the paddle into her stinging ass, as if carefully aiming his final blow. He lifted the paddle and swung.

A shout popped out of her mouth uncontrollably at the impact. He caught her as her body lurched forward.

"*Shhhh,*" he soothed. "This part is done."

She cried out shakily as he turned the paddle and began to rub the fur over her burning bottom. It felt so good. The tingle in her clit had become a plaguing, burning ache. She longed to touch herself, apply pressure. Was the paddling at Ian's hand responsible for her stark arousal, or was it the stimulation cream he'd applied? Just thinking of him rubbing the emollient on her clit with his thick, long finger made her moan. She felt feverish. Suddenly, he stopped stroking her ass with the fur and encouraged her to stand with the hand on her shoulder.

She turned toward him at his urging, feeling strange . . . dazed . . . aroused. He was no longer holding the paddle.

She just stood there, feeling overwhelmed, as he gently brushed her hair away from her face.

"You did extremely well, Francesca. Better than I'd ever dreamed of," he murmured, his thumbs brushed against her cheeks. "Are you crying because it hurt?"

She shook her head.

"Why then, lovely?"

Her throat was too constricted to speak. Besides, she didn't know what she would say, even if she could.

He cradled her jaw with his hands. Being overweight for most of her life, and tall for a woman, she usually felt huge and ungainly. But Ian was much larger than her. Next to him, she felt small, delicate . . . feminine. She suddenly realized his hands shook.

"Ian, your hands are trembling," she whispered.

"I know. I suspect it's from too much restraint. I'm doing everything in my power not to bend you over this very second and fuck you raw."

She blinked in shock. He seemed to notice and closed his eyes briefly, as if in regret at what he'd said.

"I would like to spank you over my knee now. It would please me a great deal to have you lay in my lap, at my mercy. But you are very tender. If the paddling was too much, I won't insist that we continue."

"No. I want to continue," she whispered hoarsely. She looked into his eyes. *I want to please you, Ian.*

His eyelids flickered. He continued to stroke her cheeks with the pads of his thumb, studying her closely.

"All right," he said finally, sounding resigned. "But come over to the fire first."

She followed him, but he detoured to the bathroom.

"I'll be right back," he said.

She waited by the fire, the heat from it combined with her body's arousal creating a strange sense of lassitude and excitement. He returned a moment later carrying a large comb.

"Let me comb your hair and let it dry a little by the fire."

She glanced at him in puzzlement. He gave her a small, sheepish smile.

"I have to do something to calm myself down a little."

She returned his smile shakily and, at his urging, turned her back to him. The paradoxical sensation of relaxation and sharp anticipation grew as Ian parted her hair into portions, gathered handfuls of it and slowly, sensually drew the comb through it. Her head drooped.

"Are you sleepy?" he murmured from behind her. His voice itself seemed to make her nipples prickle in awareness. The tingling burn on her clit was amplifying. *Wicked cream.*

"No, not really. It just feels good."

He drew the comb from root all the way to the drying ends that hung just above her waist. "I've never seen hair the like of yours. Rose gold," he mused gruffly. He caressed her tingling bottom, making her shiver, and exhaled as if in defeat. He set the comb on the mantel. "So much for the idea of that calming me down. Better just continue. Follow me."

He walked to the couch and sat on the middle cushion, his thighs slightly spread. He glanced down to his lap in a silent command. Her self-consciousness returned with a fury. She was naked and he was clothed and she had no idea what she was supposed to do. She swallowed nervously when she saw his erection pressed against the crotch of his pants, the shaft of his cock running along his left thigh. Staring at the sight as if mesmerized, Francesca came down on the sofa on her hands and knees, bridging his thighs, then began to lower. He opened his hand along her ribs and hip, guiding her into the location he wanted.

When she was settled, the lower swells of her breasts were pressed against his outer left thigh, her belly was draped across his thighs, and her bottom curved over his right thigh. He swept his hand along her waist, hip, and ass, and she felt his cock move against her ribs.

"This is the exact position you will take for an over-the-knee spanking. Do you understand?" he asked, his warm hand now caressing her ass. The nerves there still prickled, not uncomfortably, from her paddling.

"Yes," she said, nodding at the same time. Her hair fell into her face.

"There's just one other thing," he said. He carefully smoothed back her hair and gathered it at one shoulder. He lightly pushed with his hand at the back of her skull, and her forehead pressed into the soft fabric of the couch. "I will often blindfold you for a spanking—I want you to be totally focused on my hand, the feeling of your punishment . . . my arousal. But for now, keep your face down and close your eyes."

She clamped her eyelids shut and squirmed in his lap. She felt him go still.

"What? Did that arouse you?"

"I . . . I guess so," she said, confused. She supposed he was right. A stab of lust had gone through her at his words. Why would that be? "It must be the cream," she muttered.

He resumed stroking her ass. "Let us pray it's more than

the cream," he murmured, and she heard the smile in his voice. "Now stay completely still, or I will spank you harder."

He lifted his hand and slapped her right buttock, then her left, then her right in quick succession, the cracking noises echoing in her ears even when he paused. She bit her lip to stop herself from moaning. He was obviously experienced at spanking; his strokes were precise, firm, quick but unhurried. He landed another flurry of blows, covering all of her ass and upper thighs. Her bottom began to burn in a different way than it had from her paddling. Ian's hand created a slow, simmering kind of heat that resonated off her skin. She also learned quickly enough where he liked spanking her most—on the round lower curve of her buttocks. Every time he smacked her there, his cock lurched against her and she felt the tension leap in his thighs. His slapping hand grew every bit as hot as her ass. Heat resonated from his cock, as well, through the fabric of his trousers and into her skin.

He landed a slap on the bottom curve of her ass, then suddenly grabbed the entire buttock and lifted his groin, grinding her against his cock. Her shaky moan mingled with his low, feral growl. Her clit went from a burn to a sizzle at the pressure and the sharp awareness of his arousal. She felt dizzy, fevered, like she was on fire from the inside out. She wanted nothing more than to twist in his lap and get pressure on her clit . . . to hump against his cock like a wild, shameless thing. He lowered his hips and resumed spanking her. When he paused after a rapid round of slaps and again molded a buttock greedily into his palm, her control broke.

"Oh, Ian . . . no. I'm sorry, but I can't do this anymore,"

she moaned, writhing in his lap. He stilled, her ass cheek still squeezed in his palm.

"It's too painful?" he asked tautly.

"No. I can't stay still anymore. I *burn*."

For an anxious few seconds, he didn't move. Then he let go of her ass and slid his hand between her thighs. She whimpered in frantic agony when his fingertips skimmed across her outer sex. His cock leapt against her.

"*Christ* . . . you're soaking wet," she heard him utter. He sounded stunned. She was too excited to be embarrassed . . . too far gone. She gasped when he put a hand on her shoulder, urging her upward.

"Come here," he ordered in a hard tone.

Oh, no. Had she irritated him again? She pushed herself onto her knees with his assistance.

"Straddle my lap," he ordered.

Her nearly dried hair scattered around her shoulders and back as she did his bidding. He placed his hands on her hips, settling her hot, burning bottom on his thighs. He smoothed her hair behind her shoulders, exposing her breasts. His gaze fixed on them, his upper lip curling slightly in a snarl.

"Look at that," he said under his breath. "Your nipples are nearly as red as your ass." His gaze flickered up to her face. "So are your cheeks, Francesca . . . and your lips. You enjoyed being punished, lovely. And that pleases me so much. It's going to be so good fucking your wet little pussy."

Her sex clenched painfully. He opened his large hands around her ribs and lowered his head, bringing her breasts to him. She tensed, expecting the delightful, forceful suck he'd treated her nipple to in the workout room, but instead, he pursed his lips slightly, kissing first one turgid nipple, then the other sweetly. "So perfect," he whispered. His hands moved rapidly. Her excitement spiked when she realized he was unfastening his pants. He slipped just the crest of her breast between his lips, sucking lightly and whipping the flesh with his wet, warm tongue.

Her clit sizzled, tormenting her. Her hips twitched in his lap. She couldn't control herself. She clutched onto his head and made a wild, fevered sound in her throat. He lifted his head and glanced up at her face.

"It's all right," he soothed, his blue eyes alight with lust. He moved his hand, sliding it down her heaving belly. She whimpered when he slid his finger between her creamy labia. He touched her clit. That's all. One touch.

She exploded like a cache of dynamite.

She hardly knew what she was doing, so much pleasure swamped her existence at that moment. For a moment or two, he continued to stroke her clit as climax thundered through her. Distantly, she was aware of him cursing harshly and pushing her closer to his body, as if he wanted to absorb her shudders of orgasm. She shook against him, helpless in the face of roaring pleasure.

He shifted his hand. She cried out when she felt him push a thick finger into her vagina.

The next thing she knew, she was sprawled on the couch next to Ian, and he was staring down at her as she gasped for air.

"You've never been with a man. Have you?"

Her soughing breath froze. It hadn't really been a question but an accusation.

"No," she said, resuming her panting. Why was he looking at her like that? "I *told* you."

Fury sparked in his eyes. "When exactly did you tell me you were a virgin, Francesca? Because I sincerely doubt I would have let such a crucial piece of information slip my mind," he snarled.

"There—before we came into the room tonight," she said, pointing stupidly at the door to his bedroom. "You asked if I'd ever done this before, and I said—"

"I meant had you ever let a man punish you. Dominate you. Not— *fuck*," he muttered in a blistering fashion. He stood jerkily and began to pace in front of the fireplace, raking his fingers through his short hair. He looked a little demented.

"Ian, what—"

"I knew this was a mistake," he muttered bitterly. "Who did I think I was kidding?"

Her lips parted in dawning shock. He thought this had been a mistake? He was rejecting her? *Now?* Fresh images and sensations bombarded her consciousness, memories of how wild she'd been, how out of control with lust and need.

She relearned a painful childhood lesson at that moment, one that she would have done well to recall tonight. It caused no greater shame than to express need, to make oneself vulnerable, and then to have that pure, honest emotion thrown back at you as if it was garbage.

Tears blinding her eyes, she reached desperately for the cashmere throw blanket at the corner of the couch. She whipped it around her naked body before she stood. Ian came to a halt when he saw what she was doing.

"What are you doing?" he barked.

"I'm leaving," she replied, stalking toward the bathroom.

"Francesca, stop right this second," he commanded, his voice quiet . . . intimidating.

She paused and glanced back at him. Hurt and fury rose in her, tightening her throat. "You just lost the right to order me around," she grated out.

He blanched.

She turned just in time to prevent him from seeing the gathered tears spill out of her eyes. Ian Noble had seen enough of her vulnerability for one night.

He'd seen more than enough for a lifetime.

# Part Three

## Because You Haunt Me

# Five

Two days later, Ian watched out the window of his limo as Jacob Suarez turned down a street lined with attractive brick townhomes. An associate had informed him that David Feinstein had inherited the residence from his deceased parents, Julia and Sylvester, but that David could likely have afforded the affluent Wicker Park residence on his own. Feinstein's art gallery was doing very well. Apparently Francesca's roommate possessed excellent taste and good business sense along with a refined, quiet, thorough manner that appealed to many wealthy art connoisseurs.

Ian had also been admittedly relieved to learn that David—or "Davie," as Francesca called him—was gay. *Not that her housemates' sexual preferences mattered much*, Ian thought, as Jacob came to a halt. He'd proved firsthand the other night that Francesca's housemates weren't touching anything they shouldn't.

He'd learned firsthand that he *had* been touching things he shouldn't, he added to himself, with the result that he was wearing a frown by the time his driver opened the car door for him.

The image of Francesca's shattered expression as she'd left his bedroom the other night burned his consciousness for the thousandth time. He'd watched, fuming silently, as she'd fled the penthouse, wanting to stop her but knowing by the fixed, stubborn expression on her beautiful face that she wouldn't listen to him at that moment. He'd been furious at her for putting them in this situation, and furious at himself for seeing only what had been convenient for him to see.

Yes, he'd understood she was innocent, but not to *that* degree. He'd known it was best just to let her go. For good.

Yet here he stood.

He rapped at the dark green painted wood door with a strange sense of resigned determination. From where did this strange obsession come? Did it have to do with the fact that Francesca had caught him unaware in her painting, years ago? Her possession of him had been fleeting, but alarmingly concise.

He wanted to both punish her and possess her in turn for her innocent infraction.

He understood from Mrs. Hanson that Francesca hadn't been to the penthouse to paint. Her avoidance of his residence made him angry—irrationally so, but logic didn't seem to be quieting the emotion. Ian still hadn't decided, as he knocked again on the door, if he was here to apologize and assure Francesca that she would never again be bothered by his attentions, or if he wanted to convince her at all costs to let him touch her again.

The friction of his uncustomary ambivalence had him so

wound up and frustrated, even Lin, who was usually a soothing balm to his occasional bad moods, was steering clear of him like a category-five hurricane.

The front door swung open and a brown-haired man of medium height, who looked younger than his twenty-eight years, regarded him somberly. He must have recently come from his gallery, because he was dressed for work in a dark gray suit.

"I'm here for Francesca," Ian stated.

Davie glanced into the interior of the house anxiously, but then nodded once and stepped back, granting Ian entrance. He led him into a tastefully decorated living room.

"Have a seat. I'll see if Francesca's home," Davie said.

Ian nodded and unbuttoned his jacket before he sat. He distractedly picked up a catalog from the cushion next to him, listening all the while to the sounds in the large town-home, not hearing footfalls on the stairs. The pages of the catalog had been folded back, as if someone had recently been studying the contents. It was a listing of paintings that would be going up for sale at a local auction house.

Davie reentered the living room a minute later. Ian glanced up and set aside the catalog.

"She says she's busy," Davie said, looking vaguely uncomfortable with his messenger errand.

Ian nodded slowly. It'd been what he'd expected.

"Will you please do me the favor of telling her that I'll wait until she isn't busy?"

Davie's Adam's apple bobbed when he swallowed. He left the room again without replying and returned a minute later, still with no Francesca. He gave an apologetic grimace. Ian smiled and stood.

"It's not your fault," he assured. He held out his hand. "I'm Ian Noble, by the way. We've never been properly introduced."

"David Feinstein," Davie said, shaking his hand.

"Would you sit with me for a bit while I wait?" Ian asked.

Davie looked a little nonplussed by the hint that Ian was, indeed, staying, but was too polite to argue. He sat in a chair across from the coffee table.

"I can understand why she's upset with me," Ian said, crossing his legs and once again picking up the catalog.

"She's not upset."

Ian glanced up at Davie's words.

"She's furious. And hurt. I've never seen her so hurt."

He paused, waiting for the sting that resulted from Davie's honesty to fade. For several seconds, neither of them spoke.

"I treated her in a manner I shouldn't have," Ian admitted finally.

"Then you should be ashamed," Davie said, anger ringing in his quiet voice. Ian recalled that he'd said something similar to Davie and Francesca's other two roommates at the tattoo parlor.

"I am," Ian said, listening carefully. He closed his eyes briefly in regret at what he heard. He thought of Francesca's freshness the other night, her sweetness. The memory of her pussy had been somehow lodged in his brain like a tenacious virus, only growing more vivid as he tried to rid himself of it: the silky, rose-gold hair between lithesome white thighs; creamy, plump labia; the slickest, tightest little slit he'd ever touched. He recalled spanking her and how he'd loved it . . . how *she* had. "Unfortunately," he continued, addressing

Davie, "my shame wasn't sufficient to keep me away. I'm beginning to think no amount of it would."

Davie looked startled. He cleared his throat and stood.

"Maybe I'll just go and see how Francesca is coming along on that . . . project she's working on."

"Don't bother. She's not here anymore," Ian murmured.

Davie did a double take and paused next to his chair. "What do you mean?"

"She snuck out the back door about twenty seconds ago, if I'm not mistaken," he said, idly flipping the pages of the catalog. He took advantage of Davie's apparent shock to hold it up.

"Yours?" Ian asked.

Davie nodded.

"I see what you must have been looking at. When did Francesca paint it?"

Davie blinked and seemed to come to himself. "About two years ago. I sold it at Feinstein last year. I was glad to see it come back on the market at this estate sale auction. I'd like to get it back, sell it for a price that's worthy of the piece, and give the extra profit back to Francesca." He frowned. "She's had to sell a lot of her paintings over the years for practically nothing. I hate to think of what she must have let a couple of them go for before I met her. Francesca was living hand to mouth for years before we became friends. I may not have been able to sell her work for the price I think it's worth, seeing as she's still a relative unknown, but at least I gave her more than the price of a bag of groceries." He nodded at the catalog. "If I can get ahold of this particular piece, I'm convinced I can sell it for an excellent price. Francesca is starting to make a name for herself in art circles.

I'm sure the award she won from you, and the subsequent recognition, has helped."

Ian stood and buttoned his jacket. "I'm certain your support of her work has as well. You've been a good friend to her. Would you give me your card? There's something I'd like to speak to you about, but I'm running late for a meeting."

Davie looked distinctively undecided, then reached into his pocket with the air of a man who would have to confess something major to a loved one later.

"Thank you," Ian said, accepting the card.

"Francesca is a wonderful person. I think . . . I think it'd be best if you stayed away from her."

He narrowly studied Davie's anxious yet determined expression for several seconds. Davie looked away uncomfortably. Francesca's friend saw a lot more with those gentle eyes than he must typically reveal to his well-heeled clients. Bitterness rose in him at his own lack of decency by contrast.

"You're undoubtedly right," Ian said as he began to move toward the door, unable to keep the note of resignation out of his tone. "And if I were a better man, I'd follow that advice."

This is what things had come to: She was working like a thief in the night. The painting had called her back, despite the untenable circumstances surrounding it.

Francesca mixed her colors rapidly, using the glow from the small lamp she'd placed on a desk in order to see, desperate to capture the exact hue of the midnight sky before the light changed. The rest of the room was swathed in

shadow, allowing her to better see the brooding, glowing
buildings against the backdrop of a velvety night sky. She
stopped abruptly and glanced back toward the closed door of
the studio, waiting tensely, her heart starting to pound in
her ears in the eerie silence. Shadows seemed to thicken
and form at the back of the room, tricking her eyes. Mrs.
Hanson had assured her that she'd be alone in the penthouse
tonight. Ian was in Berlin, and Mrs. Hanson was going to be
visiting a friend in the suburbs.

Nevertheless, she hadn't felt alone for a second since
she'd stepped off the elevator into Ian's territory.

Could a place be haunted by a living person? It was as if
Ian lingered in the luxurious penthouse, his presence
weighing on her mind, on her very skin, making it prickle in
awareness as if from an invisible touch.

*Stupid*, Francesca chastised herself, putting brush to
canvas and making long, energetic strokes. It'd been four
nights since she'd stood naked and exposed in Ian's bedroom. He'd tried to contact her. He'd called her on several
occasions, and there had been that embarrassing episode
at her house when she'd run out the back door like a fool.
She'd been overwhelmed by the idea of seeing him
again . . . afraid.

*You're afraid of what will happen if you see him, listen to
him. You're afraid you'll end up begging him like a fool to finish
what he'd started the other night.*

Her arm made a slashing motion before the canvas.
*Never.* She'd never beg that arrogant asshole.

The hair on her arms stood up, and she glanced over
her shoulder again. Hearing and seeing nothing out of the
ordinary, she returned her focus to the painting. She

shouldn't have come back here, but she had to finish this piece. She'd never rest if she didn't, and it wasn't because Ian had already paid her. Once a painting had gotten in her blood, it gave her no freedom until it was complete.

She told herself to concentrate. The ghost of Ian—her own ghosts—made focusing a trial.

*You stood there like an idiot while he whacked you with a paddle; you laid in his lap, stark naked, and let him spank you like a child.*

Shame flooded her consciousness. Was she so desperate, following a majority of life spent overweight, to have a man like Ian show desire for her that she was willing to sacrifice her dignity? How else would she have allowed herself to be demeaned that night? How far would she have gone if Ian Noble had said he wanted it?

Her thoughts mortified her. She took out her anguish on the canvas, finally finding the coveted zone of creative concentration she desperately sought. An hour later, she set aside her paint palette and wiped the excess paint off her brush. She rubbed her shoulder to ease the tension from her almost constant sweeping strokes. Her friends were always surprised when she told them how physically taxing painting a large piece could be.

The hair on her nape stood on end and her massaging fingers stilled. She spun around.

He wore a white shirt that coalesced faster out of the shadows than the rest of his dark apparel. He was jacketless, and his sleeves had been rolled back. The gold of his watch glinted from the darkness. She stood there unmoving, feeling as if she were dreaming.

"You paint as if a demon was driving you."

"You sound as if you know what that's like," she replied in a tight voice.

"I think you know I do."

The image of Ian walking alone through the deserted streets popped into her mind's eye. She crushed down the wave of compassion and deep feeling the memory always evoked.

She let her hand drop from her aching shoulder and turned toward him. "Mrs. Hanson said you would be in Berlin tonight."

"I was called back early for an emergency."

She just stared at him for a moment, speechless, seeing the lights from the skyline reflected in his eyes.

"I see," she finally said, turning away. "I'll be going then."

"How long do you plan to avoid me?"

"As long as you exist?" she countered quickly. Hearing the hint of anger in his voice acted like a lit match to her own fury and confusion. She started to stride past him, her head lowered, but he reached out and wrapped his hand around her upper arm, halting her.

"Let go of me." Her voice sounded angry, but she was horrified to feel tears burn in her eyes. It was bad enough to see him again, but why did he have to sneak up on her like this, catching her unaware and vulnerable? "Why can't you just leave me alone?"

"I would if I could, trust me," he replied, his voice as frigid as a hard winter's frost. She twisted in order to escape, but he firmed his grip, bringing her next to his body. The next thing she knew her face was pressed to his hard chest and crisp shirt, and his arms surrounded her.

"*I'm sorry*, Francesca. Truly, I am."

For a moment, she lost all of her will and leaned into him, giving him her weight, accepting his strength and warmth. Her body shuddered with emotion. She focused on the sensation of his hand stroking her hair. Later, when she analyzed her temporary lapse, she realized that it'd been his tone that'd done it. He'd sounded as barren and as hopeless and as desperate as she felt. He wasn't the bad guy, she conceded. He hadn't demeaned her by giving her a glimpse of true desire that night.

She was just furious at him because he didn't want her. Enough to overlook her inexperience, anyway.

Emotion swelled tight in her chest. She pushed against him, finding the weight of her need unbearable. He released her slowly, still keeping her within the circle of his arms.

She lowered her head and swiped at her cheeks, refusing to look up at him.

"Francesca—"

"Don't say anything else, please," she said.

"I am not the man for you. I want to make that very clear."

"Right. Crystal clear."

"I'm not interested in the type of relationship a girl of your age, experience, intelligence, and talent deserves. I'm sorry."

Her heart squeezed in pain at his words, but she knew he was right. Ridiculous to think otherwise. He wasn't for her. How obvious could that be? Hadn't Davie been telling her that repeatedly for the past few days? She stared blankly at the pocket of his dress shirt. She longed to escape; she longed to stay there in the shadows with Ian holding her. He caught her chin and applied pressure, forcing her to look up at him. When she did so warily, she saw his slight wince.

She broke out of his arms abruptly, despising the vision of his pity. He caught her forearm, and she paused.

"I am abominable when it comes to women," he bit out. "I forget dates and appointments. I'm rude. The only thing I'm truly focused on is sex . . . and getting my way," he stated harshly, making her start and stare back at him in shock. "My work is everything to me. I *can't* lose control of my company. I *won't.* This is who I am."

"Why are you bothering to tell me this then? Why did you even come in here tonight?"

His face and jaw tensed, as if he suppressed himself from spitting out something bitter. "Because I couldn't stay away."

She wavered for a few seconds, confused. The memory of her mortification the other night swept over her once again, clearing her brain. "If you can't stay away, you're going to have to find another artist or move my work space."

"Francesca, do *not* walk out on me again," he said, his tone intimidating. Again, her feet wavered.

She barely grasped at her dignity sufficiently to make it out the door.

Several nights later, that empty ache still lingered, but Francesca had managed to compartmentalize it . . . contain it in her mind and spirit. It hurt the worst when her phone rang and she saw that it was Ian trying to contact her. It cost her more than she could put into words to ignore those calls.

It was a lot less burdensome to ignore her heartache on a rowdy Saturday night while waitressing at High Jinks. She was so busy, she had no opportunity to consider Ian or the painting or her regret as the lounge swung into high gear at about two o'clock in the morning. High Jinks was a popular last stop on the Wicker Park–Bucktown bar circuit. It catered to young urban professionals and older students. While many bars closed by two, three, or four, High Jinks stayed open until five a.m. on Saturday nights, serving devoted partiers and carousers. Saturdays always exhausted Francesca, and tested her patience, but she tried not to miss opportunities to work one; the tips were typically three times what she'd make on any other night of the week.

She set her tray down at the waitressing station and called out her order to the owner, Sheldon Hays—the older, frequently cantankerous, occasionally cuddly-as-a-teddy-bear owner, who was bartending tonight.

"You're going to have to tell Anthony to hold them at the door," she shouted over the loud music and the din of the crowd. "We've got to be at capacity."

She took a sip of the club soda she kept at the station and leaned over the bar when Sheldon waved her in, as if he wanted to say something important. "I need you to run over to the corner and buy all the lemon juice they've got on the shelf," he yelled, referring to the local convenience store that stayed open all night. "That idiot Mardock forgot to put lemon juice on the order, and I'm having a rush on sidecars."

She sighed. Her feet were already killing her, and she didn't treasure the idea of walking the required five blocks. Still . . . it'd be awesome to breathe the fresh autumn air for a few minutes and give her eardrums a break from the loud music . . .

She nodded at Sheldon and whipped off her apron. "Tell Cara to pick up my area?" she shouted.

Sheldon's nod told her not to worry, he'd take care of everything. He handed her a couple twenties from the register, and she plunged through the dense crowd.

There were only four bottles of lemon juice left on the shelf of the convenience store. The sleepy-looking cashier roused himself enough to locate another bottle in the storage room. As she walked back to High Jinks a few minutes later, carrying her purchase, she noticed the sidewalk was crowded with people walking toward their cars and the El stop. *Where are they all coming from?* Francesca thought in confusion as she reached the block where High Jinks was located. She paused at the corner as she saw a couple dozen more people exit the bar, the heavy wood door slamming shut behind them.

"What's going on at High Jinks?" she asked a passing trio of men.

"Fire in the storage room," one of the men said, his sour tone making it clear he didn't appreciate his late-night carousing being cut short prematurely for safety reasons.

"*What?*" Francesca called, but the men just passed her and kept walking. She rushed toward the bar, alarmed. She didn't smell any smoke or hear any sirens. Their bouncer, Anthony, was nowhere in sight when she opened the door and peered inside the establishment.

*No one* was in sight.

She paused inside the entrance of the bar, staring, aghast. The bar, which had been jam-packed with customers just twenty minutes ago, was now completely empty and quiet. Had she just entered the twilight zone?

She noticed movement behind the bar. Much to her

mounting amazement, she saw Sheldon calmly cleaning glasses.

"What the hell is going on, Sheldon?" she demanded as she approached. Surely he wouldn't be standing there so nonchalantly if there were a dangerous fire in the back room?

Her boss glanced up at her and set down a beer glass. "I was waiting to make sure you got back okay," he said, drying his hands on a towel. "I'll just go to my office. Give you a little privacy."

"But what—"

Sheldon pointed over her shoulder as if by way of explanation. Francesca spun around. She froze when she saw Ian sitting at one of the tables, his long legs bent before him. A large partition had blocked him from her view when she'd entered. Her heart did its typical bounce upon observing him. Even through her shock, she registered that he was wearing jeans and that there was a shadow of whiskers on his jaw. He looked very un-Ian-like, a little scruffy, a lot dangerous . . . still sexy as hell. Had he been walking the streets alone again tonight?

He pinned her with his stare as he waited calmly.

"He wants to talk to you in private," Sheldon said quietly from behind her. "He must want to *a lot.* I'm sorry if you don't want to talk to him, but he's not really the kind of man that a guy like me can refuse."

"It was his money you couldn't refuse," Francesca muttered acidly under her breath, anxiety and irritation spiking her tone. *What was he doing here? Why wouldn't he leave her alone so that she could finish the process of forgetting him? Had he actually gone to the trouble of closing down this bar because he wanted to* speak *to her?*

*You'll never forget him. Who are you kidding?* she thought bitterly as she turned to deposit the lemon juice on the bar. Sheldon responded to her frown with a sheepish "what's a man to do?" glance before he walked toward his office. She could only imagine what Ian had paid the bar owner to get him to clear the place out on his most lucrative night.

She took her time unloading the grocery sack and lining the bottles of lemon juice on the counter, her neck prickling with awareness of his gaze on her. Let him put up with the inconvenience of having to wait for a few seconds longer. He couldn't have everything in the moment that he wanted.

*He cleared out the entire bar just to talk to me?*

She silenced the excited voice in her head with effort. When she could think of nothing else to do to avoid him, she turned and slowly walked to him.

"Out slumming, are we? This is going a little far to convince me that you don't disdain a cocktail waitress's service, isn't it?" she asked sarcastically as she approached.

"I didn't come here to have you serve me. Not tonight."

Her gaze shot angrily to meet his stare at his innuendo. She expected to see his usual subdued amusement at her defiance. Instead, she saw fatigue and . . . was it resignation? In *Ian Noble*?

"Sit down," he said quietly.

They regarded each other silently for a moment once she'd sat. A thousand questions zoomed around her brain, but she stifled them. He'd behaved outrageously, clearing out hundreds of people from the bar and shutting down a business in order to see her at the precise moment he desired it. He was going to have to be the one to break the silence after all that; she refused.

"It just won't do," he said. "I know that I'll hurt you. I know there's a good chance you'll end up despising me . . . fearing me, even. But I still can't stop thinking about you. I must have you. Completely. Frequently . . . and at all costs."

She listened to her heart drumming in her ears for several strained seconds, trying to gather herself. How could she be so furious at a man and still want him so much it was like some kind of biological mandate, like breathing?

"I'm not for sale," she finally said.

"I know that. The cost I'm referring to can't be paid with money."

"What are you talking about?"

Leaning forward, he rested his forearm on the table. He wore a dark blue cotton T-shirt shirt with short sleeves. The Rolex was absent. She recalled vividly how stirred she'd been the first time she saw his large hands and muscular forearms. She still was. More so now that she knew what he could do with them.

"I suspect I'll lose a bit of my soul in this thing with you. I already have, just by the fact of my being here tonight," he spoke intently, his stare boring into her. "I know I'll take a piece of yours."

"You know no such thing," she countered, even though she feared he was right. "Why are you so convinced that you'll hurt me?"

"Many reasons," he said so surely that her heart sank another inch. "I already told you one—I'm a control freak. Did you know that when I sold Noble Technology Worldwide in a public offering, I was offered the job of CEO?" he asked, referring to the hugely successful social-media company that he'd founded and built, then sold. "It was a very cushy position, but I turned it down. Do you know why?"

"Because you couldn't stand the idea of a board of directors being able to veto your decisions?" she asked irritably. "You have to be in complete control at all times, don't you?"

"That's right. You've come to understand me better than I'd realized." Why was his smile both bitter and pleased? "I'll tell you something else that you should know. I was with a virgin once. She became pregnant and I ended up marrying her. It was a catastrophe. She couldn't abide my controlling manner, and I'm not just talking about in the bedroom, although that arena was bad enough. She thought I was the worst kind of pervert."

Her lips parted in amazement. There could be little doubt, given his intense, almost angry expression, that he was telling the truth.

"What happened to the baby?" she asked, her brain sticking on that morsel of unexpected information about Ian Noble's life.

"Elizabeth lost it. According to her, it was because of me."

She stared, seeing the disdain in his expression, the flicker of anxiety in his eyes. He was quite sure that Elizabeth had been wrong in her assertion. Still . . . the seed of doubt remained.

"By the end of our marriage, my wife was afraid of me. I believe she considered me the devil incarnate. Perhaps she was partially right. But mostly, I was a fool. A twenty-two-year-old fool."

"And I'm a twenty-three-year-old one," she replied.

His expression flattened; his brow furrowed. She could tell he hadn't quite understood her meaning. Some instinct inside her warned her of what he was about to say. The sinking feeling of inevitability she also experienced told her, loud and clear, how she would respond.

His mouth hardened. "To make things clear—I want to possess you sexually. Totally. On my terms. I offer you pleasure and the experience. Nothing else. I have nothing else *to* offer."

She swallowed with difficulty upon hearing the words she'd both anticipated and dreaded. "You make it sound like you want to do this to get me out of your system."

"Perhaps you're right."

"That's not very flattering, Ian," she said, sounding exasperated when she was truly stung.

"I didn't come here to flatter you. I will make the experience as rich and rewarding as I can for you, but I'm not offering you false promises. I respect you that much, at least," he added under his breath.

"And this experience will end whenever you've had your fill?"

"Yes. Or whenever you have, of course."

"When will that be? After one night? Two?"

His smile was grim. "I think it might take longer than that to purge you from my mind. A good deal longer. But again, I can't say for certain. Do you understand me?"

Her heart now threatened to burst out of her rib cage, as if it were on the front line of the war that raged inside her. It was a mistake, and she knew this. And yet . . .

"Yes," she said. The tension coiled tighter with every erratic beat of her heart.

"And do you agree to this?"

"Yes." *What the hell was she doing?*

"Look at me, Francesca."

She looked up, her chin tilted at a defiant angle. His gaze ran over her, searching. "I told you once before that you shouldn't let your anger make you foolish," he said softly.

This, more than anything, infuriated her.

"If you think I'm too much of a child to make a wise decision, then you shouldn't have asked the question," she grated out. "I'm giving you my answer. It's up to you whether you accept it or not. *Yes,*" she repeated.

He closed his eyes briefly.

"All right," he said after a moment, calmly, and it was as if she'd imagined all the conflict in him. "That's settled then. I have an important meeting in Paris on Monday morning that I can't delay. I'd like to leave first thing in the morning."

"Okay," she said dubiously, thrown off by his abrupt change of topic. "So . . . I'll see you when you get back."

"No," he said, standing. "Now that things have been decided, I can't wait much longer. I want you to come with me. Can you get away for a few days?"

*Was he serious?*

"I . . . I think so. I don't have class on Mondays, but I have one on Tuesday. I suppose I could miss one class, though."

"Good. I'll pick you up at your house at seven o'clock tomorrow morning."

"What should I bring?"

"Your passport. You have one, don't you?"

She nodded. "I studied for a few months in Paris during my senior year. It's current."

"Just your passport and yourself then. I'll supply everything else you need."

She countered her breathlessness at his reply with practicality. "Can't we leave later? It's nearly three o'clock in the morning already."

"No, seven o'clock. I have a timetable. You can sleep on the plane. I have work I need to do on the flight anyway." His gaze flickered over her face as he stood. His hard expression softened slightly. "You *will* sleep on the plane. You look exhausted."

She started to say that he looked tired as well, but realized he no longer did. All the fatigue she'd sensed in him at the beginning of their conversation seemed to have vanished . . .

Now that he'd gotten his way.

"Come here, please."

Something about his quiet, authoritative tone made her breath freeze in her lungs. She'd just agreed to stop running from him, and he knew it. Did he want to prove his power over her?

She stood up and approached him slowly. He opened his hand at the side of her skull, his fingers furrowing through her upswept hair. His gaze traveled over her face, those dark-angel eyes glittering with an emotion she couldn't understand.

He lowered his head and covered her mouth with his. He bit at her lower lip and she opened, gasping. His tongue sunk into her mouth. Heat rushed through her sex. Ah, God. *This,* she could understand. Wisdom shriveled in the heat of this kind of desire. She moaned, the freshness, the immediacy of her need stinging her like a slap against tense muscle.

By the time he lifted his head a moment later, things were damp and warm between her thighs.

"I want you to know," he said next to her quivering, sensitized lips, "that I would have stopped it if I could. I'll see you in a few hours."

She stood there, unable to take a full breath until after the front door of the bar had slammed shut behind him.

# Six

Francesca got into bed that night, but she never dropped off into sleep. Her mounting excitement wouldn't let her. She got up before her alarm went off, made and drank coffee, ate some cereal, and showered. Staring into her closet, she felt a sinking sensation. What did she have to wear that was suited to a getaway with Ian Noble?

Since absolutely nothing she owned was probably appropriate, she ended up picking her favorite pair of jeans, boots, a tank top and a sage-green tunic that did good things for her complexion. If she couldn't be sophisticated, she might as well be comfortable. She took time styling and straightening her long hair—which was rare for her to do—and applied some mascara and lip gloss. She studied herself in the mirror when she was done, shrugged, and left the bathroom.

It would have to do.

Despite the fact that he'd told her she wouldn't need anything, she did pack a duffel bag with underwear, a few changes of clothing, jogging apparel, some toiletries, and her passport. She set her bag and her purse by the door and walked into the kitchen, where Davie and Caden sat at the kitchen table. Davie was always an early riser, even on a Sunday, but Caden was not. Francesca recalled that he was burning the midnight oil this weekend to get a project done for work.

"I'm glad I caught you guys," she said, pouring herself another cup of coffee, even though she knew she shouldn't drink it; nervousness about Ian being there in a few minutes was starting to make her stomach roil. "I'm going away for a few days," she said, turning to face her friends.

"Going to Ann Arbor?" Caden asked before he sliced his fork into a syrup-drenched waffle. Her parents lived in Ann Arbor, Michigan.

"No," she said, avoiding Davie's curious stare.

"Where, then?" Davie asked.

"Um . . . Paris."

Caden stopped chewing and blinked at her. She started when she heard a brisk knock at the front door. She set down her coffee cup on the counter with a loud thud, causing coffee to splash up on her wrist.

"I'll explain when I get back," she assured Davie as she used a towel to dry her forearm. She began to edge out of the kitchen.

Davie stood. "Are you going with Noble?"

"Yes," Francesca said, wondering why she felt so guilty at the admission.

"Then call me as soon as you can," Davie insisted.

"All right. I'll call you tomorrow," she assured.

The last image she saw as she left the kitchen was Davie's

worried expression. *Damn.* If Davie looked concerned, it was usually with good reason.

*Was this one of the stupidest choices she'd ever made in her life?*

She flung open the front door and all of her thoughts about Davie and wisdom versus foolishness vanished. He stood on the front steps, wearing a pair of dark blue pants, a white button-down shirt open at the collar, and a casual hooded jacket. Well, even if he did look good enough to eat, at least he wasn't wearing one of his immaculate suits, given how she'd dressed.

"Are you ready?" he asked, his blue eyes running over the length of her.

She nodded and reached for her duffel bag and purse. "I . . . I didn't know what to wear," she said, shutting the door behind her.

"Don't worry about it," he said as he took her bag. He glanced back at her as she followed him down the steps. Her heart leapt when he gave her one of his rare smiles. "You're perfect."

Her cheeks turned hot at his compliment, and she was glad he turned away. He introduced her to his driver, Jacob Suarez, a middle-aged Hispanic man with a nice smile. Jacob immediately took and stowed Francesca's bag while Ian opened the car door for her.

She slid onto one of the sofalike seats, absorbing the luxurious surroundings of the elegant limo. The impressions that struck her the most were the cushy, buttery softness of the seat and the smell—leather mixing with Ian's spicy, clean male scent. The screen on the built-in television monitor was off, but Ian's laptop was opened on the table between the two leather seats. Classical music resounded sedately from the surround sound stereo. Bach—the Bradenberg concertos, she recognized after a few seconds. It seemed a perfect choice for Ian—the man and the music were both mathematically precise and intensely soulful. A chilled, newly opened bottle of her preferred brand of club soda sat on the table near his computer.

Ian removed his jacket and slid into the seat across from her.

"Did you sleep much?" he asked her once he was settled and the car began to move smoothly down the street.

"A little," she lied.

He nodded, his gaze skimming over her face. "You look pretty. I like your hair that way. You don't usually straighten it, do you?"

Her cheeks warmed again, this time in embarrassment. "It takes a lot of time."

"You have a lot of hair," he said, a small smile playing on his lips. Perhaps he noticed her blush. "Don't worry, I'm not complaining. I'm fond of every strand of it. Would you mind very much if I worked?" he asked her with abrupt reluctance. "The more I can get done here and on the plane, the better I can totally focus on you when we get there."

"Of course," she assured, set a little off balance by his rapid change of topic.

She didn't mind him working. She liked being able to watch him while his singularly intense focus was elsewhere. *He wore glasses?* She watched him don a pair of sleek, stylish lenses. His fingers flew over a keyboard fast enough to make the most proficient administrative assistant envious. Strange . . . to think that those large, masculine hands could move with so much fleet precision.

He would use those hands to make love to her sometime very soon. She couldn't believe it. Her first lover was going to be Ian Noble.

A heavy, warm sensation settled in her lower belly and sex. She took a swig of her icy club soda and forced herself to stare out the window. A swarm of questions buzzed in her head. By the time they'd passed the Skyway and headed several miles into Indiana, she couldn't contain one any longer.

"Ian, where are we going?"

He blinked and glanced up, giving her the impression of rising out of a deep trance of concentration. He glanced out the window.

"To a small airport where I keep my plane. We're nearly there," he said, hitting a few buttons on his computer and lowering the monitor.

"You own a plane?"

"Yes. I have to travel quite a bit, sometimes on the spur of the moment. A plane is an absolute necessity."

Of course, she thought. He would never be satisfied waiting for anything.

"I want to show you something tonight in Paris," he said.

"What?"

"It's a surprise," he said, his shapely, firm lips forming a small smile.

"I don't really like surprises," she said, unable to look away from his mouth.

"You'll like this one."

She looked up into his eyes and saw the sparkle of amusement there, along with something else . . . white-hot heat. She had a feeling his stark declaration about her desires was dead-on.

As usual.

A few minutes later, she stared out the window, her mouth hanging open. "Ian, what are we *doing*?" she exclaimed as Jacob drove them up a ramp.

"Driving onto the plane."

They rose into the sleek jet that sat on the tarmac of a small airport. She felt like Jonah going into the belly of the whale. "I didn't know you could do that."

She stared at him, stunned, when he chuckled, the low, rough sound causing the skin at the back of her neck and along her arms to prickle in awareness. He reached for her hand across the table and drew her onto the seat next to him. He placed his hand on her jaw, lifted it, and swept down to cover her mouth with his, sandwiching her lower lip between his own, nibbling at her. He dipped his tongue into her mouth and moaned, his coaxing kiss transforming into a voracious one.

He lifted his head when he heard Jacob's door slam. The car had come to a full halt. She stared up at him, half-slain by his unexpected kiss.

He leaned up and grabbed his briefcase at the same moment Jacob rapped once and then opened the door. Francesca followed him out of the car, feeling dazed, excited, and extremely aroused.

The jet was unlike anything she'd ever seen. They took an elevator up to a second level and entered a luxurious compartment with a wet bar, a full entertainment center and shelving unit, a built-in leather couch, and four luxurious, wide chair recliners. Expensive drapery covered the windows. She would never have guessed in a million years she was on a plane.

She followed Ian into the compartment, her hand in his. "Would you like something to drink?" he asked politely.

"No, thank you."

He chose a pair of recliners that faced each other, a table between them.

"Sit there," he said, nodding at the chair to the left. "There's a bedroom, but I'd prefer if you rested here. The chair fully reclines, and there's a blanket and pillows in that drawer there," he said, pointing at the gleaming mahogany entertainment center.

"There's a *bedroom?*" she asked, experiencing a ridiculous wave of embarrassment at just saying the word.

He sat in his own chair, immediately pulling his computer and some files out of his briefcase. "Yes," he murmured, glancing up at her. "But I would prefer if you slept where I can see you. You are free to use the bedroom, however, if you prefer. It's in there," he said, pointing to a mahogany door. "And so is the bathroom, if you should need it."

She turned away so that he wouldn't notice her breathless reaction to his words. She returned a moment later carrying the soft blanket and pillow she'd retrieved from the drawer. He said nothing, but she noticed his small smile while he started up his computer.

She sat and studied the electronic control panel on the arm of the lounger, figuring out how to recline it. She started to do so.

"Oh, and Francesca?" Ian asked, not looking up from his computer screen.

"Yes?" she asked, lifting her finger from the control button.

"Take off your clothes, please."

For several seconds, she just stared. Her heartbeat began

to throb in her ears. Perhaps he'd noticed her frozen state, because he glanced up, his expression calm. Expectant.

"You can put the blanket on while you sleep," he said.

"Then why do you want me to take off my clothes, if I'm going to be covered up anyway?" she blurted out, confused.

"I'd like to know you're available to me."

Liquid heat surged through her sex. *God help her.* She must be as much of a sexual deviant as Ian was, to respond so wholly to a few uttered words.

Slowly, she rose on trembling legs and began to strip.

He hit the Send button on his computer, zooming off a detailed memo to his senior staff. For the fiftieth time in the past five minutes, he glanced over at the outline of the shapely feminine form curled beneath the blanket. The tiny, even rise and fall of the cover told him she still rested soundly. He could have guessed within seconds the precise moment Francesca had finally succumbed to sleep about five hours ago. He was that aware of her. If he was having trouble concentrating—if he suffered—he could blame no one but himself. He'd been the one to insist she take off her clothes. He'd been the one to sit and stare, hypnotized, as she'd removed item after item, while his mouth went bone-dry and his heartbeat began to throb along the shaft of his cock.

Every time he recalled her lowered gaze and pink cheeks, her long, glorious hair swishing next to her narrow waist, her bare, thrusting breasts and luscious, fat nipples, legs that could make a man weep they were so long, shapely, and supple—and worst of all—the soft-looking, red-tinted, golden hair at the juncture of her thighs, the amount of it sparse enough so that he could clearly see her plump labia and slit, the blood began to pound fiercely again in his cock. Since he was thinking of the vision constantly, he'd pretty much sustained an erection for the past five hours.

It would be hell not to touch her until tonight, but he'd promised himself to make this experience as special for her as he could. An even worse torture would be to touch and not take her. He whipped off his glasses and stood.

It would be a delicious torture. And he was used to suffering.

He lowered onto the seat next to her. She lay on her side, facing him, her face still and lovely in repose. Her lips were a shade deeper in color than their usual lush pink hue. His cock leapt against the restraining fabric of his boxer briefs. Was she, by chance, aroused as she slept?

He grabbed the blanket at her shoulder and gently, slowly lowered it all the way to her knees, teasing himself as her splendor was fully revealed inch by tantalizing inch. He smiled to himself when he saw that her nipples were, indeed, puckered and tight. What sorts of erotic journeys did an innocent like Francesca take in her sleep? His gaze flickered and stuck on the trim, strawberry-blonde thatch of hair between her white thighs. Was that moisture gleaming in the slit? Surely it was his imagination . . . wishful thinking after hours of tortuous arousal.

He spread his hand over the smooth expanse of her flat belly. She said that she'd been overweight as a child, but he could see no evidence of it. Losing the weight so young must have saved her from stretch marks. Her skin looked flawless. She shifted slightly in her sleep, her face tightening momentarily, before she sighed and sunk back into slumber.

His hand lowered across her satiny, warm skin. He reached, sliding his finger into that silky hair, burrowing it between those sex lips that had been haunting him night after night.

He grunted in satisfaction. It hadn't been his imagination. Her juices coated his finger. He moved, finding her clit, teasing it with his fingertip, calling her to him from the realms of her dreams. He spread his hand for a moment over her outer sex, arousal stabbing at his cock. Things were warm, wet, and divine in the crevice.

His gaze was on her face when she opened her eyes. For a second, they just stared at each other as he stimulated her clit with his finger. He watched as fresh color rushed into her cheeks and full lips.

"Is this what you wanted me available for?" she muttered, her voice low and thick with sleep.

"Perhaps. I can't stop thinking about your pussy. I'm looking forward to spending as much time as possible buried in it." He flicked her clit with extra pressure, and watched, fascinated, as she gasped and bit her fleshy lower lip. Christ. He was going to kill himself feasting on her. She was a never-ending orgy of delight all encapsulated in one gorgeous, fascinating woman.

"Roll onto your back," he said, his finger still plucking and stroking between her creamy labia, his gaze intent on her face as he tightly examined her subtle reactions to his manipulations, gauging her . . . learning her. His hand moved with her as she lay on her back. "Now spread your legs. I want to look at you," he instructed gruffly.

She widened her slender thighs. His gaze fixed between her legs, he reached for the control panel, lowering the footrest of her recliner. He knelt before her, his body between her spread knees. He removed his hand and stared at her sex, utterly spellbound.

"I usually ask women to shave for me," he said. "It increases the sensitivity. Makes a woman totally available to me."

"Is that what you'd like me to do?" she asked. His gaze zoomed up to her face. Her dark, velvety eyes shone with arousal.

"I don't want you to change a thing. You have the prettiest pussy I've ever seen. I may be demanding, but even I know better than to mess with perfection."

Her throat convulsed as she swallowed. He reached and used his fingers to widen her sex lips, exposing glistening dark pink folds and the tiny slick opening to her vagina. His cock lurched viciously, knowing precisely where it wanted to be at that moment. He longed to push his tongue into that hole, as well, to have her juices sliding down his throat. He craved it.

But if he tasted her, he'd take her, there and now. That was a certainty.

He reluctantly rose and sat again next to her on the wide seat of the lounger. He leaned down and kissed her parted lips lightly as he resumed stroking her clit.

"Does this feel good?" he asked, his gaze running over her flushed face.

"Yes," she whispered, the fervency of her response convincing him as much as her pink-stained lips, cheeks, and heaving breasts. He flicked at her clit, giving it a rapid, gentle, back-and-forth lashing with the ridge of his forefinger. She gasped, and he smiled. She was so wet that he could hear himself moving in her creamy flesh.

"You're so responsive. I can't wait to see what heights of pleasure I can evoke out of your beautiful body."

He rubbed her clit hard, pulsing her.

"Oh . . . Ian," she moaned, twisting her hips, lifting her pelvis against his hand to increase the pressure.

"It's all right, lovely," he whispered next to her mouth, plucking at her lips as she panted. "I grant you what I deny myself for now. Come against my hand."

He watched, raging in an inferno of arousal, as the tension in her sleek, soft body broke, and she cried out in pleasure. He smelled it-the unique perfume that rose off her skin when she climaxed. Unable to stop himself, he seized her mouth with his own, silencing her whimpers almost angrily, slaking his thirst on her sweetness.

When her shudders of orgasm finally quieted, he tore his mouth from hers and buried his head in the crook of her shoulder and neck, panting nearly as much as she was. After a moment, he acknowledged that he wouldn't be able to quiet his raging erection while inhaling her intoxicating scent.

He straightened and rose, walking back over to his lounger.

"We'll be arriving in Paris soon," he murmured, tapping his keyboard and noticing that the finger he'd used to make her come still gleamed with her abundant juices. He closed his eyes briefly to shut out the arousing image. It lingered, seemingly burned into the back of his shut eyelids. "Why don't you go into the bedroom, wash up, and change."

"Change?" she asked.

He nodded and dared to look at her naked beauty flushed from climax. *Christ,* she was beautiful: the dark eyes of a nymph, the pale, soft skin of an Irish maid, the lithe, voluptuous body of a Roman goddess. He resisted a nearly imperative, dark urge to pounce and sink his cock into the heaven of her like some kind of wild animal.

"Yes. I'm taking you out to dinner," he said, shortly, instead.

"You bought me something to wear?" she asked, nymph eyes going wide in surprise.

He smiled grimly and returned his attention to his work with monumental effort. "I told you I'd give you everything you needed, Francesca."

She must be becoming jaded, because when she saw the opulent, surprisingly large aircraft bedroom suite, she wasn't stunned. Maybe that was because she was getting to know Ian better and knew he'd never be satisfied with anything but tasteful perfection. She opened the closet door, as he had instructed her to do, and saw a black knit evening dress hanging in the closet.

"Lin says to tell you that everything else you'll need is either inside the top drawer in the bureau in the closet or on top of it," Ian had said a moment ago. "She says the temperature in Paris will be a pleasant sixty-five degrees tonight, so the hosiery is optional," he added, glancing at his cell phone, clearly reading a text from his efficient assistant.

Inside the built-in mahogany drawer, she found an exquisite black lace panty-and-bra set. She held up another ebony lace item, confused, before realizing it was a garter. A wave of embarrassment went through her at the thought of Lin arranging to have this intimate apparel made available to her. Perhaps she ran such errands for Ian all the time?

Her fingers ran over the last item in the drawer—silk stockings. She glanced nervously at the closed door to the bedroom and stuffed the garter back into the drawer. More than likely, Ian would want her to wear them, but she had no idea how to put on a garter and stockings. Besides, Lin had said hosiery was optional, hadn't she?

On top of the bureau were two boxes—one made of cardboard and one of leather. She opened the shoe box first and gave a muted *oooh* of pleasure when she saw a black suede, super-sexy pair of pumps nestled in tissue. Francesca wasn't a shoe hound by any stretch of the imagination—her jogging shoes were the most prized and expensive item of clothing that she owned—but a woman's heart must beat in her breast after all, because she couldn't wait to try on the sophisticated heels. She noticed the brand and winced. The shoes probably cost more than she paid for three months' worth of rent.

Feeling both thrilled and wary, she opened the last box. The pearls shone luminously against the black velvet lining. The necklace was an exquisite double strand, the earring studs simple. Both items epitomized understated class.

Was this all part of her payment for agreeing to let Ian possess her sexually for a period of time? The thought sickened her a little.

Setting aside the leather box, she hurried to the bathroom and dropped the blanket she'd wrapped around herself. A hot shower would ground her, help her cast off this surreal sense that kept creeping upon her stealthily. She twisted a towel around her head to keep her hair dry and turned on the water.

She walked out of the bathroom several minutes later, her skin gleaming with the scented moisturizer she'd found on the counter. She still hadn't decided about what to do with all the expensive clothing and jewelry Ian had provided.

"We're about an hour out. We got lucky. Conditions were perfect," an electronic-sounding male voice said, making her start in shock. She realized it was the pilot, who spoke through a microphone somewhere. She thought of Ian out in the other compartment, glancing up, rising out of his concentration as he worked when he heard the pilot.

He expected her to wear the clothing he'd bought for her. He would be irritated if she refused. She didn't want to do battle with him. Not tonight. Besides, hadn't she agreed to this mad venture?

*Hadn't she sold her soul to the devil in order to fully experience his touch?*

She discounted the melodramatic thought and went over to the drawer and withdrew the silk-and-lace panties.

Twenty minutes later, she walked out of the bedroom, feeling extremely self-conscious and quite sure she was going to fall on her face in the luscious heels she wore. Ian gave a brief sideways glance when she approached, then did a double take. His expression went flat as his gaze ran over her.

"I . . . didn't know what to do with my hair," she said stupidly. "I have some plastic clips in my purse, but they didn't seem—"

"No," he said, standing. Even wearing the heels, she was still a good three or four inches shorter than him. He reached out and ran his fingers through her unbound hair. At least she'd straightened it this morning, and it wasn't too wild after her sleep. It looked smooth and lustrous next to the black dress after she'd combed it, but even Francesca—a complete fashion idiot—knew that the outfit she wore called for an upswept style. "We'll get you something suitable to put it up tomorrow. But for tonight, you can wear it down. A crown of glory like that is never out of place."

She gave him an uncertain smile. His blue-eyed stare flickered over her breasts, waist, and belly, making her flush with heat. Francesca had been part horrified, part thrilled to see how closely the thin knit wraparound dress hugged her figure. The dress was elegant sexiness defined—or at least it would have been on somebody else, she amended as she studied Ian's face anxiously.

Was he pleased? She couldn't quite tell from his shuttered expression.

"I'm not going to keep any of these things," she said quietly. "They're too much."

"I told you that I could offer you two things in this venture."

"Yes . . . pleasure and experience."

"It gives *me* great pleasure to see your beauty revealed. As for you, the clothing is part of the experience, Francesca." His gaze sunk over her, and he released her hair, his jaw looking tight. "Why don't you just enjoy it? God knows I will," he said roughly before he turned and walked into the bedroom, closing the door behind him with a brisk click.

An hour and a half later, Francesca sat in the midst of the Palais-Royal, at a private table at the historic Le Grand Véfour restaurant. She was so overwhelmed by the voluptuous

artwork, the sumptuous food, the anticipation of what was
to happen later that night . . . by Ian's steady, heavy-lidded
gaze on her that she could barely swallow the food, let alone
appreciate it as she should have.

The entire experience was a barely restrained seduction.

"You hardly ate," Ian said when the waiter came to clear
the remains of their entrées.

"I'm sorry," she said sincerely, cringing inwardly at the
mere thought of how much money and effort had been
wasted on her sublime meal of beef bourguignon and mashed
potatoes with oxtails and black truffles that was about to be
tossed into the garbage. The waiter spoke inquiringly to Ian
in French, and he replied in kind, never removing his gaze
from her. One thing was for certain: She'd barely been able
to take her eyes off him ever since he'd emerged from the
plane's bedroom earlier, wearing a modern version of a
classic tuxedo with a black necktie instead of a bow, a pristine
white shirt, and a handkerchief tucked into his pocket. He'd
turned every head in the exclusive restaurant while escorting
her to the table.

"Are you nervous?" he asked quietly once the waiter had
walked away.

She nodded, intuiting his meaning. She stared at his
long, blunt-tipped fingers idly circling the base of his
champagne flute and repressed a shiver.

"Would it help you any to know that I am as well?"

She blinked and looked into his face. His blue eyes were
like gleaming crescents beneath hooded lids.

"Yes," she blurted out. And after a pause, "You *are?*"

He nodded thoughtfully. "With good reason, I think."

"Why do you say that?" she asked in a hushed tone.

"Because I'm so excited to have you, there's a chance I'll lose control. I never lose control, Francesca. Never. But I might tonight."

A thrill of anticipation went through her at the hint of dark warning in his tone. Why did the thought of seeing Ian undone by passion stir her to her very core? She glanced up in surprise when the waiter returned and placed a beautiful dessert before her and a silver coffee service before Ian.

"Est-ce qu'il y aura autre chose, monsieur?" the waiter asked Ian.

"Non, merci."

"Très bien, bon appétit," the waiter said before he walked away.

"I didn't order this," Francesca said, staring dubiously at the dessert.

"I know. I ordered it for you. Eat some. You're going to need the energy, lovely." She glanced up from beneath her lashes and saw his small smile. "It's the house specialty, *palet aux noisettes*. Even if you were stuffed to the gills, you'd want this. Trust me," he urged softly. She picked up her fork.

She gave a small moan of sensual delight a moment later as the combination of cake, chocolate mousse, hazelnuts, and caramel ice cream blended on her tongue. He smiled, and she smiled back impishly, forking another portion with more enthusiasm.

"You speak French very well," she commented before she slid the fork between her lips.

"There's no reason I shouldn't. I'm a French citizen, as well as one of the United Kingdom. It's a tie-up as to whether my native tongue is French or English. The townspeople spoke French where I grew up; my mother English."

She paused in her chewing, recalling what Mrs. Hanson had told her about Ian's grandparents finally finding their daughter in northern France and discovering a grandson as well. She longed to ask him more about his past.

"You never speak of your parents," she said cautiously, taking another bite.

"You never speak of yours, either. Aren't you close with them?"

"Not really," she said, hiding her scowl at the realization he'd changed the topic away from himself. "My whole life I thought they disapproved of me because I was overweight, or so I thought. Now that I'm not overweight anymore, I've had to come to the conclusion that they just don't get me. Period."

"I'm sorry."

She shrugged, toying with her fork. "We get along all right. We're not feuding or anything dramatic. It's just . . . painful to be around them."

"Painful?" he asked, pausing as he raised his cup to his mouth.

"Not *painful*, I guess. Just . . . awkward," she said, lifting her fork.

"Don't they appreciate what a gifted artist you are?"

She closed her eyes briefly in gustatory bliss as the flavors melted on her tongue. "My artwork just annoys them. My father more than my mother," she said after she'd squeezed every last bit of sweet succulence out of the confection and swallowed. She slicked her thumb along her lips, capturing a dollop of milk-chocolate mousse with the tip of her tongue. God, it was delicious.

She glanced up when Ian tossed his napkin on the table.

"That's it. Time to go," he said, pushing his chair back.

"What?" she asked, startled by his abruptness.

He came around to help her with her chair. "Never mind," he said grimly, taking her hand. "Just remind me the next time I'm grasping for restraint not to order you chocolate."

Pleasure flooded through her at his comment, the potency of it far greater than even that conferred by the delectable *palet aux noisettes*.


"Where are we staying?" Francesca asked him several minutes later as Jacob zoomed down a darkened, nearly deserted Rue du Faubourg Saint-Honoré. Unlike their trip from the airport to the restaurant, when he'd sat next to her in the limo, her hand fast in his, Ian now sat across from her, his manner distant as he stared broodingly out the window.

"At the Hotel George V. But we're not going there yet."

"Then where—"

The car slowed. He nodded significantly out the window. Her eyes widened as she recognized the shape and ornate architecture of the Second Empire building that overtook the entire city block.

"*The Musée de St. Germain?*" she asked, joking. She was familiar with the museum of Greek and Italian antiquities from her undergraduate days of study in Paris. The museum was housed in one of the few remaining privately held palaces left in the city.

"Yes."

The laughter died on her lips. "Are you serious?"

"Of course," he said calmly.

"Ian, it's past midnight in Paris. The museum is closed."
Jacob halted the limo. A moment later, the driver rapped
once on the back door before he opened it. Ian got out and
took her hand as she alighted on the tree-lined, dimly lit
street. He smiled when she stared dubiously up at him, and
then took her hand.

"Don't worry. We won't stay long. I'm as eager to get
back to the hotel as you are. More so," he added under his
breath. He guided her onto the sidewalk and to a door
couched within a deep stone arch. Much to her surprise, an
elegant man with salt-and-pepper hair immediately answered
when Ian knocked on the thick wooden door.

"Mr. Noble," he greeted with what appeared to be a
mixture of pleasure and respect. They entered, and the man
closed the door behind them before tapping his fingers over
a keypad. Francesca heard a lock click loudly. A green light
began to blink on what appeared to be an elaborate security
system.

"Alaine. I can't thank you enough for this special favor,"
Ian greeted warmly when the other man turned. The two
men shook hands within a dimly lit, white marble entryway
as Francesca glanced around, confused but curious. This was
*not* an entrance on the public tour.

"Nonsense. It is nothing," the man said in a hushed tone,
as if this were some kind of clandestine nighttime mission.

"How is your family? Monsieur Garrond is well, I trust?"
Ian asked.

"Very well, although we are both like displaced cats at the
present moment as we have major renovations done on our
apartment. We're getting too old to have our routines
disrupted, I'm afraid. How is Lord Stratham fairing?"

"Grandmother says he's a bear following his knee surgery, but his stubbornness is an asset in this case. He's recovering well."

Alaine chuckled. "Please give both of them my regards the next time you see them."

"I shall, but you will likely see them before I do. Grandmother plans to attend the opening of the Polygnotus exhibit next week."

"We are fortunate," Alaine said, beaming, and Francesca couldn't help but feel he meant it entirely. His gaze landed on Francesca with polite interest. She clearly sensed his intelligence and curiosity.

"Francesca Arno, I'd like you to meet Alaine Laurent. He's the director of the St. Germain."

"Ms. Arno, welcome," he said, taking her hand. "Mr. Noble tells me you are quite a talented artist."

Warmth rushed through her at the knowledge Ian had complimented her behind her back. "Thank you. My work is nothing to what you come into contact with every day in your work here. I loved coming to the St. Germain when I was an undergraduate studying in Paris."

"It's a place of inspiration as well as art and history, no?" he said, smiling. "I hope the piece that Ian shows you tonight will provide its own special inspiration. We are quite proud to have her here at the St. Germain," he said mysteriously. "I will leave you to your own devices then. I have everything arranged for you. Please be assured that you won't be disturbed. I have shut off surveillance of the Fontainebleau salon for your short visit to afford you some privacy. I'm working in the east wing, if you should need me," Monsieur Laurent said.

"We won't. And I want to thank you again for this consideration. I know it was an unusual request," Ian said.

"I have complete faith that you wouldn't make it without excellent reason," Monsieur Laurent said smoothly.

"I will call you when we are finished with the viewing. It won't be long," Ian assured.

Monsieur Laurent gave a slight bow that seemed completely natural and graceful and walked away.

"Ian, what are we doing?" Francesca whispered heatedly as he started to lead her down a dim, arched passage in the opposite direction from which Monsieur Laurent had departed.

He didn't immediately reply. It was difficult to keep up with his long-legged stride in her stiletto heels. They quickly started to penetrate the passages into the bowels of the huge, venerable building, eventually entering museum areas that she recognized. It was a salon-style museum versus a gallery. The St. Germain's interior as a palace residence had been preserved. Walking through the rooms gave the impression of going back in time to a posh, elegant, lived-in seventeenth-century palace showcasing priceless furnishings and incredible pieces of Grecian and Roman art.

"Do you want me to paint something else for you, and the inspiration is here at the St. Germain?" she prodded.

"No," he said, not looking at her as he pulled her along, the sound of her heels on the marble floor echoing off the high ceiling and sweeping marble arches.

"Why are you in such a hurry?" she asked incredulously.

"Because I told myself I wanted to give you this experience, but I'm also eager to get you alone at the hotel." He'd said it so matter-of-factly that she was rendered speechless as they passed salons to her right and left, the images of frozen statuary only increasing her sense of unreality. She'd thought things had been surreal all day, but walking through a mostly deserted, hushed palace's halls at Ian's side had her truly disoriented. He marched into a familiar long, narrow salon and suddenly came to a halt.

He'd stopped so suddenly, she nearly spilled forward in her high heels, her hair falling into her face. She noticed where Ian was staring and glanced up, dazed. Her mouth fell open in awe.

"Aphrodite of Argos," she gasped.

"Yes. The Italian government has sent her on loan to us for six months."

"*Us?*" she whispered in a hushed tone as she stared at the priceless statue of Aphrodite. Moonlight shown through the arched column of skylights built into the ceiling, bathing the salon and statue with soft luminescence. The gracefully twisted torso and sublime expression worked into the cold white marble was breathtaking as it glowed from the draped shadows.

"The St. Germain Palace belongs to my grandfather's family. James Noble is the patron of the museum. His collection is one of his many contributions to the public—an offering to those who share in his love of antiquities. I sit on the board for the St. Germain, as does my grandmother."

She stared up at him, his open admiration and reverence as he studied the statue taking her by surprise. *Pleasant* surprise. He was typically so stoic. There were depths to Ian Noble she couldn't fathom.

"You adore this piece," she stated more than asked, recalling the miniature of it in his Chicago penthouse.

"I would own it if I could," he admitted. His smile struck her as a little sad. "But you can't own Aphrodite, can you? Or so they tell me."

She swallowed. A strange, light-headed feeling came over her as she stood there with this compelling, enigmatic man.

"Why do you love this particular piece so much?" she asked.

He glanced down at her, moonlight making his bold features as compelling as Aphrodite's.

"Aside from the artistry and beauty? Maybe because of what she's doing," he said.

Her brows knitted together as she looked again at the statue. "She's bathing, isn't she?"

He nodded. She sensed his gaze on her face. "She's partaking of her daily ritual of purity. Every day, Aphrodite washes herself clean and arises anew. It's a nice fantasy, isn't it?"

"What do you mean?" she asked as she looked up at him, ensnared by his shadowed visage and the moonlit gleam in his eyes. He reached up. His fingertips were warm on her cheek, but she shivered nonetheless.

"That we could wash away our sins. I just keep compounding mine, Francesca," he said quietly.

"Ian—" she began, compassion going through her at his tone. Why was he so convinced he was tainted?

"Never mind," he said, interrupting her. He turned to fully face her, putting his hands on her waist and pulling her against his body. Her eyes widened. With her heels on, she was aligned higher on his body than usual. She could feel his firm testicles pressing against the top of her mons and the dense ridge of his cock riding along his left thigh. *How could he possibly be so hard when they'd barely been touching? Was this Aphrodite's work?* She wondered in a flight of fancy.

His hand opened along the side of her jaw, lifting her face to the moonlight. Her heart started to drum out a primal beat against her breastbone. He thrust his hips, making the air pop out of her lungs at the evidence of his full arousal. His fingers flexed into her hip. His head dipped, and he brushed his lips against hers, as if he tried to inhale her gasp.

"God I want you," he said almost angrily, before he captured her mouth with his, his tongue parting her lips. Coming into full contact with him was like suddenly being submerged in a fire. The sheer force of him, his taste, inundated her. She staggered slightly in the heels, and he caught her tighter against him, her body molding against stark, unrelenting muscle and rigid male arousal. She'd never experienced so much concentrated male desire. Had this inferno been building in him all day? All week?

She moaned into his mouth, her female flesh melting against his hard male heat. His hands shifted to the belt of her wrap dress. When he sealed their kiss roughly a moment later, Francesca felt dizzy with excitement. He stepped back. The sides of her dress gaped open, exposing her bare skin to moonlight. He pushed the material aside, exposing her near-nude body. His gaze ran over her. Her breath stuck in her lungs when she saw the reverence in his rigid features mingling with blazing lust. His nostrils flared slightly.

"I want you to remember this for the rest of your life," he said abruptly.

"I will," she replied without hesitance—who could

possibly *forget* such a charged experience?—although she was bewildered by the meaning behind his words.

"Sit here," he said, putting his hands on her hips.

She opened her mouth to express her confusion, but he was guiding her to the marble pedestal surrounding Aphrodite. She sat and felt the cold, hard marble beneath the thin fabric of her dress. Ian put his hands on her knees and spread them. He knelt before her.

"Ian?" she asked confusedly.

Were his hands shaking as he slid her panties down her thighs and over her knees? Her sex clenched tight in rising anticipation.

"I thought I could wait. I can't," he muttered, and she heard the harsh regret in his tone. He looked into her face as his hands caressed her thighs and hips, and she felt herself heating the cool marble. "If I don't taste you now, I think I'll die. And I if taste you, I won't be able to stop. I'm going to have to fuck you here and now."

"Oh, God," she moaned shakily. She felt the increasingly familiar surge of liquid heat between her thighs. His dark head lowered to her lap. His hands parted her farther for his ravishment. Her eyes sprang wide at the sensation of the tip of his warm, sleek tongue burrowing between her labia, rubbing and stabbing at her clit.

She grasped at his thick, crisp hair and whimpered. Her head fell back. In the hazy midst of her voluptuous ecstasy, she glimpsed Aphrodite watching her initiation with calm, supreme satisfaction.

# Part Four

## Because You Must Learn

# Seven

She felt herself melting on the cold marble slab, losing all sense of self, living only to experience the next electrical thrust, the next sensual slide of Ian's tongue on her sex. She tangled her fingers in his hair, loving the texture. How did human beings manage to live and work and sleep and eat when so much distilled pleasure was available to them?

Perhaps *he* was the answer to her question. Everyone didn't have such a talented, glorious lover available to them. For surely Ian's tongue and mouth must be the most skilled on the planet at giving pleasure . . .

He urged her with his hands, and she leaned farther back on the pedestal, bracing herself with her hands, tilting her pelvis to a more accommodating angle. His low growl of satisfaction vibrating into her flesh was her reward. He spread her thighs even wider, burrowing, seeking. Her cry echoed off the high vaulted ceiling when he plunged his tongue deep into her slit.

"Ian!"

He tongue-fucked her, slow and languorous at first, but as the seconds passed, more lustily as her hips began to bob back and forth against him. He groaned, spreading his large hands across her hips, his fingers biting into her buttocks, and held her steady for his consumption. She gasped when he spread his mouth over her entire sex, his tongue lodged deep inside her vagina, and used his upper lip to apply a steady pressure on her clit. He twisted his head sharply, side to side between her thighs, stimulating her precisely. Her eyes sprang wide.

She stared up at the goddess of sex and love, transfixed, as she shuddered in violent orgasm.

Ian held her to him, his mouth moving with constrained force, his tongue delving, urging every last blast of pleasure out of her sweet, quivering body. When she quieted, he took another moment to lick up the juice of his labor. He'd known she'd be delicious from the taste of her mouth and skin, but he hadn't been prepared for the sheer decadence of her pussy.

He was full-out drunk on her, and yet he wanted more.

His raging cock had other things in mind, however. He gathered her to him, pressing a damp kiss against the erotic harbor of her taut belly. He stood, wincing at the ache in his cock. Her sublime taste had temporarily sated his lust. It came roaring back as he stared down at her near-naked body sprawled on the pedestal, moonlight shimmering in her dark eyes and glistening on her wet, spread pussy.

He lifted her, liking the way she curled against him. She could be so stubborn at times, willful. It moved him to have her lay her head on his shoulder so trustingly.

It made him want to wholly possess her all the more.

He took her to a low, tufted velvet chaise lounge positioned several feet in front of Aphrodite—a recliner fit for a king, if Ian recalled correctly. Instead of setting her on it, he placed her on her feet. He quickly removed her dress and draped it on the back of a nearby armchair. Next, he removed his jacket. She gave him a puzzled glance when he carefully spread it on the cushion of the chaise.

"Louis XIV once lounged on this piece. Grandmother would strangle me if I ever . . . spilled on it."

His small smile widened when he heard her low, rich laughter. He put his hands along her jaw and lifted her face for his voracious kiss, eating her mirth hungrily. His cock lurched when she shyly, curiously licked at his lips, tasting herself.

"That's right. Why shouldn't you taste something so sweet?" he rasped as he regretfully released her in order to locate a condom. The storm brewing in him was starting to tear at him from the inside out. He couldn't trust his sanity, couldn't trust anything if he didn't get inside Francesca soon . . . very soon. "Lie down on the chaise," he directed, his voice sounding tight to his own ears.

She reclined on his spread jacket, her legs and belly looking pale in the moonlight and contrasting with the black lining of his jacket. The chaise was armless, long, and wide, with a curved backrest. She lay so that her body was on the flat portion, the top of her head against the back, her calves resting at the end of the piece of furniture. Her loveliness bit at him, making him grind his teeth.

He began to unfasten his pants hastily. He shoved his trousers down his thighs and peeled his boxer briefs down over his erection. He paused while rolling on the condom a moment later when he noticed her huge eyes fixed on his cock.

She was afraid of him.

"It'll be all right. I'll go slow," he assured, whisking the tight rubber down farther over the shaft.

"Let me touch you," she whispered.

He froze, fisting the base of his cock. It throbbed and twitched in his hand at the unexpected sweetness of her request. He graphically pictured her doing what she requested, the agony of feeling her fingers on him, her lips, her tongue—

"No," he said more harshly than he intended. Regret lanced through him when he saw her startled expression. "I have to be in you now," he said more quietly. "I must. I've waited so long. Too long."

She just nodded her head, her large, dark eyes glued to his face. He kicked off his shoes, removed his socks and stepped out of his pants. His shirt was a burden. He unbuttoned it, but he couldn't keep his gaze off her spread thighs and glistening pussy. He was too crazed to remove the garment all the way. He came down over her, his knees near the bottom corners of the wide chaise, his hands just above her shoulders. He knew he should put his knees between her opened thighs, but something made him spread around her, planting his legs outside of hers, completely encompassing her.

So beautiful . . . and his for the taking.

"Reach for the back of the chaise," he directed.

She looked confused by his request but followed his direction nonetheless, her acquiescence making his cock throb where it hung between his thighs, heavy . . . burning.

When her arms were above her head, gripping the roll of the back of the lounge, he gave a small grunt of satisfaction.

"I would like to restrain you, but since I can't here, you must keep your arms behind you, do you understand?" he asked tensely.

"I would rather touch you," she said, the movement of her dark pink lips enthralling him.

"I would much rather you did, as well," he assured grimly, taking his cock into his hand. "And that is why you will keep them above your head at all costs."

She was finding it difficult to take a full breath, lying there, gripping desperately onto the wood rim of the chaise, staring up at the very image of primal male beauty. She wanted to touch Ian so much, but instead stared in rapt fascination as he touched himself. He slid his palm along the thick shaft in preparation to enter her. Her vaginal muscles clenched tight in arousal and anxiety. He looked so large, so heavy, so ripe with his desire.

At the last second, he seemed to reconsider and released his cock. It hung heavily between their bodies. He reached for the silk bra and opened the front clasp. Fresh liquid heat surged at her sex when he peeled the cups back, baring her breasts. She saw his cock twitch in the air.

"Venus," he said roughly, a small smile quirking his mouth. She waited, her breath held in her lungs, hoping he'd touch the exposed, tingling skin of her breasts and the prickling nipples, but he didn't. Instead, he grasped his penis again. Pushing one of her knees back to open her farther for him, he pressed the head of his penis against her slit. She bit her lip to stifle a cry. He grunted—whether in arousal or dissatisfaction she couldn't say—when he flexed his hips and the tip of him slid inside her.

"Ah, Jesus, you're going to try me," he muttered.

She saw how rigid his shadowed features were, the flash of his white teeth as he grimaced. Wanting to give him relief more than anything at that moment—wild to give him pleasure—she thrust up with her hips. She yelped at the sudden stab of pain, barely noticing when Ian gave an intimidating growl and slapped the side of her hip in warning.

"Stay still, Francesca. What are you trying to do, kill us both?"

"No, I just . . ."

"Never mind," he said, and she realized his breath was coming in erratic puffs. "Is it better now?" he asked between pants after a moment.

She realized he was referring to the pain she'd experienced. How had he known it'd been so sharp? It suddenly hit her that his penis was halfway inside her body. Her muscles stretched and thrummed around the throbbing flesh. It felt a little uncomfortable, but the sharp pain had passed.

*Ian inside her. Fused to her.*

"It doesn't hurt," she whispered, awe tingeing her tone.

She saw his throat convulse as he swallowed. He removed his hand from her knee and reached between her thighs.

"*Oh,*" she moaned when he began to press and rub against her clit with his thumb. He seemed to know the precise amount of friction to make her squirm in pleasure. The fullness of his embedded cock providing an upward pressure on her clitoris added another dimension of excitement.

"Stop squirming," he grated out, his tone a mixture of exasperation, fondness, and arousal near the breaking point. His manipulations were making her burn unbearably. He pressed with his hips. His groan seemed to rip at his throat as his cock drove almost completely into her. Only enough room for his hand between her thighs remained. Pain splintered through a thick, dense sensation of pressure and pleasure as he continued to stroke her.

"*Ian*," she cried out.

He thrust slightly with his hips, pressing his hand more firmly against her clit, and then bumping against it with his pelvis . . . once . . . twice. She mewled and began to shake in orgasm, her vagina clenching around him. This time, even through the waves of pleasure rushing around her, she knew that his growl was from arousal. She was still coming when he removed his hand from her pussy and braced himself with his arms. He grunted as he withdrew and sunk into her again.

"Ah, God, your *pussy* . . . better than ever I imagined," he groaned almost incoherently as he stroked her again, long and hard. "The only thing better is going to be having you raw."

She still whimpered as shudders of climax quaked her body. Ian made her tremble even more as his thrusts grew more demanding, his pelvis began to slap against hers in a demanding rhythm. He paused a moment later, fully embedded in her body, and ground his testicles against her spread outer sex. She cried out in excitement.

"I don't want to hurt you, but you've been driving me mad, Francesca," he hissed.

"You're not hurting me."

"No?"

She shook her head.

She sensed the tension increase in his body. He began to fuck her again, his hips driving his cock like a fluid, thrusting piston this time. She bit off a scream, but it burned in her throat. She realized he'd been restraining himself before, but he fucked her thoroughly now . . . and not just thoroughly—with a skill that stunned her. His motion was subtle and raw at once, controlled yet wild. It felt as if he beat pleasure into her, stroked her flesh to flesh until she knew she'd burst into flame any moment. She began to bob her hips in a counter-rhythm, small cries popping out of her throat each time they crashed together with a sharp smacking sound of skin and against skin.

"Jesus," he groaned a moment later, sounding miserable and ecstatic at once. He shifted on the chaise, and drove into her with such force that the top of her head bumped against the back cushion. She dazedly realized he'd spread his legs entirely over the chaise and that his feet were now planted on the floor. He reared over both her and the chaise lounge and thrust, teeth bared in a snarl.

"Ian, let me let go of the chair," she begged when he crashed into her again and again and she felt another climax looming over her just as Ian did. She longed to touch him so much.

"No," he said tensely. He pushed off his planted feet and drove into her, grunting when their bodies smacked together. A cracking sound exuded from the chaise, but thankfully the priceless piece of furniture didn't collapse into a heap of splinters and velvet with them on top of it. Her head bumped against the cushion, her breasts bounced high with each forceful thrust of his large body, the sensation exciting and dizzying her. He lifted a hand and reached between their bodies, opening her labia wide, before he rotated his hips, grinding his balls against her exposed outer sex, circling his engorged cock subtly against her vaginal walls. "Not until you come again, lovely."

It didn't really feel as if she had a choice. The pressure he'd built in her was unbearable. A cry of disbelief burbled out of her throat as bliss shook her once again. He gave a savage grunt of satisfaction and began to fuck her faster than before, letting the wildness he contained so carefully overtake him.

She cried out in protest when he withdrew his cock abruptly and pressed his knees onto the chaise, straddling her. His breath sounded ragged and erratic. She stared up at him, her climax waning in his absence, bewildered by his actions. She watched in the light from the dim emergency lighting as he used his hand to pump his cock.

"Ian?"

His groan sounded like the depth of agony, the height of bliss as he began to ejaculate. An ache opened up inside her at the sight of him spending himself while separate from her. She lowered her arms slowly, feeling stunned, help less . . . very aroused at the vision he made.

A moment later, he dropped his hand and hunkered down over her, his muscles bunched tight, gasping for breath. She'd thought he was beautiful as he reared over her, possessing her body and soul, but he was beyond that as he knelt over her, shaking and undone by his desire.

She reached for him, sliding her hands beneath his collar and stroking his powerful shoulder muscles. A shiver went through him at her touch, thrilling her.

"Why—"

"I'm sorry," he gasped. "I started to worry . . . pregnant."

"It's okay, Ian," she whispered. Compassion filled her at the realization of how starkly anxious he was at the smallest chance that he would have unintentionally impregnated her. She carefully moved back the opened placket of his shirt and held it behind him with one hand. With her other hand at his back, she urged him down to her gently.

"Come here," she insisted when she felt him resist. He hesitated for a moment, but then he came down over her, his solid, heavy weight pressing into her body striking her as a miracle.

"I was so primed for you. I haven't . . . there hasn't been anybody else for weeks now. Not typical for me. I could feel it building up inside me, and I was worried . . . the condom wasn't enough. Stupid," he muttered between pants.

She kissed his shoulder and stroked his broad, heaving back. Something full and inexplicable swelled in her chest at his admission that he'd abstained from his usual sexual practices.

Had *she* had something to do with his abstinence?

No. Surely not.

It frightened her a little, his complexities, his determined loneliness. She continued to caress him as he came back to himself, her gaze glued to the enigmatic face of their on-looker, wondering numbly all the while if Aphrodite planned to bless or curse them.


He seemed lost in some private world on the drive to the hotel, even though he sat next to her in the back seat of the limo, his arm around her, her head resting on his chest, him stroking her hair. At first, she was worried he was regretting his momentary vulnerability back there at the museum—his admission—but then she began to relax into his silence. She watched through heavy eyelids as the lights of Paris rushed by the window, recalling all the details of what had unexpectedly occurred in that salon in vivid detail.

Surely he couldn't regret a moment of that incredible experience, could he?

The Hotel George V was just off the Champs Elysées. *To call it luxurious was a bit of an understatement*, Francesca thought as she followed Ian onto the gilt elevator. She gasped when he opened the door for her and she stepped into an antique-filled living room featuring rich fabrics, a marble fireplace, and original seventeenth- and eighteenth-century artwork.

"This way," he directed, leading her into a bedroom fit for royalty.

"Oh, it's beautiful," she murmured, touching the rich damask and silk bed coverings and gazing around the tastefully decorated room.

His gaze ran over her as he removed his jacket and hung it over a valet stand.

"The hotel was close to where my meeting is tomorrow. I have to get up early. I'll probably be gone by the time you wake up. You must look at the view on the terrace come morning. I think you'll like it. I'll order you breakfast, and you can dine out there, if you like. You look very tired."

She blinked at his change of subject. "I am, I suppose. It's been a long day. I can't believe it was just this morning that

I left High Jinks. It all seems a little . . . surreal." In truth, she felt like a different person than the one who had answered Ian's knock this morning . . . even than the one that first entered the Musée de St. Germain that night. Ian's powerful lovemaking had altered her somehow.

She glanced at him nervously, uncertain about what he wanted her to do.

"Why don't you get ready for bed," he said gruffly, pointing at the entrance to the adjoining bathroom. "Jacob brought up our things while we were at dinner. You'll find your bag in there."

"Would you rather go first?" she asked.

He shook his head as he began to remove his cuff links. "I'll use the bathroom in the other suite."

"There's another bedroom suite?"

He nodded. "Jacob usually stays there."

"But not this time?"

He glanced up at her. "No. Not this time. I wanted you all to myself."

Her pulse began to thrum at her throat as she turned and walked to the bathroom. She carefully removed the dress, bra, and pearls, Ian's words still echoing in her skull.

Looking in the bathroom mirror, she saw what Ian must have noticed as he studied her before. Her face looked pale next to her passion-stung, reddened lips. Her eyes appeared unusually large above the shadowed circles beneath them. She wanted to shower but was suddenly too exhausted. She washed at the sink instead and brushed her teeth. She stared in rising dread at her nylon duffel bag sitting on a stool with a gold pouf cushion. It looked woefully out of place in these surroundings.

Just like she did, no doubt.

After an evening like she just experienced, she felt ridiculous putting on the yoga pants and Cubs T-shirt she'd brought as a substitute for pajamas. She applied moisturizer and ran a comb through her hair before she walked out of the bathroom. She went still when she saw Ian standing in profile by the lush sofa, tapping on his cell phone. Her gaze ran over him in covetous awe. He wore nothing but a pair of black pajama bottoms that rode low on his lean hips. The upward slant of his torso from narrow waist to a broad, powerful chest, back, and shoulders struck her as sublime. There wasn't an ounce of fat on him. He was so disciplined, she could just imagine what his workout routine was like. The short, dark hair at his nape and temples was slightly damp from his wash.

She'd never seen a more beautiful man in her life. She was certain she never would again.

He glanced around and saw her standing there. She shifted awkwardly on her feet beneath his laserlike stare. He abruptly looked away and resumed his task.

"Why don't you get into bed?" he asked, tapping out a message.

She started to remove the decorative pillows and pull down the decadently luxurious bedding.

"Take off your clothes," he said from across the room when she started to get into bed. She paused and glanced back at him. He hadn't looked up from his phone. Her breath started to come erratically as she began to undress.

Why didn't he look at her like he had on the plane when she stripped, his gleaming blue eyes tracking her every move?

She got into bed and pulled a sheet and blanket over

herself. Ian remained on the other side of the room, only his thumbs moving. Her eyelids grew heavy; the bed was very soft and warm. She drifted.

There was a click, and her eyes flew open. Ian had shut out the light. She felt the mattress sink beneath him as he got into the bed next to her. He came down on his side, pulling her into his arms, her back to his stomach. She could feel that he still wore the pajama bottoms, also . . . that he wore nothing beneath the thin garment.

Suddenly, she was wide awake.

"How come you get to wear pajamas, and I have to be naked?" she asked into the darkness.

He brushed her hair off her shoulder and stroked her, sending tendrils of pleasure through her.

"I'll often be dressed while you're naked."

"That doesn't make any sense," she said, her breath hitching when his long fingers brushed over the top curve of one of her breasts. She felt his cock stir next to her bottom. Her clit twanged in pleasure, as if in response.

"It pleases me to be able to touch you in any way, at any time that I desire it."

"While you get to remain clothed and in control?" she asked, a hint of anger entering her tone.

"While I get to remain clothed and in control," he repeated in affirmation.

"But—"

"There's no 'but' about it," he said as he caressed her ass, a smile in his voice. His cock batted against her, and he sighed, withdrawing his hand. "You shouldn't be complaining, Francesca," he chastised, settling her more firmly against him. "My control is already whisper thin when it comes to you. You need only look at tonight to have your proof of that."

"It was amazing," she whispered, awe filtering into her tone.

He went still for a moment, and then reached between her thighs. She gasped in excitement when he pushed his fingers gently between her legs and cupped her sex, the gesture both tender and baldly possessive.

"I power drove you like I might have the most experienced of women, and you . . . a virgin," he murmured, a thread of anger in his voice.

She flushed with heat at his crude words. *Power drive* was right. She'd been completely at his mercy lying on the chaise lounge, and loving every minute of his masterful possession.

"I'm not a virgin anymore," she said shakily. "We could do it again, and you wouldn't have to worry so much this time."

His cock lurched against her again. For a few seconds, she sensed his tension . . . his indecision.

He slowly removed his hand from her sex. "No. Tomorrow is soon enough. I have many things I want to teach you. You deserve at least one night to recover."

"What things?" she whispered.

"You'll find out soon enough. Now go to sleep. I have a big day planned for you tomorrow."

Hearing that hardly made her sleepy. Nevertheless, after a minute, she found herself relaxing against Ian's body, taking comfort in his hard, warm presence.

Ian rose out of a deep sleep and dark, sensual dreams to find Francesca's naked body plastered against him, a raging hard-on pressed against her soft, curving bottom, his hand filled with a firm breast.

*Jesus.*

He grimaced as he twisted his torso to see the clock, keeping a hand on Francesca's hip the whole time, keeping her lush ass in close contact with his cock. She sensed his movement and twitched her hips in her sleep, making him grind his teeth at the stimulation on his erection.

He picked up his phone and shut off the alarm that was about to go off at any second. Instead of getting up, like he should have, he set the phone back on the bedside table and whisked his pajama bottoms down below his balls, freeing his swollen cock from the material. He pulled Francesca closer, flexing his hips and burrowing his cock deeper in the sweet, warm cleft between her ass cheeks. God, it felt good, he thought as he pushed the thick column of his erection even deeper, sandwiching himself between her buttocks. The sexual excitement that had built in him as he held her naked body all night—that had been building ever since he'd exploded in climax at the St. Germain— swelled high and strong. He held her hip steady and flexed his hips, snarling at the pleasure that tore through him as his cock burrowed once more between the satiny-smooth, firm globes.

He became aware that she rustled next to him. He heard her gasp and softly say his name, but he was so caught up in the unexpected deliciousness of the early morning sexual spell she'd cast upon him, all he could do was thrust and grunt and take his pleasure. His cock felt huge and tight, exquisitely sensitive as he drug it back forth between the warm, snug crack of her ass. She tried to reach around to touch him, but he caught her hand and placed it next to her belly, holding it there as he continued his mad humping of her sweet bottom.

Since when could he become so sexually frantic just from the feeling of a woman's ass?

"Give me a moment," he said harshly, continuing to stroke her rapidly. "It's not going to take much more."

Sure enough, he broke in climax just a few thrusts later. He ground his teeth together and watched himself come onto her lower back and the upper curve of her right ass cheek. *Jesus, what she does to me,* he thought as he tensed and ejaculated, tensed and ejaculated, wondering wildly if the shuddering pleasure would ever end. He slumped over her, breathing heavily. She whimpered when he leaned back to grab some tissues, and he dried his abundant emissions from her skin.

He glanced up and did a double take. She'd turned her head on the pillow. Her cheeks were a brilliant pink, her lips flushed red. He tossed aside the wet tissues and leaned over her.

"Did that arouse you?" he asked, kissing her lips softly. "Letting me use your body for my pleasure?"

"Yes," she said next to his lips.

"Just for that, you get to come, too, lovely," he said.

He slid his fingers between her clenched thighs and found her delightfully creamy. She gasped, turning her head away from him, pressing her cheek to the pillow. He smiled as he slid his finger between her labia and diddled her clit.

"I want to be able to come inside you, Francesca. All over

you," he murmured, leaning over, breathing next to her ear. "Wouldn't you like that, too?"

"Oh, yes."

"You're going to have to go on birth control, then."

"Yes," she soughed as he rubbed her gently . . . firmly. Persuasively.

He watched her profile closely as he stimulated her, fascinated by the flutter in her delicate eyelids and the deepening of color in her cheeks. Her parted lips beckoned him.

"I'm going to restrain you later," he murmured. "And teach you how to please me even more than you already do. Will you like that?"

"Yes," she said, her trembling lips killing him. He plucked at them as he rubbed her clit harder. She bobbed her hips against him, and he gave her what she needed, moving his entire arm as he stroked her forcefully. "I *want* to please you, Ian."

"You do," he growled, kissing her roughly, abusing her lush mouth a little. A lot. "And you will."

She cried out and quaked against him. He nursed her through her climax, excitement and anticipation mounting in his body as he thought about coming to the suite later and finding her there, ready to submit to his desire . . . to her own.

He kissed her neck while she quieted, occasionally lapping at the sweet taste on her skin. Her soft moan vibrated into his lips.

"The laws are a bit more lenient in Paris regarding birth control. I know a pharmacist who can get us several months' worth. You could get started right away," he murmured.

He paused in his ravishment of her neck when he felt her stiffen.

"I wouldn't have to see a doctor?"

"Eventually, when you return stateside, yes. But the sooner you get started, the better. I could have Jacob pick up the delivery, and you could start on the pill this very day. I spoke with the pharmacist. You don't have any health risks, do you? High blood pressure, history of stroke?"

"No, I'm perfectly healthy. I just had a physical last month." She was turned in profile to him. She tilted her chin and regarded him with dark, soft eyes. "Of course I'll start on the pill. I know how important it is to you, Ian."

"Thank you," he said, dropping a kiss on her mouth, thinking all the while that she didn't know the half of how important it was.


Francesca snuggled in bed as Ian got up to get ready for his meeting, lazy and content in the aftermath of kisses and climax. She dozed, opening her eyes sleepily a while later to see Ian standing at the edge of the bed looking down at her, looking awesomely gorgeous in a dark suit, starched white shirt, and pale blue silk necktie, his spicy aftershave tickling her nose.

"Would you like me to order breakfast for you?" he asked, his hushed, deep voice striking her like a caress in the luxury-draped, still room. "You could have it out on the terrace? It's a beautiful day."

"I'll order it. You don't have to," she said, her voice rough from drowsiness.

He merely nodded and stepped back as if to go. He

hesitated, and suddenly swooped down, kissing her hard on the mouth.

There was no doubt about it. Ian's kisses were just more . . . *sexual* than anyone else's. Not that she had much experience, but still. How could that swift kiss immediately make her recall what it'd been like to have his mouth on her nether lips, worshipful . . . demanding?

She watched him walk away a moment later, looking so tall and commanding in his dark suit, feeling a strange mixture of joy and regret. After he was gone, she showered and washed her hair, letting it dry as she sat out on the sunny terrace that overlooked the Paris skyline and the famous art deco fountain of the Three Graces. She ordered room service and ate her breakfast outside, as Ian had suggested, the whole experience in the lap of luxury striking her again as incredible.

Afterward, she contacted Davie. Mostly, she tried to assure her friend that she was safe and happy to be in Paris with Ian. Davie seemed less than thrilled by her little adventure. In fact, his concern highlighted some of the things that'd been easy for her to forget when Ian was next to her, making love to her, making her forget everything but her desire for him.

She remembered how Ian had paid her in full for the painting, knowing full well she'd never refuse to finish it. She recalled in detail how he'd shut down the bar and said he wanted to possess her sexually in order to get her out of his system.

She thought of how he'd persuaded her to start taking the pill later that day.

Wait . . . *when* had she made a coherent decision about

such an important choice about her body? It'd just happened, somehow, while Ian had been kissing her and coaxing her and making her scream in pleasure.

A lead weight sank in her belly.

No. It hadn't been like that.

*Had it?*

Fortunately, she had the excuse of the long-distance price tag to cut her call short with Davie. Toward the end of their conversation, she began to worry her friend would start to hear the anxiety seeping into her voice.

Feeling restless, she pulled out her jogging clothes, pausing when she realized Ian hadn't given her a key to the suite. She called down to the front desk, relieved to find an attendant that spoke English. The woman assured her that her name was down as a guest and she may pick up a card key at the front desk if she showed her identification.

She changed and took to the streets of Paris, running the narrow back roads for miles and then along the tourist- and shopper-crowded Champs-Elysées, past the Arc de Triomphe. By the time she returned to the hotel, she'd pounded out a lot of her anxiety and worries on the pavement. Jogging always did calm her.

*Of course* Ian hadn't been manipulating her about the birth control. She wanted to be risk free in regard to pregnancy as much as he did. Why had she thought otherwise?

She was feeling easygoing and peaceful until she opened the door to the suite and saw Ian pacing tensely in front of the marble fireplace, the energy pouring off him, reminding her of a caged tiger. He had his phone pressed to his ear. He paused and looked back at her.

"Never mind," he said, his mouth pressed into a hard line

as his gaze ran over her. "She just walked in." He tapped his finger on the phone panel and set it on the mantel.

"Where have you been?" he asked. Her spine stiffened at his accusatory tone. He walked toward her, his eyes gleaming like banked flames.

"Jogging," she said, glancing down at her shorts, T-shirt, and running shoes as if to say, *Hello, isn't it obvious?*

"I was worried. You didn't even leave a note."

Her mouth fell open. "I didn't think you'd be back before I was," she exclaimed, stunned by his restrained fury. "What's *wrong* with you?"

His facial muscles tightened. "I'm the one who brought you to Paris. I'm responsible for you. I'd prefer it if you didn't just run off like that," he snapped, turning and stalking away from her.

"I'm responsible for *myself*. I've been doing a pretty good job of it for the past twenty-three years, thank you very much," she replied irritably.

"You're here with me," he said, whipping around.

"Ian, that's ridiculous," she cried. She couldn't believe he was being so irrational. What was behind his anger? Was he so controlled, so fastidious about his plans, that he couldn't allow for a spontaneous decision, like her morning run? "You can't actually be *mad* at me for going jogging."

A muscle jumped in his cheek. Behind the glint of anger in his eyes, she saw a shadow of helpless concern. God, he really *had* been worried about her. *Why?* Despite her irritation at him, her heart went out to him. He walked toward her. She resisted an urge to step back, he looked so intense.

"I'm angry because you left without leaving word where you were. If you'd brought it up earlier, it might have been different, although I would have said that I preferred you didn't go traipsing around a strange city by yourself. This isn't Chicago. You barely speak the language."

"I lived in Paris for several months!"

"I don't like it when someone I'm responsible for suddenly disappears," he said through a stiff jaw.

His gaze dropped over her, and she suddenly felt self-conscious of the clothing she wore—a jogging bra, a tight T-shirt, and shorts. Her nipples pulled tight when his stare lingered on her breasts.

"Go and shower," he said, turning and walking toward the fireplace.

"Why?"

He rested a forearm on the mantel and glanced back at her. "Because you have a lot to learn, Francesca," he said, his tone more subdued. She swallowed thickly.

"Are you going to . . . to punish me?"

"I was very worried when I came back to an empty hotel suite. I expected you'd be here waiting for me. So the answer is *yes*. I am going to punish you, and then I'm going to fuck you for my pleasure alone. If you haven't learned the lesson after that, then maybe I will punish you again. However long it takes for you to learn that I don't like it when you're impulsive."

Her nipples pulled even tighter against the tight fabric of her jogging bra even as her ire rose. Her sex flushed with heat.

"You can punish me if you want, but I'm not letting you do it because I went jogging. That's just stupid."

"Believe whatever you like. But you *will* go and shower and put on a robe. Nothing else. Wait for me in the bedroom," he said, turning away and picking up his phone again. He punched out a number and greeted someone briskly in French before he began making several queries. She'd been dismissed.

She faltered where she stood, burning to tell him to go and *fuck* his fucking shower and his fucking robe and his godforsaken high-handedness.

Another part felt bad for having unintentionally caused that shadow of fear in his eyes.

Another part still was excited by what he'd said. She'd thought incessantly of the time that he'd paddled and spanked her, and each time regretted that things had come to an unnatural halt.

She *wanted* to see how Ian culminated such arousing proceedings. She *wanted* to please him.

*But at what cost?* she wondered anxiously as she walked to the bedroom, resigned to the fact that she would do his bidding.

Why *must* he be such a puzzle?

Why must he turn *her* into one . . . even to herself?

# Eight

After her shower, she sat nervously on the plush sofa in the sitting area of the bedroom suite, her anger mounting. How dare he make her wait like this? Wasn't it just like him to yank her strings in this way?

He was yanking her strings in more ways than one. She had an urge to run to the bathroom and lock the door and another one to grind her sex against the cushion of the sofa. The waiting was pissing her off, but for some damnable reason she couldn't comprehend, it was making her aroused as well . . . the anticipation . . . the excitement mixed with a potent dose of anxiety about what he planned to do to her.

She jumped when the door to the bedroom suite opened abruptly and Ian walked into the room. He glanced at her where she sat before he walked over to the valet stand and hung up his suit jacket. He opened the doors to a highly glossed antique cherry wardrobe and bent as if reaching for something. She strained, trying to see what he was doing, but the door blocked her view. When he started to straighten, she turned, not wanting him to know how focused she was on his every move.

. So she was shocked when he walked around the couch a moment later and set a black crop on the coffee table. She stared wide-eyed at the two-inch-by-four-inch supple leather slapper at the end of the long, thin rod, her heart starting to pound against her breastbone.

"Don't be afraid," he said softly.

She looked at him. "But it looks like it will hurt."

"I've punished you before. Did it hurt?"

"A little," she admitted, her gaze dropping to one of his hands, which held what appeared to be a pair of cuffs, the hand straps made of soft-looking black leather.

*Oh no.*

"Well, it wouldn't be much of a punishment if it didn't sting a bit, now would it?" She stared up at his handsome face, mesmerized by the sound of his low voice . . . compelled. "Stand up and take off the robe."

She didn't break his stare as she stood, somehow taking courage from some unspoken message in his eyes. She dropped the discarded robe onto the cushion. His gaze dropped over her, his nostrils flaring slightly. She shivered.

"Would you like me to turn on the fire?" he asked, referring to the gas fireplace.

"No," she said, thrown off emotionally by the combination of his polite query and his intention to punish her. She walked to the mantel.

"Keep your back to me," he ordered when she started to turn to face him. She longed to twist her chin over her shoulder to see what he was doing behind her, her anxiety and excitement mounting, but she restrained herself with effort. Was that because she once again didn't want to give him the satisfaction of knowing she was curious, or because she somehow sensed he wouldn't want her to gawk over her shoulder?

She started when he wrapped his hands around one of her wrists.

"Easy, lovely," he murmured. "You know I'd never really harm you. You must trust me."

She said nothing, her mind racing as he buckled one of the cuffs snuggly around her right wrist. "Now you may face me," he said.

She turned, her nipples pulling tight when she realized how close he stood. He must notice. There was no way she could hide her arousal as he fastened her other wrist into the cuff, his lowered head just inches from the tingling, prickling crests. The position of her arms as he cuffed her wrists together plumped her breasts. When he'd finished, her hands were bound together in front of her mons. He stepped back. Her nipples pinched even tighter when she noticed his gaze glued to them.

"Now lift your wrists and place them behind your head," he instructed. He watched her while she complied. "Push back your elbows and arch your back a little. I want your muscles stretched tight." She strove to do as he asked, thrusting her breasts forward and her elbows back, noticing the slight snarl shape of his mouth when she did so. The position left her feeling extremely naked and exposed. Then he turned away. "It will amplify the sensation," he explained, his back to her as he walked over to the coffee table.

"Of pain?" she asked, her voice shaking from a potent brew of anxiety and anticipation as she watched him walk over to the coffee table. Was he getting that scary-looking crop?

He was coming toward her again, but she didn't see the crop. Her heart knocked on her stretched rib cage like it was asking to get out when she saw the familiar little white jar. He unscrewed it and dipped a thick forefinger into the cream.

"I told you before that I would prefer if you didn't fear me," he said.

She gasped loudly, shuddering when he immediately plunged his finger between her labia and began to coat her clit with the emollient that she knew would soon make her tingle and burn . . . and want.

She bit her lip to prevent from crying out and noticed he watched her with a tight focus.

"But I want to emphasize, this is a punishment never-theless," he stated firmly.

"*I* want to emphasize that while I give you permission to punish me," she said before air puffed out of her throat as his finger rubbed the cream with bull's-eye accuracy. "I'll still go jogging—or do anything else I damn well please—without asking for your permission."

He dropped his hand and walked away. She stifled a cry of deprivation. He turned and came toward her again, now carrying the crop. She couldn't take her eyes off the wicked-looking device gripped in his large, masculine-looking hand. It looked as if it would hurt more than the paddle or Ian's hand.

"Spread your thighs . . . *if you damn well please*," he added softly.

She blinked at his words, her gaze zooming up

incredulously to meet his stare. Heat rushed through her sex when she saw the glimmer of amusement and the heat of arousal in his eyes . . . when she absorbed the edge of a dare to his tone.

If she agreed to what he'd demanded, it would be because *she* wanted it. And her impulsive statement of defiance just now was proof of that. Frustration went through her when she recognized how he'd tricked her into compliance and revealed her own desire in one fell swoop.

She widened her stance, glaring at him all the while.

"Your anger tautens your muscles as greatly as the position. It doesn't displease me, strangely enough," he murmured, the tilt of his mouth indicating he was laughing silently, not only at her but at himself. He lifted the crop, and all of her irritation was crowded out by stark anticipation. Wasn't he going to slap her bottom with it, like he had with the paddle? Her abdomen muscles jumped in excitement when he ran the leather slapper over her belly. An erotic sensation swooped through her sex when he rubbed it sensually over her hip. He lifted the crop.

*Snap. Snap. Snap.*

She gasped, feeling the sting of the slapper lingering on her hip. It quickly faded to a tingling sensation of heat.

"Too much?" he murmured, his gaze running over her face and then her breasts. He smoothed the leather across her ribs over the globe of her right breast. She moaned uncontrollably when he pressed the slapper against her nipple and rubbed. "Your pretty nipples are telling me all is well." He lifted the slapper and popped the side of her breast, then the bottom curve, and then the puckered nipple, his actions quick, firm, and concise.

Something ignited inside her. Liquid heat rushed between her thighs, the strength of her reaction shocking her nearly as much as the fact that he'd just spanked her breast. Her eyes clamped tight as shame struck her. What sort of a deviate was she, to have such an overwhelming reaction to something so sick?

"Francesca?"

She opened her eyes at the sound of his taut tone.

"Are you all right?"

"Yes," she told him, her mouth quivering uncontrollably. The clit stimulant seemed to be doing its job with even more vigor than when Ian had paddled her, making her clit sizzle with excitement.

"Bad or good?" he demanded roughly.

"I . . . *bad*," she whispered, shame and arousal vying for control of her mind and body. His expression stiffened. "And *good*. So good."

"Damn it," he muttered, his eyes blazing, although she had the distinct impression he liked her answer instead of being angered by it. He brought down the crop again, popping the underside of her other breast, making the globe jiggle slightly. She bit her lip, but her moan vibrated in her throat. "I'm going to turn your ass red for that, you little . . ."

She never learned what sort of a "little" she was, because he popped a nipple again and again, his actions gentle, but firm enough to cause a burning sting that made Francesca grit her teeth and clench her eyes shut. Without thinking, she thrust her breasts forward.

"That's right, present yourself to me," she heard him mutter as he popped the underside and side of her breast

several times. "Now . . . tell me what you damn well please
at this moment?" he murmured, sliding the crop sensually
across both of her breasts. Her eyes still clamped shut, she
was exquisitely attuned to the sensation. God, her clit was
screaming for attention between her thighs.

"Francesca?" he asked sharply.

Oh, no. He wasn't going to make her say it. He slid the
leather slapper across a nipple and made a twitching movement, stimulating her all the way to her core. She gasped.

"It would please me if you . . ."

He twitched the slapper on her nipple again, and she
trembled.

"Just say it. There's no shame in it," he said, his voice
sounding hard and soft at once.

Her jaw tightened, torn between speaking the truth and
swallowing it. He massaged her nipple briskly with the
leather.

"It would please me if you slapped me . . . between my
thighs."

She opened her eyes warily when he lifted the nipple and
didn't speak. "*What?*" she asked after a moment, unable to
read his rigid expression.

He shook his head slowly, and she realized he was
stunned. His nostrils flared, and he suddenly looked fierce.
Her heart sank. It suddenly struck her that he hadn't been
expecting her to say that.

"I . . . well, anywhere . . . I . . . I'm sorry. Ian?" she
asked, bewildered by his reaction, not sure what she was
supposed to say.

"Don't ever apologize for being beautiful," he said, before
he stepped forward and placed his hand along the side of her

jaw. He seized her mouth with his own, pillaging it with his shaping, firm lips and plunging tongue. His taste—his forceful possession—had just started to make her intoxicated, when he lifted his head. "You tempt me beyond reason." Francesca panted against his lips. His tone had sounded like an accusation, but it began to dawn on her that in this situation, at least, it definitely indicated he was pleased.

Heat flooded her sex, his pleasure somehow her own.

"But I won't be sidetracked."

"I wasn't trying to sidetrack you—"

"I *will* finish this punishment," he said as if steeling himself, ignoring her outburst. He kissed her once softly on the mouth. "Now bend over and present your bottom. You may keep your thighs together since your hands are restrained. I'm going to have to make your sweet ass burn for making me worry like that."

Something in his tone made her think he was going to punish her harder than he had that first time. She lowered her arms, bending and placing her restrained hands on her knees. He immediately began to rub the leather slapper over her ass cheeks in a sliding caress. She recalled how Ian had told her to arch her back slightly. Her sex clenched tight; her supersensitive nipples prickled as she thrust them forward.

He paused in his caressing of her bottom with the slapper. She glanced sideways at him anxiously.

He muttered a blistering curse. She watched in mounting arousal as he began to unfasten his pants hastily. Instead of drawing them down his thighs, he left them around his hips, merely reaching inside the open fly to draw out his rigid erection with what appeared to be considerable effort. He let the heavy weight of it fall once it was free, the bunched boxer briefs and fabric from his pants keeping it suspended at a horizontal angle from his body.

She stared at his cock in amazement. She'd never seen it this close before. He'd never really let her. It stunned her how beautiful it was. How did he walk around with something so obvious, so *large*, between his legs all the time? Granted, he usually wasn't this hard . . . but still. It seemed incomprehensible to her, the sheer flagrancy of his sex. She stared, spellbound, at the thick, lengthy staff with several swollen veins running along it, feeding his arousal; the tapered, succulent head that made her mouth water; the shaved, full testicles.

"I should have blindfolded you," he muttered dryly. "Look down at the floor, lovely." She did so, having trouble catching her breath. He rubbed the crop against her bottom. "Are you ready?"

"Yes," she squeaked. *Was she?*

He popped her ass with the slapper, and she squealed. Perhaps he was learning to differentiate her sounds of excitement versus her sounds of pain, because he continued to smack her, landing the popper on different patches of skin each time, heating her entire ass. Once he'd spanked both buttocks entirely, he began again. The slapping of her already spanked skin *did* sting. She gritted her teeth, the unbearable sizzle of her clit helping her endure the slight burn of discomfort. Why did the slapper seem to be stimulating her nipples at such a distance? And why in the world did even the soles of her feet start to burn as he continued to punish her bottom?

"*Oooh,*" she moaned when he landed a blow that particularly smarted.

"Bend all the way over and put your hands on top of your feet."

He'd spoken so sharply, she couldn't help but turn to look at him. She moaned shakily when she saw he fisted his cock in his hand and was stroking himself as he continued to spank her. Even though his gaze remained on his task, he must have noticed that she looked.

"Head down," he rasped.

She bent farther, stretching her hamstrings, staring blindly at her hands when she lay them flat on top of her feet. Did his low grunt sound pleased? Her thoughts suddenly scattered when he used his large hand to pull back her ass cheeks, exposing her wet outer sex to the cool air.

She cried out sharply when he tapped the slapper over the delicate, aroused tissues. He pressed harder with his hand, peeling back her buttocks and sex lips.

*Pop.*

Her knees buckled at the concise tap on her swollen clit. She suddenly understood the full value of the crop as a sex toy: small, precise, *lethal*—at least in Ian's hand.

He hastily put his hand on her shoulder, steadying her as orgasm slammed into her like a tidal wave. She keened, losing herself for several seconds, lost in the grip of an explosive climax. Distantly, she was aware that Ian held her against him as she quaked, one hip pressed against his body, the other held by his hand, his fingers moving busily between her legs, making her cry out sharply in sustained ecstasy.

Ian was now urging her with his hands, guiding her several feet, as the shudders waned.

"Bend over and put your forearms on the seat of the chair," he said tautly from behind her. She dazedly leaned

BECAUSE YOU ARE MINE

down over the wide, plush cushion of the Louis XV chair. She felt Ian moving behind her, his pants brushing her ass, then the tip of his erection. Fresh excitement pierced through her satiated befuddlement.

He had suspected she was going to kill him, but he hadn't expected her to do it so precisely . . . so cruelly. He wildly sought and found a condom and rolled it on.

*It would please me if you slapped me . . . between my thighs.*

He'd almost had a heart attack when she'd said it. He'd been trying to tease her into begging him to slap her gorgeous nipples, which she'd clearly been enjoying as much as he had.

Then she'd opened her pink lips and said *that*. And he'd said he was punishing her for the sin of impulsivity. Who the fuck did he think he was kidding?

He put one hand on her hip, steadying her, and took his cock in his hand.

"I'm going to fuck you now. Hard," he said, staring down at the erotic contrast of her reddened bottom and her pale back and white thighs. "I won't wait for you to come, lovely. You've done this to me, and you have to accept the consequences."

He used his hand to peel back an ass cheek and open her vagina, pushing the head of his cock into her tiny slit. He felt himself stretching her. Her heat penetrated the condom. He grasped her hips to steady her as he thrust into her to his balls, but she jolted forward nevertheless. Her hands scrambled to find a hold. He waited until she'd grabbed the wooden sides of the back of the chair, his mouth twisted in a grimace of restraint.

He began to fuck her, drawing his cock back until only the head was submerged, and then driving back into her until their skin smacked together and a little cry popped out of her throat. His world narrowed down to the vision of her naked, submissive beauty, the sharp, nearly unbearable friction of her squeezing, hot channel taunting him, milking him . . . killing him.

Through the haze of his rabid need, he became aware that his powerful thrusts into her soft, warm body were causing the chair to hop and scoot slightly on the Oriental carpet. It wasn't Francesca's fault—he was completely to blame—but he growled like a deprived animal anyway.

"Stay right there," he grated out, lifting her hips more firmly in his grasp and serving her pussy to his raging cock, slapping her ass against his pelvis and thighs, too far gone to care if he was making her spanked bottom burn in discomfort. God, it felt so good. He slammed her against his pelvis, his cock jerking viciously at her farthest reaches.

His roar of release scored his throat as orgasm tore through him.

Francesca just lay there with her hot cheek pressed against the soft fabric of the chair, her mouth gaping open in wonder at the sensation of him coming inside her. All that power, rocketing into her, detonating inside her. She thought she'd remember the first time she felt Ian succumbing to pleasure while harbored deep inside her body for the rest of her life.

His grunt sounded like it tore at his throat. It felt like something vital was being ripped out of her when he withdrew abruptly.

"Francesca," he said at the same moment he lifted her into a standing position, her back against his front, and turned her toward the couch. They walked—staggered more like it—their bodies not breaking contact while they walked the short distance to the sofa. Ian fell onto the cushions, bringing her with him. He lay on his left hip, her back pressed against his tie and the buttons of his dress shirt. His warm, sticky, still-formidable cock pressed against her lower spine.

They both just panted and gasped for a minute. She became transfixed by the sensation of his warm breath striking her neck and shoulder.

"Ian?" she asked after his breath had grown more even and he began to languorously stroke her waist and hip.

"Yes," he replied, his voice low and rough.

"Are you really angry with me?"

"No. Not anymore."

"But you were before?" she persisted.

"Yes."

She twisted her chin. His face looked subdued as he watched his hand moving up and down the naked side of her body.

"I don't understand. Why?"

His hand faltered and his mouth went tight.

"Please tell me," she whispered.

"My mother used to run away occasionally when I was a child," he said.

"Run away?" she asked slowly. "Why? Where did she run to?"

He shrugged. "God knows. I'd find her different places— staggering down a country road, trying to feed leaves to a panicked puppy, bathing naked in an ice-cold river . . ."

A shiver of horror went through her as she studied his impassive face.

"She was mentally ill?" she asked, recalling what Mrs. Hanson had told her.

"Schizophrenic," he said, lifting his hand from her hip and brushing back his short bangs off his forehead. "Disorganized type. Although she could be quite paranoid at times, as well."

"And was she . . . was she like that all the time?" Francesca asked through a throat that had gone tight.

His blue eyes flickered over her face. She quickly hid her concern, intuiting he'd take it for pity. "No. She wasn't. Sometimes, she was the sweetest, kindest, most loving mother in the world."

"Ian," she called softly when he began to sit up. She sensed his withdrawal and hated knowing she'd caused it.

"It's all right," he said, swinging his long legs onto the floor, his profile to her. "Maybe it'll help you understand better why I really would prefer that you don't disappear like that."

"I'll be sure and leave a note or call if something similar happens in the future, but I have to make my own choices," she said, studying him nervously. She would *not* promise to always be waiting around for him in order to help him manage his anxiety.

His head swung around. She sensed his irritation. Was he going to tell her that she damn well better do what he demanded, or their arrangement would come to a halt? "I would prefer that you just sat tight if a similar situation arises," he said.

"I know. I heard you," she said softly. She sat up and brushed her mouth against his hard jaw. "And I'll keep your preferences in mind before I make my own choice."

He closed his eyes briefly, as if gathering himself. Would she never cease to annoy him?

"Why don't you get cleaned up and we'll go out for a spell," he said stiffly as he stood and started out of the room, presumably to go to the other suite and clean up. Relief swept through her when she realized he wasn't going to fly her back to Chicago this instant for not doing precisely what he wanted, when he wanted it. Admittedly, so did a tad of triumph.

"You're not going to try and teach me anymore . . . try to convince me it's your way or the highway?" she asked, unable to keep a smile from pulling at the corners of her mouth.

He glanced over his shoulder. She saw the flash in his blue eyes that reminded her of heat lightning—like a storm brewing and mounting in the distance. Her smile faded.

When *would* she learn to keep her big mouth shut?

"The day isn't over yet, Francesca," he said, his voice a low, caressing menace, before he turned and walked out of the room.

# Part Five

## Because I Said So

# Nine

When she walked into the living room of the suite after cleaning up and dressing, she found Ian sitting at a desk, his computer open, his phone next to his ear.

"I've gone over his background extensively. His experience is steeped in venture-capitalist and fly-by-night Internet companies. He hasn't got a stitch of financial discipline," she heard him say. He glanced up and noticed her walk into the room. His eyes remained on her as he spoke. "What I actually told you is that you may hire whomever you wanted from a pool of acceptable CFO candidates, Declan. You have yet to supply me with that pool, so until you do, don't start the hiring process, especially with a joker like this." Another pause. "That may be true for all the other companies in the world, but not for one of mine," he said, his voice like dry ice, before he said good-bye briskly.

"Sorry about that," he said, standing and removing his glasses. "I'm having a hard time staffing a start-up company."

"What sort of a company is it?" Francesca asked,

interested. He never really spoke to her much about his work.

"A social-media–gaming concept that I'm test-driving in Europe."

"And you're having trouble finding the executives you want?"

He sighed and stood. He looked regal casual—a new term she made up on the spot to describe Ian's apparel when he wasn't wearing his typical suit. Today, it involved a cobalt-blue V-neck lightweight sweater, a white dress shirt beneath showing at the collar, and a pair of black pants that did god-awful sexy things for his narrow hips and long legs.

"Yes, among other things," he admitted, tapping on his computer keyboard. "It's usually that way, though. Unfortunately, my youth-oriented market appeals to the wild-gunslinger variety of executive who likes to spend my money merely because it's there."

"And while you may be liberal in your product and marketing ideas, you're a rigid financial conservative?"

He looked up from his computer before he closed the monitor and walked toward her. "Do you know very much about business?"

"Not an iota. I'm a walking financial disaster. Ask Davie. I can barely swing my rent every month. I was just guessing about your business style from what I know of your personality." He paused a few feet in front of her and raised his eyelids slightly, his manner one of amused expectancy.

"Personality?"

"You know," she said, her cheeks heating. "The control-freak thing."

He smiled and reached up to her touch her cheek, as though tracing the path of the warmth.

"I'm not afraid to spend money—and a lot of it—I just want to know it's for an excellent reason. You look very pretty," he said abruptly, changing the subject.

"Thank you," she murmured, glancing down in embarrassment at the simple long-sleeve cotton shirt she wore tucked into low-riding jeans with her favorite belt. She'd left her hair down but pinned back the front to keep it off her face. "I . . . I didn't bring that much to wear. I wasn't sure what you wanted to do this afternoon."

"Ah . . . speaking of which . . ." Ian dropped his hand from her cheek and checked his watch. As if his focus on the time had made it happen, a knock resounded on the suite door. He strode across the room and opened it. An attractive woman in her forties, wearing a chocolate-brown dress and stunning lizard-skin heels entered the suite. Francesca stood there, bewildered, as Ian exchanged greetings with the woman in French and then waved toward Francesca significantly.

"Francesca, this is Margarite. She's my shopping assistant. She speaks French and Italian, but not English."

Francesca exchanged greetings with the woman in the limited French she knew. She looked at Ian with a question in her eyes when the woman withdrew a tape measure and what looked like a wooden ruler contraption from the posh handbag she was carrying. She approached Francesca, smiling.

"Ian? What's going on?" she asked, brows furrowed as she watched Margarite set down the wooden contraption and her handbag and whip the tape measure in her hand. She walked up close to a bewildered Francesca. Her eyes went wide in incredulity when the woman stretched the measure around her hips, then quickly moved it around her waist.

"Lin Soong has an uncanny ability to guess people's ready-to-wear clothing sizes, and she's even a crack shot at foot sizes. She's the one who ordered the clothing you wore last night, and she seemed up to her usual standards. However, I thought it'd be better to get more precise measurements for some tailored clothing," Ian said casually from across the room. She looked up, aghast, when Margarite matter-of-factly stretched the tape measure around her breasts. Ian was in the process of stuffing some files into his briefcase, but paused when he saw her expression.

"Ian, tell her to stop this," she mumbled under her breath, as if muting her voice would lessen the likelihood of Margarite taking offense, forgetting the woman didn't speak English.

"Why?" Ian asked. "I want to make sure your new wardrobe fits you perfectly."

Margarite was retrieving the wooden contraption, which Francesca now realized was a foot-measurement device. She walked past the smiling woman, her expression strained, and approached Ian.

"Stop this. I don't want any new clothes," she hissed, glancing back uncomfortably at a politely-confused-looking Margarite.

"I might want you to attend some events with me that require more formal attire," he said, zipping his briefcase closed briskly.

"I'm sorry. I guess I won't be able to go if you don't think my appearance is suitable."

He glanced up sharply at the tone of her voice. His nostrils flared slightly when he finally took note of her anger.

Margarite made a query in French from across the room. Ian's stare felt like it had weight, but Francesca held it determinedly. He walked past her and addressed Margarite rapidly in French. The woman nodded in understanding, smiled warmly at Ian, grabbed her purse, and took her leave.

"Would you mind telling me what that was all about?" he asked her once he'd closed the door after a departing Margarite. His tone was cool, but his eyes gleamed with anger.

"I'm sorry. It was a generous offer on your part. But I know what type of clothing you'd probably tell Margarite to buy or have made. I'm a graduate student, Ian. I can't afford things like that."

"I know that. I'm purchasing them for you."

"I told you I wasn't for sale."

"I told you that this sort of thing is the type of experience I can offer you," he snapped back.

"Well, I'm not interested in that 'sort of thing.'"

"I made it clear that this would be on my terms, Francesca, and you agreed. I'll accept your stubbornness in small doses, but you go too far this time," he said as he stalked toward her, clearly infuriated at her resistance.

"No. *You* go too far. I spent almost my entire life having authority figures tell me my appearance was wrong and try to alter it. Do you really think I'm so stupid as to give you permission to start doing the same thing now? I am who I am. If you don't want to be around me this way, I'm sorry," she said, her voice shaking.

He came to a halt. She wished he wouldn't look at her with that laser stare of his that seemed to see so much. Tears unexpectedly filled her eyes. It hurt, for some reason, knowing that he'd prefer she was different. She knew that was irrational—he hadn't said he wanted to alter *her*, just her clothes—but she couldn't seem to prevent the swelling of emotion. They stood there in silence while she tried to contain it.

"Never mind," he said quietly after a moment while she stared blankly out the sun-filled terrace windows, her arms crossed beneath her breasts. "Perhaps we can discuss it later. I don't want to argue with you right now. It's a beautiful day. I'd like to enjoy it with you."

She glanced at him hopefully. Was he really willing to forgive her for refusing his generosity? She dropped her arms.

"What . . . what were you planning on doing?"

He closed the distance between them. "Well, I was planning on a little shopping and a late lunch, but now that I hear your opinion on the matter, I think a change of plan is in order."

She hid her grimace. She knew he didn't like to change his plans.

"What about a quick tour of the Musée d'Art Moderne and a late lunch instead?"

She studied his impassive face closely, searching for clues as to his mood and finding none. "Yes. That would be wonderful."

He nodded once and held out his arm toward the door. She walked past him, halting when he called her name suddenly, as if he'd been hesitating about saying something before, but now it popped out of him. She looked back.

"I want you to know that I am far from being critical of your appearance. Whether you're in pearls or your Cubs T shirt, I find you to be extremely attractive. Perhaps you haven't noticed?"

Her mouth fell open in shock. "I . . . I have noticed. Really. I just meant—"

"I know what you meant. But you're an extremely beautiful woman. I would like you to own that, Francesca."

"It seems more like *you* want to own it . . . for however long it's convenient to you," she couldn't stop herself from saying.

"No," he said so harshly she blinked. He inhaled slowly, looking as if he regretted his outburst. "I admit, you probably have good reason for believing that, given what you know of me . . . what *I* know of me, even. But I find I truly would like you to see yourself clearly . . . to recognize your power."

She just stared at him, her mouth hanging open, confused by the message in his eyes.

She was still bewildered when he took her hand and led her out of the suite.

Francesca had to keep repeatedly reminding herself that it was a purely sexual agreement she had with Ian, because in truth, she couldn't have imagined a more romantic day in her life. At her request, they left Jacob to his own devices and walked the streets of Paris, Francesca experiencing a ridiculous amount of excitement and euphoria at the sensation of her hand enfolded in Ian's, frequently glancing sideways to assure herself that she really was being escorted around the most romantic city in the world by the most appealing, compelling man she'd ever seen.

"I'm starving," she said honestly after their brief and enjoyable tour of the Musée d'Art Moderne, where she'd continued to be amazed by the depth of his artistic knowledge and innate taste. He'd been the ideal companion—considerate of her desires for what she wanted to view, interested in what she had to say, revealing more of his dry, sharp wit and sense of humor than he ever had before with her. "Can we eat here?" she asked, pointing at the attractive little sidewalk bistro they passed on Rue Goethe with outdoor seating.

"Lin has arranged a private table for us at Le Cinq," Ian said, referring to the ultra exclusive, pricey restaurant in their hotel.

"Lin Soong," she mused, watching a couple seated at a nearby table, the woman picking at her food idly with her fingers while she laughed at something her companion had said. "She's extremely efficient at planning things, isn't she?"

"The best. That's why I employ her," he said crisply before he gave her a sideways glance. She looked at him in surprise a moment later when he paused before the entrance to the little bistro and waved his hand to enter, his expression one of subdued amusement.

"Really?" she asked excitedly.

"Certainly. Even I can be spontaneous once in a while. In very small measures, anyway," he added drolly.

"Will miracles never cease?" she teased. He blinked, looking slightly surprised, when she went up on her toes and kissed him on the mouth before they sat at one of the outdoor tables.

"Would you like anything else to drink besides club soda?" Ian asked politely when the waiter came to their table.

She shook her head. "No, just that, thank you."

Ian placed their order and they were left to each other's company. She smiled at him from across the table, feeling very happy, admiring how electric blue his eyes looked even though they sat in the shadow of the canopy above them.

"You mentioned to me once that you didn't really bloom and come into your own until you went to college. How is it that you never ended up in a serious relationship with a man in all the intervening years?" he asked.

She avoided his gaze. Her experience with dating—or lack of it—was not really the sort of thing she wanted to discuss with a sophisticated man like Ian.

"I just never really clicked with anyone, I guess." She glanced up cautiously and saw that he continued to regard her expectantly. She sighed. He wasn't going to drop the topic. "I wasn't interested in most guys in college, not in a romantic sense, anyway. I like hanging around men, as a rule. I get them better than women. Women are all like . . . *'How do I look? Where'd you get those jeans? What are you wearing on Friday night so we can all look the same?'"* She rolled her eyes.

"But when it came down to it with men . . . to the . . ." she faded off, having difficulty finding the right words.

"Dirty details?" Ian supplied quietly.

"Yeah, I guess so," she admitted, falling silent for a moment while the waiter served their beverages. They both placed their orders for lunch. After the waiter left, he glanced at her again as if waiting.

"I don't know what you want me to say," she said, blushing. "Men are okay to party with, and to hang out with, and to have fun with, but for me, I was never really . . .

turned on," she said, her voice dropping into a whisper, "by any of them. They were too young. Too annoying. I got sick of them always asking me what I wanted to do for a date," she said in a burst of honesty. "I mean . . . why did *I* always have to be the one to decide?" She did a double take when she noticed his small smile. "What?" she asked.

"You're a natural sexual submissive, Francesca. A more natural one I've never seen. You're also singularly bright, talented, independent . . . full of life. A unique combination. Your frustrations in dating likely stem from the fact that men were striking the wrong chord with you, so to speak. There are probably only a handful of men on the planet that you would submit *to*." He picked up his glass and watched her over the rim as he took a sip of ice water. "Apparently, I'm one of those men. I consider myself to be very lucky for it."

She made a scoffing sound, all the while studying him nervously. Was he *serious*? She recalled how he'd used the word *submissive* that night he'd spanked her in his penthouse. She didn't like what the word implied about herself, and had been regularly pushing it out of her awareness ever since then.

"I don't know what you're talking about," she said dismissively. This time, however, she couldn't stop thinking about what he'd said, couldn't stop recalling her exhausted disgust when a man on a date had to drink too much before he made a move on her sexually, when he behaved indecisively or immaturely. . . .

. . . when he acted the exact opposite of Ian.

His brow quirked up slightly, as if he'd seen the pieces lock together in her brain.

"Can we please talk about something else?" she asked, staring out at the people strolling by on the sidewalk.

"Of course, if you wish," he agreed, and Francesca suspected his acquiescence was so easy because he knew he'd already made his point.

"Look at that," she said, nodding to three young people whisking past the bistro on motor scooters. "I always wanted to rent one when I was in Paris. They look so fun."

"Why didn't you?" he asked.

She really blushed this time. She glanced around, hoping like crazy she'd see their waiter coming with their entrées.

"Francesca?" he asked, sitting forward slightly.

"I . . . uh . . . I . . ." She closed her eyes briefly. "I don't have a driver's license."

"Why not?" he demanded, looking puzzled.

She tried to shrug off her mortification, not sure why she was feeling it so strongly with Ian about this particular topic. All of her friends knew she didn't drive. *Lots* of people in the city didn't. Caden, for instance, didn't have a car.

"In high school, I didn't really have anywhere I needed to drive *to*, and my parents didn't push it. I opted out of driver's ed," she said hurriedly, praying he didn't observe her sidestepping of the truth.

The truth was, she'd been at her heaviest when she'd been sixteen. She daily thanked God her body had been youthful enough to sustain the abrupt weight loss she experienced at eighteen. Much to her amazement, there had been no lasting scars from those weight-laden years of her life. The weight had melted off her as if it truly had been a traumatic experience she could heal from versus a measurable biological event.

But Sweet Sixteen had been Miserable Sixteen to Francesca. She'd been slated to take driver's ed with three other girls in her gym class, three girls who—by a horrible stroke of fate—regularly bullied her. Gym class had already been a daily torture for her. The idea of spending an hour in confined quarters with three sneering girls hiding their laughter at every clumsy move she made, and a young male gym teacher vaguely sympathetic to the other girls' disdain, had been too much for her. Her parents had suspected this was the reason for her avoiding driver's ed, and hadn't insisted she take the class.

They were likely just as mortified by the idea as she had been.

"By the time I moved to Chicago, there was absolutely no reason to get a license. I can't afford a car, the parking, or the insurance, so it became a moot point," she explained to Ian.

"How do you get around?"

"The El, my bike . . . my feet," she said, grinning.

He shook his head once, briskly. "That's not acceptable."

Her grin faded. "What do you mean?" she asked, offended.

He gave her an exasperated glance when he noticed she'd once again taken umbrage. "I just mean that a young woman like you should have the very basics of control in her life."

"And you think driving is a basic of control?"

"Yes," he replied so matter-of-factly that a surprised laugh popped out of her throat. "It's a developmental milestone, getting your driver's license, no different than taking your first step . . . or learning how to control your temper," he added significantly when she opened her mouth to argue. The arrival of their entrées temporarily postponed their charged conversation.

"There's a reason for all the sayings, you know," Ian mused a moment later, lazily watching her pour salad dressing onto her greens. "The ones about being in the driver's seat, driving your fate, power driving . . ."

Her gaze flew up to meet his stare at the last, recalling vividly how he'd described his claiming of her at the St. Germain last night. His small smile told her he knew she was remembering.

"Why don't you let me teach you how to drive?" he asked.

"Ian—" she began, feeling frustrated and a little helpless.

"I'm not saying it to control you. I'd like you to feel more in control over your life, in fact," he interrupted, cutting his chicken fillet briskly. He glanced up when she didn't speak. "Come on, Francesca," he coaxed. "Be a little impulsive."

"Oh, *ha ha*," she said sarcastically, but she couldn't help but smile at his goading. She melted a little when he grinned back, a devilish, sexy gleam in his eyes. "You act like you're planning on teaching me to drive here in Paris after we finish lunch."

"That's because I am," he said, picking up his phone.

They lingered at the bistro, talking, sipping coffee, and waiting for Jacob to arrive with the car Ian had requested.

"There he is," Ian said, his gaze on a shiny black BMW sedan with tinted windows. She'd listened to him ask Jacob to lease an automatic-transmission vehicle and bring it to the bistro address. Now here was Jacob, not a half hour later. It was so strange to consider the things one could do on a whim when money was no object.

She couldn't believe she'd let him talk her into this.

She smiled at Jacob as he handed Ian the keys. "Aren't we going to drop you off?" she asked the driver when he turned to walk down the sidewalk.

"I'll just walk to the hotel. It's not far," Jacob assured cheerfully before he waved and turned away.

Ian opened the passenger-side door for her. She was relieved that he wasn't going to start teaching her to drive on the busy Paris streets. Even so, she was convinced that a disaster was about to occur.

"This is an extremely nice car," she said, sitting on the passenger side and watching while Ian adjusted the driver's seat for his long legs. "Couldn't you have rented a banged-up car? What if I wreck this one?"

"You won't wreck it," he said as he began to drive down the shaded street. Clouds were rolling in, hiding the gorgeous golden sunshine they'd relished the entire autumn day. "You have excellent reflexes and good eyes. I noticed during our little fencing match."

He glanced quickly to the side and caught her staring at him. She blinked, her gaze bouncing off him. She'd only seen him drive one other time—that night he'd yanked her out of the tattoo parlor. Maybe he was right about power and driving. He seemed utterly in control as he maneuvered skillfully through Paris traffic. She couldn't remove her gaze from his large hands grasping the leather wheel, his touch light but sure, like a lover's. For some reason, it made her think of what that crop had looked like in his grip earlier. She shivered.

"Is the air-conditioning too much?" he asked solicitously.

"No. I'm fine. Where are we going?"

"Back to the Musée de St. Germain," he murmured. "It's

closed on Mondays. There's a rather large employee parking lot in the rear, where we can practice."

Francesca had a vision of ramming the car directly into the elaborate palace's wall and couldn't decide if she was glad or uneasy that Ian's grandfather owned the property. It would be a miserable way for the venerable earl to learn of her existence.

Twenty minutes later, she sat behind the wheel of the sedan while Ian sat beside her in the passenger seat. It felt very strange—firstly to be in the driver's seat, and secondly because the wheel was on the opposite side of the car than it would be in the States.

"I think those are all the basics," Ian said after pointing out the key control mechanisms and pedals to her. "Keep your foot on the brake and shift the car into drive."

"Already?" she squeaked nervously.

"The object is to make the car move, Francesca. You can't do that while it's in park," he said dryly. She did what he'd said, her foot jammed against the brake.

"Now ease up on the brake, that's right," he said as the car began to inch forward in the empty parking lot. "Now begin to experiment with pressing on the accelerator . . . easy, Francesca," he added when she pressed too far and the car jolted forward. She slammed her foot on the brake even more aggressively, and they both flew forward against their seat belts.

Damn.

She glanced at Ian nervously.

"As you can see," he said wryly, "the pedals are very sensitive. Keep experimenting. It's the only way you'll learn."

She clenched her teeth together this time and cautiously

touched the accelerator. When the car began to respond to her subtlest urging, a thrill went through her.

"Very good. Now turn to your left and circle around," Ian instructed.

She used too much gas on the curve.

"*Brake.*"

Again, she jolted them against the seat belts.

"I'm sorry," she squealed.

"When I say *brake*, I mean apply your foot gently to the brake to slow down. If I want you to stop, I'll say *stop*. You have to slow on a turn or you'll lose control. Now again," he said, not unkindly.

He was so patient with her for the next half hour, she was a little amazed, especially because she *really* was a bad driver. Her jerky stops and accelerations smoothed out quite a bit under Ian's tutelage, however, and she was starting to feel euphoric piloting the sleek, responsive vehicle.

"Now park in that end spot there," he requested, pointing. Rain began to spatter on the windshield as she did a neat turn into the parking spot and cried out in triumph. "Very nice," Ian complimented, smiling at her when she turned to him. "We'll practice more when we get to Chicago. I'll have Lin forward the rules of the road so you can study on the plane home tomorrow, and you'll be ready to take the test in a week or so."

She was so excited, she didn't comment on his meticulous planning of the details of her life. She held on to the wheel and stared out the front window, grinning. Learning to drive had been a much more liberating experience than she'd imagined. Or was she just euphoric because Ian had been the one to patiently instruct her?

"You see, it's not so hard," he said as rain began to fall rapidly on the windshield in fat drops. "Turn on your wipers and lights. It's really starting to come down. Here," he said, pointing to the respective controls. "Good. We'll just try one other thing before the storm hits full force. I want you to back out of the spot and turn the car to the left. That's correct," he said as she began to go in reverse. "Use your mirrors. No . . . no, the other way, Francesca." She fumbled, confused as to how to move the wheel while going backward to get the desired result. Meaning to brake, she hit the accelerator hard at the same moment that she twisted the wheel in the other direction. When the car lurched, she slammed down on the brake, with the result that the car swung around on the wet pavement in a complete circle.

Electricity seemed to spark in her veins at the unexpected, abrupt exhilaration of movement . . . of losing control.

She whooped.

The vehicle came to a brain-rattling halt, causing her hair to fling forward onto the wheel when the seat belt caught her. She experienced a sudden, strange kinship with the car—as if it were alive and had just revealed a rebellious streak. She snorted with laughter

"Francesca," Ian said sharply.

She ceased her laughter and looked over at him wide-eyed. He looked stunned and a little ruffled. "I'm really sorry, Ian."

"Put the car in park," he said briskly. Was he angry with her? He hated disorder, despised when she lost control. She followed his instructions quickly, feeling a little breathless and dizzy, not sure if her reaction came from the car whipping around in a tight circle or the glint in Ian's eyes just now.

"I told you this was a bad idea," she muttered, turning the key in the ignition so as not to cause any further unintentional havoc.

"It wasn't a bad idea," he said, his mouth set in a hard line. Her breath froze in her lungs when he reached for her, his fingers furrowing into her hair, turning her face toward him. The next thing she knew, he'd leaned over and captured her mouth. The adrenaline rush that had gone through her when the car spun around on the wet pavement was nothing compared to the surge of excitement at Ian's unexpected kiss. She melted against his heat, his taste inundating her, the demanding thrusts of his tongue overpowering her senses. He applied a suction so precise, liquid surged between her thighs as if he'd somehow conjured it with his mouth. She was panting by the time he lifted his head a moment later.

"You're so beautiful," he said roughly.

"I . . . I what?" she asked, still bewildered and stunned by his kiss.

He smiled and stroked her cheek softly. "Get into the backseat and take off your jeans and panties. I have to taste you. Now."

She stared at him openmouthed and then looked out the car window anxiously.

"No one is around. Even if someone did pass by or someone studied the museum surveillance, the windows are tinted. Now do as I say," he said gently. "I'll join you there in a moment."

She unbuckled her seat belt, her breathing still erratic,

and opened the driver's-side door. A steady rain had started to fall, so she slammed the door shut quickly and dashed for the rear. She felt extremely awkward and excited when she got into the plush interior of the rear of the cab. Ian was still sitting in the passenger seat, his head lowered. She wondered if he was tapping his fingers on his cell phone, and felt sure that he was.

Slowly, she began to unbuckle her belt and unfasten her button fly.

When she'd removed her jeans and panties, she sat there feeling foolish. He didn't move. Her pussy tingled against the taut, smooth seat. She shifted restlessly, wincing at the pleasurable friction of her sensitive tissue against cool leather. What was Ian *doing*? She opened her mouth to tell him she'd removed her jeans, but he abruptly whipped off his seat belt.

She didn't think she drew a breath until he joined her a moment later in the shadowed interior of the cab. He slammed the door closed. With him on the seat with her, the space suddenly felt smaller and more intimate. In the distance, thunder rumbled and rain pitter-pattered on the roof.

He glanced over at her, wiping his hand over his slightly rain dampened, dark hair.

"You know what I want," he said quietly. "Lie back and make your pussy available to me."

His deep voice echoed around her head in the ensuing silence. Her sex throbbed and prickled with excitement. She couldn't help but recall the pure, distilled pleasure he'd given her last night with his mouth. She did her best to find a position to accommodate him. For once, he wasn't instructing her. He just watched as she leaned against the door and spread her thighs as wide as she could, given the barrier of the backseat. Her heart was pounding against her breastbone by the time she settled. Her anticipation was so sharp, it pressed down uncomfortably on her chest. He sat unmoving, his gaze glued between her thighs.

Suddenly he sat forward and pushed on her outer knee, sending her sandal-covered foot to the floorboard of the car, spreading her wider. The vision of his dark head lowering between her legs was so exciting, she bit off a moan before he ever touched her.

She whimpered when he placed his entire opened mouth over her outer sex. It felt hot and wet and unbearably exciting. He moved his lips erotically against her clit, applying a taut pressure, and then parted her labia with his sleek tongue. He shifted, burying his face more intimately in her sex, lashing at her clit more forcefully than he had last night, rubbing it, circling it, pressing it so ruthlessly that she screamed and bucked her hips.

He held her steady with his hands, forcing her to take her pleasure full-on. She grabbed onto his head, feeling herself burn and melt beneath him. He ate her with a tight focus, his actions almost angry they were so relentless, as if her pussy had done something to offend him . . . like he needed to show it who was master.

*He was,* Francesca thought through a haze of sexual heat. Her head fell against the window with a thud, but she was heedless. How could she experience discomfort when she was swimming in bliss?

What sort of a fool was she to take him as a lover? When he walked away from her, she'd never be satisfied with another. She'd be ruined for life.

He used his fingers to part her sex lips. He lifted his head and began to whip her clit hard, pressing and agitating until she called out to him in a frenzy of lust. The vision of him tonguing her sex was indecently lewd . . . unbearably exciting. Her fingers gripped in his short hair, and she cried out sharply.

She exploded in climax, holding on to his head as if she thought she was drowning and he was her only lifesaver. He continued to eat her as she shook, keeping her right on the crest of her climax for what seemed like forever, demanding she give him his due. Just when she fell limp, thinking he'd squeezed every last blast of pleasure from her, he'd move his head or his tongue in such a way that she shuddered again.

He coaxed one last shiver out of her a moment later, before he lifted his head. Her vagina clenched tight when she saw that his lower face glistened with her juices. She panted for air as he regarded her soberly.

"I want to be able to do that to you," she whispered, meaning it with every ounce of her spirit. What a powerful gift he had the power to give. She wanted to reciprocate.

"Have you ever? Used your mouth to pleasure a man?"

She shook her head. He grunted, and she couldn't tell if he was pleased or irritated. Perhaps both.

"I didn't think so. You'll learn, but those aren't the type of lessons that should be given in the backseat of a car," he said before he sat up. She watched as he closed his eyes tightly for a second and put his hand over his mouth. He dropped his hand and glanced over at her, his distracted gaze once again fixing on her pussy and narrowing. Again, he clamped his eyelids shut.

"Get dressed," he said grimly, reaching for the car door. "I'm taking you back to the hotel, and you're going to deliver on your promise."

The stark anticipation she'd experienced when he'd told her to get into the backseat began to mount again as she reached for her clothing.

# Ten

Ian didn't say anything on the rainy drive home, and
Francesca was too keyed up to push any conversation. It was
as if something had happened back there in the car that she
couldn't understand. Some sort of nameless, thick tension
seemed to fill the air between them. She would have thought
it was the low pressure from the storm but knew it didn't
exude from rain clouds.

Ian was the source.

When they arrived at the hotel and pulled beneath the
entrance canopy, a young, energetic valet greeted Ian by
name. Ian gave him some directions about returning the car
to the rental agency in English and then handed him the
keys along with a wad of cash.

"Thank you, Mr. Noble," the valet gushed appreciatively
in heavily accented English. "Never worry that the car will
be returned very fast. I'll see to it myself."

"*You don't have to worry. The car will be returned very
quickly,*" Ian said distractedly as he took Francesca's hand.

"Yes, as you say. *You don't have to worry. The car will be returned very quickly,*" the young man repeated aloud, and then several times under his breath.

"I won't give it another thought, Gene," Ian said with a small smile. The short conversation with the valet seemed to lighten his mood a tad. He noticed her raised eyebrows and curious expression when they got on the elevator. "I told Gene I'd try him out in my mailroom if he learned English. He has an aunt and uncle in Chicago and a big American dream."

She smiled as they stepped off the elevator. "Watch out, Ian."

He glanced sideways at her as he used the card key to the suite.

"You're exposing your soft spots."

"You think so?" he asked unconcernedly as he held the door open for her to enter. "I think I'm being very practical. I've observed firsthand what a hard worker Gene is. He scrambles to please when others shuffle."

"And of course you always want those who are most willing to please you."

"Yes," he said, ignoring the sarcasm in her voice. He'd led her to the bedroom suite and now turned to face her. "Are you struggling with that, Francesca?"

"With what?" she asked, confused.

"With entering into an agreement where the primary goal is to please me."

"I do this to please myself," she said, lifting her chin.

His amused glance ran over her face. "Yes," he murmured, touching her jaw with gentle, blunt-tipped fingers. She shivered. "And that's what makes you so special. Because pleasing me does please you."

She frowned. Something about what he'd said encroached on that uncomfortable topic of domination and submission.

He smiled and dropped his hand. "I would prefer you didn't struggle so much with the basics, lovely. There's nothing shameful about your nature. In fact, I find you exquisite. You really have no idea why I had to have you at all costs, do you? There's a quality in you that only a man like me can see . . ." He tapered off when he noticed the bewilderment on her face. He exhaled heavily. "Perhaps time is what is needed in your case. That, and practice."

She blinked when she saw the gleam in his eyes.

"Please undress and put on a robe. Brush your hair, but then restrain it at the back of your head. Sit at the corner of the bed. I'll be with you momentarily. We need a few things for this very important lesson."

*You really have no idea why I had to have you at all costs, do you?*

Ian's words kept echoing in her head as she did the things he'd asked, plus brushed her teeth. Sitting and waiting at the corner of the bed definitely ratcheted up her anxiety. She wasn't pleased, necessarily, that she was so eager to please Ian sexually, to give him the type of pleasure he could give her, but she was honest enough to admit it was true to herself. She had no right to mentally cast aspersions on Ian for his preferences when she herself possessed equally dark desires.

Her thoughts were cut short when Ian walked into the room wearing only the black pants, his torso and feet bare, and carrying a small plastic bag. She watched him, growing breathless at the vision of his near nudity. Would he ever allow her to touch and caress and pet all those sleek, bulging muscles and smooth skin? His nipples were tiny and almost always erect, as far as she'd observed. He set down the bag on one of the chairs at the end of the bed. He took out something with straps she couldn't identify, along with something she did recognize: the leather handcuffs. He stepped toward her, the items in his hands.

"Why do I have to wear the handcuffs for this?" she asked, disappointment filtering into her tone. She'd thought she was finally going to get the opportunity to touch him.

"Because I say so," he said gently. "Now stand up and remove the robe." She came down from the corner of the bed and untied the robe. The air felt a little chilly on her naked skin. Her nipples pulled tight as she tossed the robe on the end of the bed.

"It's cool, but I think what I have in mind will be making you very warm very soon. Turn your back to me," Ian said.

Once again, she had to resist a strong urge to gawk over her shoulder and see what he was doing back there. "Put your wrists together at your back," he instructed. Her clit pinched in excitement when she felt him buckle the restraints around her wrists, binding her arms behind her back. "Now turn around." She let out a small gasp when she saw the white jar that he held. Heat rushed between her thighs. She was becoming conditioned to that little jar of cream. Her body responded just upon seeing it. Ian paused, seeming to notice her reaction as she eyed the emollient.

"I'm acquainted with a doctor of Chinese medicine in Chicago who recommended this stimulant, but I'd never used it before you. I'm getting the distinct impression that you approve of it," he said, his full lips shaping into a small smile. He stepped toward her and she held her breath, knowing what was to come. He plunged his finger between her labia and rubbed her clit, covering it with the stimulant. She bit her lower lip to prevent herself from crying out in excitement. Maybe it was her imagination of what was to come, but she already began to burn.

He dropped his hand. She watched anxiously as he picked up the item with the black straps that she'd noticed earlier. There was a thin cord attached to it as well, with a small control panel.

"What's that?" she asked, slightly alarmed.

"It's something designed purely for your pleasure, lovely. Don't be afraid," he said as he came toward her. "It's a hands-free vibrator," he explained, sliding the adjustable straps around her hips and tightening them. She stared down in mixed fascination and arousal as she saw him press a clear, ridged, jellylike column against her labia and clit. He set the control panel with a dial at the edge of the bed. "I don't relish making you uncomfortable, but since you are inexperienced, your first lessons at this might be more . . . trying for you until you become used to things. I want you to feel pleasure while you're learning me. It will make things easier for you. Perhaps."

"I don't understand," she said as he further tightened the straps on the vibrator until they were snug, and stepped back, examining his handiwork. It was as if she wore a skimpy pair of underwear with the little vibrator wedged between her labia. Her pussy was already buzzing just from the slight pressure and the clitoral cream, and Ian hadn't even turned on the device yet.

He regarded her soberly for a moment, her nipples pinching tight when his gaze lingered on her breasts. "I happen to be very demanding when it comes to fellatio."

"Oh," she said, unable to think of anything else to say. He'd said it almost apologetically.

"I've never taught a woman to do this. I suspect I'll be a failure at easing you into this particular activity, but I want you to know that I put considerable thought into it."

"What do you mean?" She grew increasingly confused by the moment. Were they even talking about the same thing? He'd said fellatio, so she *thought* so, but still . . .

"It's a bit of a conundrum. I can't change my demanding nature, and I doubt I could if I tried my hardest in this case, as attracted to you as I am."

She felt her cheeks heat. Sometimes, Ian could say the nicest things and not even seem aware how his casual statements affected her.

"On the other hand, I understand that how a woman is introduced to giving oral sex has a major impact on whether or not she'll enjoy it in the long term, so I had to really consider."

"I see," she whispered. She couldn't believe they were having this conversation. She hadn't really thought about the mechanics before, but Ian's cock was . . . formidable. She met his stare and saw that he'd been studying her face.

"I'm confusing you," he said, sighing. "As I said, I don't want to make you dread this. Especially since I've been fantasizing about you taking me into your mouth since I first laid eyes on you. I'll want it frequently, Francesca, and I would prefer if we found it mutually satisfying."

She blushed uncontrollably. The cream began to tickle and burn her clit.

"Okay," she said. He touched her cheek.

"Kneel," he stated simply.

He supported her at the shoulders while she went to her knees, since her wrists were restrained behind her back. She looked up and swallowed thickly. Her face was directly in front of Ian's crotch. She watched, spellbound, as he unbuttoned and unzipped his pants, revealing a snow white pair of boxer briefs. He reached down into the left pant leg of the brief and extracted the shaft of his penis. He lowered his pants and the briefs, but didn't remove them, leaving them gathered beneath his testicles. Suddenly she was just inches away from his exposed cock and shaved balls. He was hard—not iron hard like she'd seen him in the past but aroused nonetheless. He was beautiful. She licked her lower lip nervously as she studied the tapered, fat head. The thickest portion of it at the base had the circumference of a small plum. Had his cock really been inside her body? How in the world would she take it into her throat?

"You even have to be dressed for *this*?" she asked, looking up at him, her eyes wide. A shiver went through her at the sight of him standing there, so tall and commanding, his cock poking from the trousers. It was an intimidating sight . . . an intensely erotic one.

"Yes. Are you ready to begin?"

He palmed the thick shaft and moved his hand along it while she watched.

"Yes."

He released the shaft of his penis, the weight of it causing it to fall down at an angle. Her lips tingled in anticipation.

"Oh!" She jumped.

He'd turned on the vibrator. It buzzed energetically against her labia and clit. She looked up at him, stunned by the rush of intense pleasure. He studied her face closely. She felt a flush of warmth go over her chest, lips, and cheeks. It felt sinfully good. He grunted in satisfaction and stood before her again. He took his cock into his hand.

"I will teach you to use your hand with your mouth on another occasion. Today you will grow familiar with having me in your mouth," he said. She went still when he stepped nearer and brushed her lips with the tip of his cock. She parted. "Stay still," he ordered tautly. She remained immobile while he outlined her lips, the fleshy tip of his cock feeling smooth and warm against the quivering flesh. His scent entered her flared nostrils . . . musk and man. Her vagina clenched tight and she moaned softly. The stalk grew firmer and the head felt tauter against her lips. Unable to stop herself, she touched the tip of her tongue to the succulent flesh.

"Francesca," he warned, pausing in his circling motions. She looked up at him anxiously. He frowned.

"I forgot the damn blindfold again," she thought she heard him mumble under his breath. "Spread your lips wide."

She opened as far as she could. He inserted the tip of his cock into her mouth. "Use your lips to cover your teeth," she heard him say through the bang of her heartbeat against her eardrums. "Make them into a stiff ridge. The harder you can squeeze, the greater pleasure you will give me." She clamped him as hard as she could when she heard that. He grunted. "Good. Now bathe the head with your tongue," he said from above her.

She eagerly did what he said, becoming even more excited as she watched him move his hand up and down the shaft.

Was there anything more erotic in the world than seeing Ian touch himself?

"That's right. Learn my shape. Press hard." She followed his instructions eagerly. "Yes. *There*," he said, his voice sounding a little rough when she charted the thick rim beneath the head and pushed against the tiny slit. She was rewarded with a few drops of pre-ejaculate. His taste spread on her tongue, unique . . . addictive. She pressed more forcefully. He growled softly and pushed another inch of his cock into her mouth. He opened his hand at the back of her head, holding her steady. He retracted and flexed his hips, sawing his cock just an inch or two back and forth, again and again.

"Now suck," he said tautly.

She squeezed him with her rigid lips and applied a firm suction.

"Ah, yeah. That's a good little student," he said raggedly from above her as he continued to thrust between her lips.

The vibrator was killing her. She couldn't escape from the persistent buzz on her sizzling clit. Like yesterday, she felt her nipples and the soles of her feet begin to burn as well. Her lips, too, felt overly sensitive, stretched as they were around the thick stalk of Ian's cock. They were starting to hurt from maintaining a constant viselike pressure around his thrusting penis. Still, she wanted more. She needed it.

She ducked her head forward, feeling him slide along her tongue, filling her mouth. He grunted and clutched at the hair on the back of her head, halting her.

"If you are impulsive like that again, we'll stop."

She blinked open her eyelids, his sharp tone penetrating her dazed excitement. His cock throbbed in her mouth. The vibrator was about to bring her off. It was a ruthless little thing. She couldn't seem to help her reaction.

She looked up at him helplessly, unable to speak with his now-raging erection lodged in her mouth. His face darkened when he saw her expression.

"Francesca?"

She began to shudder in orgasm, her breath popping out of her lungs in little gasps that were stifled by his cock. She saw his eyes widen in disbelief before she clamped her eyelids shut, shame flooding her at her inability to control her monumental need.


Ian stared down at her, not understanding her desperate expression until she began to tremble in obvious orgasm. He'd never been in a woman's mouth before while she came. He'd never considered a woman's pleasure before while he'd been taking his own.

More fool him.

He groaned uncontrollably at the sensation of her sweet, hot mouth quivering around his cock. Unable to stop himself, he furrowed his fingers through her smooth hair and slid farther into the heaven of her. She made a squealing sound deep in her throat, the sound vibrating into his cock along with her delicate shudders of orgasm. He slid out a few inches to give her some relief. She almost pulled his trigger when she continued to pull on him with an eye-crossing suction and slapped her tongue repeatedly against the head.

He opened his mouth to rebuke her but stopped himself at the last moment, thrusting into her mouth again. What

sort of an idiot corrected something so fucking good? He let
her control the movements for a moment, watching her in
intense arousal as she ducked her head, sliding his cock back
and forth between her pink lips energetically.

"That's right," he murmured. "Just take as much as you
can." A thrill went through him. Her obvious enthusiasm
went a long way to making up for her inexperience. And she
was strong. She gripped him like a vise. Her suction was
exquisite, but still he challenged her.

"Suck harder," he said, beginning to thrust his hips in
rhythm with her bobbing head. He growled, low and feral,
when she surpassed his expectations. He watched as her
flagrantly pink cheeks hollowed out, and he felt them touch
the sides of his thrusting cock.

It was too much. He pulled back gently on her hair. Her
eyelids opened sluggishly, and she looked up at him, the
vision of her spread, cock-ravaged lips and dark eyes shining
with arousal scoring his consciousness.

"You must take me deeper," he said gently. "Breathe
through your nose. If it feels uncomfortable for a moment,
know that I won't let it continue for long. Do you
understand?"

She nodded, the trust and arousal he saw in her velvety
eyes making him clench his jaw hard. He held her stare as he
thrust forward and felt the tight ring of her throat enclose
the tip of his cock. A shudder of pleasure went through him.
She blinked and gagged but contained herself sufficiently
not to balk. He groaned and slid out of her throat. "That's
right. Breathe through your nose," he soothed even as he
thrust into her again. This time, he grimaced when his cock
leapt in excitement while lodged in her throat. "I'm sorry,"

he rushed to say as he withdrew. He cringed inwardly when he saw two tears run down her cheek.

"Are you all right?" he asked.

She widened her eyes as if to reassure him, and nodded, causing his cock to bob. He grimaced as pleasure stabbed through him at the sign of her eagerness . . . her generosity. Thank God, because she was loveliness personified. He knew he wouldn't stop. He knew he couldn't.

He held her head with both hands, holding her stare as he thrust shallowly in and out of her clamped lips, drying the teardrops on her cheek with his thumbs. The glow of arousal had only grown stronger in the dark orbs of her eyes in the past several minutes, but he saw something else there; something that seemed to bless his sin.

"You please me beyond measure," he said.

He held her steady and thrust into her throat yet again. He lost himself for a minute, everything going black as he took his pleasure in Francesca's sweet mouth and she granted every one of his desperate, depraved wishes. His eyes sprang wide when he felt her shudder while he was thrust deep. He started to withdraw in deference to her discomfort but realized she wasn't gagging.

"*Sweet Francesca*," he grated out, emotion swelling high, bewildering him, when he realized she was coming yet again.

He exploded into her throat, roaring as brutal pleasure tore through him. Even so, he still had the presence of mind to withdraw, coming as he thrust on her tongue. His face clenched tight as he watched her, unable to look away from the spellbinding image of her flagrantly pink cheeks, the helpless expression in her shiny dark eyes as she succumbed to the bliss of having pleased him so well.

Her slender throat convulsed as she swallowed. He continued to shudder and come, unable to stop the scorching waves of pleasure even though Francesca appeared to be having difficulty keeping up with his ejaculations. His suspicion was confirmed when she moaned, her clamping hold on his cock loosening momentarily, and some of his semen spilled from the corner of her lips.

He gasped uncontrollably and clenched his eyes shut, another sharp jolt of climax shaking him, the vision of her burning into his brain. How could an innocent make him so helpless, flay him to the bone, turn him inside out until he felt as raw, as naked, as exposed as he insisted she become for him?

The wild thought made him crack open his eyelids. His clawing hands had loosened her rose-gold hair from the clips at the back of her head. Mussed tendrils of the silky stuff fell down around her white shoulders and brushed her cheek. Her eyes were like dark beacons. He stared down at her lush, erotic beauty like she was the first thing a recovering blind man saw.

He slowly withdrew his cock from her mouth. Her sustained suction caused a wet, popping sound when he cleared her lips. He briefly shut his eyes at the cruelty of being separated from her warmth.

Neither of them spoke as he helped her to her feet and unbuckled the handcuffs. She whimpered softly when he turned off the vibrator.

"I had it on too high for you," he said, his voice sounding flat to his own ears, perhaps because he knew he lied. The vibrator wasn't *that* concise or powerful. She'd come repeatedly while he'd ravished her, while he'd used her mouth for his pleasure, because she was so sweet and so responsive and . . .

. . . *far more than you ever expected or planned for.*

He paused in the action of loosing the straps of the hands-free vibrator.

"Ian?" she asked. He winced when he heard the raspy sound of her voice.

"Yes?" he asked, avoiding her gaze as he mechanically began to replace the things he'd brought into the room back into the bag.

"Is . . . was everything all right?"

"It was fantastic. You once again surpassed my expectations."

"Oh . . . because . . . you seem sort of . . . unhappy."

"Don't be ridiculous," he said quietly, readjusting his clothing and zipping his pants. He looked at her, determinedly ignoring her flagrant beauty and the confused expression in her dark eyes. "Why don't you shower in here, and I'll use the other bathroom? Afterward, I'll order us dinner."

"Okay," she said, the uncertainty in her voice cutting at him.

Still, no matter how sharp the sting, he started to walk out of the room. He stopped abruptly and turned, his control faltering. She hadn't moved. He held out his arms.

"Come here," he said.

She flew across the room. He hugged her to him tightly, inhaling the scent of her hair. Her breasts were a delicious, erotic fullness pressed against his ribs. He wanted to tell her how exquisite the experience had been—how exquisite *she* was—but for some reason, his heart began to beat uncomfortably hard. He didn't like the way he'd felt exposed there at the end . . . weakened by his need for her.

Still, her mouth tempted him. He kissed her with focused restraint, aware of her probable soreness. Her sweet sigh against his mouth made him want to take her over to the bed and spend the night with his lips and nose buried in her silky, fragrant skin. The fantasy of doing just that plagued him.

Instead, he gave her a final kiss and released her, needing to prove to himself he still had the ability to walk away.

# Part Six

## Because You Torment Me

# Eleven

The next morning, Francesca placed the pill on her tongue and tipped some water between her lips, swallowing. She glanced at herself in the bathroom mirror, looking away quickly when she registered her reflection. Seeing herself take the birth-control pill brought last night back to her in a vivid rush: Ian taking her for a private dinner for two with a breathlessly romantic view, her confusion by his aloofness, her sharpness in response to his withdrawal even while he was seemingly so solicitous . . .

. . . their spat and his walking away.

Why was she even bothering to take the birth control after the way Ian had behaved last night? She really was mad—both in the crazy and angry definitions of the term—for agreeing to this venture with him. Her stupidity had never been more evident than since he'd first walked away after such an incredibly erotic and intimate experience yesterday.

It'd been incredibly erotic and intimate to *Francesca*, anyway. Ian must have considered it par for the course.

*Or another example of the good service he deserved.*

Anger flared in her at the incendiary thought.

True, he'd spent time with her after they'd . . . done what they'd done—she didn't know what to *call* it, precisely. She would have said made love, but Ian clearly wouldn't agree. After he'd instructed her on how to give him pleasure with her mouth? After they'd brought each other off? After he'd made her lose herself so greatly in need, that it was now difficult to look at her own reflection in the mirror?

He not only had spent time with her, to a casual observer, he'd treated her to a once-in-a-lifetime experience. After they'd both showered in separate bathrooms, he'd reappeared, looking extremely handsome in a pair of gray pants that highlighted his long legs and narrow hips, a light blue button-down shirt and sport jacket.

"Are you ready? We're having dinner at Le Cinq," he said, standing in the entry to the bedroom suite.

She gasped and looked down at herself in alarm. "I thought we were ordering food here in the suite. I can't go to Le Cinq dressed like this!" she exclaimed, recalling everything she'd read and heard about the exclusive restaurant housed in the hotel. Why had Ian changed their plans? He'd said they'd just order the food in. Did he perhaps think that the atmosphere of the private suite was suddenly too intimate?

"Certainly you can," he'd said, his manner all brisk British aristocrat. He'd held out his hand expectantly before he registered her disbelief. "I've requested a private outdoor terrace for us."

"Ian, I can't! Not like this," she'd protested, sweeping her hand over her attire.

"You *will*," he'd said, giving her an amused glance. "We won't be seen by the other patrons. And if a single nose is turned up at your Cubs T-shirt, I'll deal with the offending nose personally."

What he'd said had been assuring, and even sweet, but with her growing awareness of him, Francesca still sensed the distant preoccupation that had descended upon him after their electric, erotic encounter earlier.

Feeling extremely doubtful, she'd hurried into her shoes upon Ian's request, and put her hand in his. She'd trailed him into the elevator and down corridors, the whole time hissing worried protests behind him that they'd kick her out of the luxurious restaurant for showing up in jeans and a T-shirt. Ian had never replied, just led her on without comment.

The smiling maître d' of the posh restaurant had greeted Ian like an old friend. Francesca had stood there awkwardly while the two men exchanged conversation in rapid French, wishing the sleek marble floor would open up and swallow her. The maître d' had only smiled broadly at her, however, when Ian introduced her, making her blush when he took her hand and brushed his lips across her knuckles like she was Cinderella on the night of the ball instead of awkward, T-shirt-wearing Francesca Arno.

She'd stared in openmouthed amazement a moment later when the maître d' led them onto a candlelit private terrace with a stunning view of the glowing lacework steel Eiffel Tower. Two heat lamps had warmed the pleasant, cool autumn evening. The table had been a glittering visual delight of flame, crystal, and gold dinnerware and a lush flower arrangement of white hydrangeas.

She'd looked over at Ian in surprise and saw that the maître d' had left. They were alone on the terrace, and Ian was holding her chair for her.

"Did you arrange all this?" she'd asked him, looking over her shoulder to hold his stare.

"Yes," he'd said, seating her.

"You should have let me dress for dinner."

"I told you once before that a woman wears the clothes, Francesca," he'd said as he sat across the table from her. His eyes had been the color of the midnight-blue sky in the candlelight. "If a woman recognizes her power, she can present herself in rags and people will recognize her as a queen."

She'd scoffed. "That sounds like the type of thing an earl's grandson would be taught. I'm afraid I live in a different world, Ian."

They'd eaten a luxurious meal, exchanging conversation, sipping red wine, and sampling items from the sumptuous gourmet tasting menu, being waited on hand and foot by not one but two waiters, neither one of which so much as blinked an eye at Francesca's apparel. Apparently, being Ian's guest conferred a special status. When she'd shivered at a brisk breeze, Ian had stood and removed his jacket, insisting that she put it on.

Anybody else would probably have thought it a storybook romantic evening, but as the dinner progressed, Francesca's uncertainty and frustration at Ian's distance had only amplified. He was solicitous and polite . . . the perfect companion. At first, she'd blamed some of the strained atmosphere on the omnipresence of the hovering waiters during their meal, but as time wore on, she knew that wasn't it.

He'd definitely shut himself off from her after teaching her how to pleasure him. Why? Had she done it all wrong, and he was too polite to tell her the truth?

Had he perhaps had his fill of her already?

Her suspicions were confirmed when they returned to the suite later and he'd asked her if she minded if he attended to some work. She'd responded with a careless "Of course not," but her uncertainty was quickly morphing to anger. She'd gone into the bedroom and checked her e-mails on her phone.

At one point, he'd entered the bedroom, causing her heart to jump. However, he'd merely handed her a package. She'd opened it to find a three-month supply of birth-control pills inside.

"These were just delivered. Aaron, the pharmacist, says you may begin taking them immediately. I had him include instructions in English," he'd said.

"How considerate of you."

He blinked at her quiet sarcasm.

"Are you upset about my suggesting you go on the pill? I'm having the results of a recent medical exam sent to me. I'll show it to you. I want you to be reassured that I'm clean and perfectly healthy, as well. As long as we're together, I won't be with anyone else."

"That's not what I was thinking about," she said, even though relief had gone through her at his words. She should have brought up that topic before.

His gaze ran over her face searchingly. "You've noticed that I've been preoccupied this evening? I'm sorry," he said after a pause. "I needed to get some work done. I have a very important acquisition that I've been planning for ages finally coming to fruition next week."

She'd given him a bland glance. It wasn't his work that had her irritated and anxious, either, and he must know that. It was the contrast of their incredibly intimate sexual experience and his current aloofness.

He'd stared at her silently for a moment, as if gathering his thoughts. Anticipation had risen in her about what he was about to say, her sarcastic expression easing. She'd experienced an overwhelming need to take his hand in reassurance.

"Would you like me to get you a glass of water?"

She'd closed her eyes briefly as disappointment flooded her at his question.

"I told you I was abominable with women," he'd said in a harsh, restrained tone. She'd opened her eyes.

"You also once told me you weren't a nice man. I can't help but notice that neither on that occasion nor this one have you expressed an ounce of remorse for your shortcomings . . . not a hint of a struggle."

Anger had leapt in his eyes at that.

"I suppose you feel you can make me a better man," he'd said, his full lips twisting as if he'd tasted something bitter. "Take a word of advice, Francesca, and save yourself the effort. I am what I am, and I've never lied to you about being anything more."

She'd stared at his tall form as he walked out of the room, mute with rising bewilderment, anger, and hurt.

Is that what he thought? That she wanted to change him just because she was confused by his withdrawal after they'd had sex?

Or was he *right* to admonish her? He'd been completely attentive to her every wish all evening, treating her to an exclusive dining experience while overlooking the most romantic skyline in the world.

He hadn't offered her his heart; he'd promised her experience and pleasure, and he'd delivered both in spades.

Her thoughts had only tangled her up further, creating an anxious knot in her belly. She'd tried to read an e-book on her phone but mostly stewed in her confusion and hurt until she'd fallen asleep.

This morning when she'd wakened, he was nowhere to be seen. She had a vague recollection of the hard, warm length of him pressing against her at some point in the night—his arms around her, his mouth moving across the skin between her neck and shoulder in a taut, electric kiss. It was difficult, however, to determine if the stirring memory was a dream or reality.

There had been a note on the bedside table.

> Francesca,
> I had a breakfast meeting in La Galerie down-stairs. Feel free to call room service if you like. We're due to leave Paris for Chicago at 11:30. Please get packed and ready, and I'll return to the suite to retrieve you at 9:00.
> Ian

She scowled when she read the message. He'd made it sound like she was a package or a suitcase.

At ten minutes past nine, she stood in the living room of the suite, her purse and packed duffel bag on her shoulder, both regretful about leaving the exquisite Parisian suite where Ian had taught her so much about desire, and longing for the normalcy—the mundane sanity—of her everyday life.

She checked her watch and scowled. No Ian.

*Screw this.*

Feeling restless, she dashed off a quick note to Ian that she'd meet him in the lobby and exited the hotel suite. It'd get her mind off things to sit in the luxurious lobby and watch all the sophisticated, well-heeled patrons while she waited.

Downstairs, she sunk into one of the plush lobby chairs and dug into her purse for her cell phone, meaning to check messages. Something caught her attention from the corner of her eye. When she realized it was Ian's tall, singular form that had snagged her focus, she leaned back in the chair, peering around the barrier of the upholstered winged back. He was walking out of La Galerie, one of the hotel restaurants, his arm around a well-dressed dark-haired woman who looked to be in her mid-thirties. Francesca couldn't hear their conversation at this distance, but their exchange struck her as intense somehow . . . intimate.

Was that why she'd instinctively ducked back behind the barrier of the chair?

Ian reached into the handsome sport jacket he was wearing and handed the woman an envelope. She accepted it with a smile and went up on her toes, kissing his cheek. Francesca's heart leapt and then slowed to a sluggish throb as she watched Ian put his hands on the attractive woman's shoulders and kiss both of her cheeks in return.

They gave each other a smile that struck Francesca as poignant . . . sad. The woman nodded once, as if to silently reassure him everything would be all right, before ducking her head and turning to walk across the shining white marble floor of the lobby, tucking the envelope Ian had given her into the leather briefcase she carried. Ian just stood there for a moment watching the woman depart, an expression she'd never seen before on his bold, masculine features.

He looked a little lost.

Francesca leaned back in the chair, blindly staring at the extravagant fresh flower arrangement on the table before her. Her heart seemed to shrivel in her chest. It felt like she'd just walked in on him in the midst of a very personal act. She didn't understand completely what she'd just seen, but somehow she just *knew* it'd been something important to Ian . . . something charged.

Something he wouldn't have *wanted* her to see.

When she spied him walking into a jewelry shop housed in the hotel lobby a moment later, she sprang up from the chair and charged toward the elevator bank.

"Hi. I thought I'd wait for you in the lobby," she said to him a few minutes later with false cheerfulness. They'd met in front of the elevators, Francesca acting as if she'd just arrived on the lobby level.

He blinked at her unexpected appearance. "I thought I'd asked you to meet me in the suite," he said, looking a little nonplussed . . . and amazingly gorgeous. Would his dark, intense male beauty ever cease to hit her like a physical blow?

"Yes. I saw your note." She noticed his near-black brows rise in a silent challenge. "*I* left a note, too, telling you I'd meet you down here."

His full lips twitched, but she wasn't sure if it was in irritation or amusement.

"I owe you an apology for my lateness. I had an important

appointment with a close family friend who happened to be in town, at a conference. I'll just go up and get my things and join you in the lobby."

"Okay," she said, wondering all the while about the identity of this beautiful, close family friend who had the ability to pierce Ian's seemingly impenetrable emotional armor.

*Had he bought something in the jewelry store for that mysterious woman?*

Knowing she couldn't ask that question, she started to walk past him. She halted when he put his hand on her upper arm.

"I'm sorry about last night."

She just stared at him, mute with surprise at his admission and what seemed to be genuine regret in his tone.

"Which part?"

"I think you know which part," he said quietly after a moment. "I was a million miles away last night. I fear you felt abandoned."

"Wasn't I?"

"No. I'm still right here, Francesca—for whatever that's worth," he added grimly. He leaned down and seized her mouth in a kiss that was both tender and passionate. Was it her imagination or did that kiss seem to tell her something Ian couldn't say?

Francesca just stared at his broad retreating back a moment later, experiencing her typical bewilderment when it came to Ian, her heart still throbbing all the way to her clenched sex from his kiss.

Despite his earlier apology, she still sensed Ian's preoccupation as Jacob drove them to the airport and they boarded his private jet. She was torn between feeling concern for him—compassion for that lost-looking Ian she'd glimpsed in the hotel lobby—and lingering irritation at his apparent ability to shut his awareness of her out like a light.

"What's this important acquisition you said you had coming up later this week?" Francesca asked once she was seated across from him on the plane and he bent to retrieve his computer from his briefcase.

"I've been wooing a particularly coy—well, actually, annoying as hell, to be honest—owner of a company for over a year now, and it appears that we're finally getting to a compromise," he said, opening his computer. "I'm not that interested in the company itself, but the deal includes a patent on a piece of software I absolutely require for this new social-media–gaming venture I'm starting." He glanced up at her and then apologetically at his computer. "Would you mind?"

"No, of course not," Francesca said, meaning it. He may confuse and vex her, but she wasn't so clingy that she constantly required his attention. He immediately plunged into work when they arrived on the plane, reading files, typing fleetly, and occasionally making a terse phone call.

Francesca learned from a message on her cell phone that Lin Soong had e-mailed her the "Illinois Rules of the Road" manual. *When had Ian made the request of his assistant?* Last night, while he'd been ignoring her after their romantic dinner?

*Didn't that mean he'd thought about her . . . even a bit?*

And weren't those precisely the kind of slavish thoughts

a supposed submissive had, constantly gauging her world by whether or not her master was thinking about her, whether or not he was pleased by her?

Disgusted by the mere idea, Francesca determinedly turned her attention away from the compelling man who sat across from her. She e-mailed a warm thank-you message to Lin, then briskly asked Ian if she could borrow his tablet.

"Why?"

"To read something."

"The 'Rules of the Road' that I had Lin send you?"

"No," she lied without blinking. "A trashy novel."

She gave a small smile at his dry glance. He handed her the tablet without hesitation or further comment.

Fortunately, Francesca could be nearly as focused on a task when she wanted to be as Ian. She diligently memorized each rule of the road on the flight home, oddly determined to get her driver's license now that Ian had brought the issue to the forefront. The experience of being in control behind the wheel had exhilarated her. After a while, she forgot her irritation at Ian, feeling comfortable with his presence as they both attended to their separate concerns.

She napped for a while and used the restroom. In her absence, Ian had brought both of them a refreshment from the wet bar. She sipped on her chilled club soda and watched him for a moment as he worked. He really was a force of nature. If he could patent that intense focus of his, he'd be the wealthiest man on the planet.

*He already is one of them*, she reminded herself wryly with a shake of her head before she went back to studying.

When the pilot's voice came through the intercom and

told them they were beginning their descent into Indiana, Ian glanced up, blinking several times, as if seeing the world around him for the first time. He shut off his computer and raked his fingers through his short, stylishly mussed hair, making Francesca experience a sudden longing to have her fingers where his were.

"How did your studying go?" he asked, his voice sounding a little hoarse from not using it for so long.

"Excellent," she replied, not at all surprised by the fact that he knew she'd been lying about the novel. Not much got past him.

"You say that with a great deal of confidence," he said, sipping his ice water and eyeing her over the rim of the glass.

"No reason I shouldn't."

He put out his hand expectantly. She held his stare and handed him the tablet.

He began to question her on the material. Francesca rattled off the correct answers without hesitation. The pilot informed them to prepare for landing, and Ian closed the tablet, sliding it into his briefcase. His handsome face was impassive, but she had the impression he was pleased.

"I have meetings this afternoon and all of tomorrow at the office, but I'll ask Jacob to take you out for some driving practice. Another time or two behind the wheel, and you'll be ready to get your license," he stated with confidence.

Francesca ignored the flare of irritation she felt—it was as if getting her license had been added to some kind of mental checklist that he planned to complete in methodical Ian fashion. Instead of commenting on that, however, she focused on something else that he'd said that surprised her.

"This *afternoon*? What time is it in Chicago?"

He checked his Rolex. "About the same time that we left Paris: eleven forty."

"Wow, it's like we transported."

He flashed an unexpected smile. The plane dipped as they went in for a landing, amplifying the swooping sensation in her belly. That smile always made him more approachable. She had an overwhelming desire to ask about the woman she'd seen him with this morning, to ask him why he'd seemed so affected by the meeting . . .

. . . to demand that he tell her something that helped her understand the enigma of him.

But Ian had another agenda altogether.

"You mentioned being a financial disaster," he said. Francesca stared at him, openmouthed. It was as if he'd just resumed a conversation they were having yesterday, without a beat. "What do you plan on doing with the money you earned for the painting commission?"

She gripped the armrest, jolting slightly when the plane hit the runway. Ian never blinked.

"What do you mean what do I plan to *do* with it? I plan to use it for my education . . . my future."

"Naturally, but it's not as if you'll have to write a check for a hundred thousand dollars anytime soon, will you?"

She shook her head.

"Why don't you let me invest the bulk of it?"

"No," she blurted out. She saw his blank expression of incredulity at her adamancy. There were thousands of people who would be turning cartwheels at the prospect of financial wizard Ian Noble offering to invest their money for them.

"You can't leave that much money in a checking account,"

he stated as if saying the most obvious thing on the planet. "It makes no sense whatsoever."

"It makes sense to me! People like me don't invest money, Ian."

"People like you? Do you mean other fools? Because that's what you'd have to be to leave that amount of money in a checking account," he said, blue eyes sparking.

She started forward in the lounger, prepared to retort hotly, and then reconsidered. She leaned back and regarded him. He stilled when he noticed her speculative look.

"What?" he asked, slightly suspicious.

"I'll invest it myself if you teach me how."

The wary gleam in his eyes transformed into one of amusement.

"I haven't got time to tutor you." She raised her eyebrows. "Not on personal investing, anyway," he added, a sexy grin pulling at his lips. Her pulse skipped. *God help her*, he was beautiful. He unfastened his seat belt when the plane came to a halt.

"Would you really like to learn about finances?"

"Sure. I need all the help I can get."

He said nothing as he clicked his briefcase closed and stood. He donned his sport coat and came over to her, reaching for her hand. She unfastened her seat belt, and he gently pulled her up next to him.

"We'll have to see what we can manage between your other lessons," he murmured, dipping his head and fitting his lips to hers.

What *was* it about the contrast between Ian's aloofness at times and his sudden, immense heat that created such a sharp, overwhelming longing in her?

It felt strange to her a half an hour later to see the Chicago skyline set against a cornflower-blue sky. It looked the same as it always had, but she felt different. When Jacob veered the limousine onto North Avenue from the interstate, she mentally prepared herself for returning to her former life. It was hard to mentally fit *this* Francesca into the former Francesca's world. Paris had done that to her.

Ian had.

Even if he walked away today, could she really regret her sensual awakening, the widening and deepening of her world?

"Are you painting tomorrow after class?" Ian asked from where he sat across from her on the leather bench seat in the back of the limo.

"Yes," she said, gathering her purse. Jacob had just come to a stop in front of Davie's Wicker Park townhome. She glanced at Ian, feeling a little awkward at the realization that now they would return to their separate worlds. Jacob rapped once on the window, and Ian casually leaned over and rapped once back. The door remained closed.

"I would like you to have dinner with me Thursday evening," he said.

"All right," she said, both pleased and flustered by his statement.

"And on Friday and Saturday, I'd like to have you. Period."

Heat flooded her cheeks. A profound sense of relief struck her. Given the edge to his tone just now, he *definitely* wasn't finished with her yet.

"I have to work on Saturday night."

"Sunday then," he said, unconcerned.

She nodded.

"I've asked Jacob to take you driving later this afternoon, and tomorrow afternoon as well. You two can arrange a time for tomorrow. Today, he'll pick you up at four. Maybe you'd like to rest before then."

"Not likely," she said wryly. "I'm going to take a run, and then I need to get some work done for school." He regarded her silently, his face cast in the shadows of the interior of the cab. She swallowed and gathered her purse closer to her body. "Thank you. For Paris," she said in a rush.

"Thank *you*," he replied simply.

She edged toward the door, feeling self-conscious.

"Francesca." He dipped his hand into an inner pocket of his sport coat and handed her a leather box. Her breath froze when she recognized the name of the jeweler that had been in the Paris hotel.

*He'd gone into the jeweler this morning to get something for* me, *not the mysterious woman.*

"I told you that I would get you something for your hair when we arrived in Paris, but you wouldn't let me take you shopping. I hope they're to your liking. I'm not accustomed to choosing such feminine things without Lin's assistance."

Swallowing thickly, she opened the box. She gasped. Nestled in black velvet were eight large hairpins, each with a delicate crescent of stones at the tip. Once they were pushed into a twist of hair, it would appear that the upswept style glittered with diamonds. It wasn't only a luxurious gift, it was incredibly tasteful and personal.

She looked at Ian, eyes wide in amazement.

"I told the jeweler about the amount of hair that you had, and she assured me this number of pins would restrain even your glory." He blinked when she didn't speak. "Francesca? You like them, don't you?"

If she hadn't heard the hint of uncertainty in his usually level, brisk tone, she might have had the wherewithal to refuse what she suspected was a very expensive gift. As it was—

"Are you kidding? Ian, they're gorgeous." Her lips trembled as she looked back at the pins. "They're not *real* diamonds, are they?"

"If they're rhinestones, I paid a great deal too much," he said dryly, all traces of his former uncertainty gone. "Will you wear them? Thursday night at dinner?"

She looked into his shadowed face. Why was it so difficult to say no to him? It *wasn't* that need to please him that she experienced with him sexually. It was something else . . . a desire to show him that she'd found his gift thoughtful . . . beautiful . . .

. . . that *he* was beautiful to her.

"Yes," she answered, wondering how diamond-studded hair and jeans would look together.

Ian's slow smile was reason enough to accept the luxurious gift. She forced herself to look away from that addictive sight and reach for the door handle.

"And Francesca?"

She glanced back, breathless.

"Just so you know," he said, his smile now seeming to laugh at himself, "if it weren't for this damn acquisition, I'd have you in my bed right this second, and we'd be continuing your lessons with vigor."

The next several days flew by as Francesca ricocheted from homework, class, painting at Ian's penthouse, and her new driving lessons with Jacob. The latter ended up being more fun than she'd expected. Ian's driver was pleasant, fun company. Plus, Jacob possessed two important qualities for sitting in a passenger seat while Francesca piloted one of Ian's luxury automatic vehicles: nerves of steel and a sense of humor.

On Wednesday evening, she drove for the first time in the city. When she pulled up in front of High Jinks and put the car in neutral, she gave Jacob a hopeful glance, which the middle-aged driver returned with a wide grin.

"I think you'll be ready to take your test anytime you say the word."

"You really think so?" she asked.

"I really do. We'll go out to the suburbs to take the test. It'll be a lot easier taking it there than in the city."

"I feel bad about taking you away from your duties so much this week," she said, gathering her purse. She was working a shift tonight at High Jinks, and Jacob had suggested she drive herself there as part of her lesson.

"My duties are whatever Ian tells me they are," Jacob said, a sparkle of amusement in his eyes. "And he tells me my duty is to make sure you get your driver's license . . . oh, and to keep you safe at all costs in the process."

She lowered her head to hide her pleasure at his off-the-cuff comment. "He doesn't ask much, does he?" Francesca asked, thinking about the handful of times she'd *just* missed hurtling the two of them into wrecks on Chicago streets this afternoon.

Jacob chuckled. "It's been a nice break from my normal

routine. Besides, Ian has been holed up in his office since we got back from Paris, hammering out the details for a deal going down this week. He hasn't needed me."

Francesca had been glad for this tidbit of news. She certainly hadn't caught a glimpse or heard a peep from Ian since they'd returned to Chicago. His absence just made her anticipation for having dinner with him—of seeing *him*, period—on Thursday all that much sharper.

Unfortunately, he never called her to say the time he expected to see her for dinner. As a result, she did her best to focus on her painting Thursday afternoon and into the evening. Mrs. Hanson would tell him she was in the studio if he inquired. Slowly, as her work commenced, all of her fluttery, nervous excitement about spending time with Ian slipped away, and she entered the sublime zone of creative focus she craved as an artist.

When a shoulder cramp sliced through her concentration at about seven o'clock that evening, she was forced to lower her brush and consider what she'd wrought.

"It's incredible."

The hair on her arms and on the back of her neck stood up in awareness of the familiar quiet, hoarse voice. She spun around. He stood just inside the closed door, wearing an immaculately cut dark gray suit, white shirt, and pale blue tie. His hair was sexily mussed, as if he'd walked home from the office through a Lake Michigan breeze. Francesca walked over to a table in order to dry the excess paint off her brush, needing a moment to catch her breath at the sight of him.

"It's coming along. I'm having some trouble getting the light just the way that I want it on the Noble Enterprises building. I need to go over and stand in the lobby there as well, to check the light . . . see what it'll look like once it's hung."

From the corner of her vision, she saw him walking toward her, his approach like that of a sleek, powerful animal's. She placed her brush in a solvent and turned to face him. His blue eyes captured her stare and held tight.

Like always.

"The painting is amazing. I was referring to you, though. It's incredible to watch you work. It's a little like catching a goddess while she creates a small part of the world," he said, reaching up to touch her cheek, a self-deprecating smile on his full lips at his whimsical turn of thought.

"Do you really like it? The painting?" she asked, unable to pull her gaze off his mouth. He stood close enough that she caught his scent—English milled soap, the subtle fragrance of spicy aftershave, and a hint of the fresh breeze he'd just been in. Her body responded immediately, perking up in sensual awareness.

"Yes. But that's no surprise to me. I knew whatever you painted would be brilliant."

"I don't know how you could know that," she said, glancing aside in embarrassment.

"Because *you* are," he said, shifting his hand to cradle her jaw, tilting her face back up to his. He leaned down and kissed her with firm deliberation. No brushing, shaping lips this time. He almost immediately penetrated her mouth with his tongue, as if he'd craved her taste and could wait no longer. Heat and pleasure rushed through her sex when she registered his heat and flavor . . . when she acknowledged his complete dominance of her senses.

When he lifted his head a moment later, Francesca blinked open her eyelids sluggishly, still drunk from his potent kiss. At the touch of his fingers moving fleetly, unfastening the buttons of her blouse, her eyes went wide.

"Mrs. Hanson?"

"I locked the door when I came in," he said.

Liquid heat surged from her sex at the sensation of his fingers moving in the sensitive valley between her breasts. He flicked his wrist, and the front clasp of her bra snapped open. He peeled the fabric back and stared, his nostrils flaring.

"Why am I so greedy when it comes to you?"

"Ian—" she began, moved by his intensity, but he cut her off, leaning down to take a prickling nipple into his warm, wet mouth. She gasped as pleasure rushed through her sex, her hand flying to his head. He agitated and whipped at the crest with a firm, sleek tongue, and then drew on her. She moaned, her fingers clawing in his hair. He massaged her other breast, pressing the nipple against his palm, and then pinching at it tenderly with his fingers. Her head fell back as she abandoned herself to rioting pleasure.

He raised his head after a moment and studied her bared, flushed breasts. "So beautiful. I don't know why I haven't spent at least an entire day worshipping them," he murmured as if to himself, stimulating both beading nipples at once. "I want to spend a whole day worshipping each square inch of you, but there aren't enough hours in a day. Besides," he said, his mouth becoming hard. "I always lose control before I can."

"It's okay to lose control, Ian. Sometimes," she said softly. He looked up, his gaze piercing her as he continued to finesse a nipple with one hand. He began to unfasten her jeans, holding her stare all the while.

"I want to watch while you lose control. Right now," he said. He didn't shove her jeans down her thighs, just opened the button fly and slipped his long fingers beneath her panties.

"Oh!" she gasped when he burrowed between her labia and began to agitate her clit. He grunted in satisfaction.

"Creamy. Did you like having me suck on your beautiful breasts?" he muttered, his gaze roaming over her face, reading her reaction to his intimate touch.

"Yes," she whispered.

"Put your hands on your breasts. Squeeze them. It will please me," he added when he noticed her hesitation.

It was all he needed to say. She gathered her breasts in her hands, massaging them, experiencing her own flesh in a whole new way because of Ian's hot stare on her. He continued to rub her clit with expert precision. With his other hand, he cradled her jaw and caressed her tenderly with his thumb, the contrast between his demanding, intimate touch on her sex and his gentle stroking of her cheek driving her wild for some reason. His gaze flickered down to her chest. He watched as she played with her breasts for his pleasure . . . and, increasingly, her own.

"That's right. Pinch the nipples," he said, his voice growing rough, his movements between her thighs more forceful. "Now hold them up—present those pretty pink nipples to me."

Francesca blinked through a haze of rising arousal. She lifted her breasts from below, unsure of what he expected. He swept down suddenly and treated first one nipple, then the other, to a sweet, hot suck. It was too much. When she felt the scrape of his teeth against a painfully erect nipple, she broke in delicious climax. Sharp, jagged pleasure tore through her.

When she came back to herself, his hand was still moving between her thighs, but he stood erect, watching her as she came. Slowly, his hand fell away from her sex.

"Forgive me. I thought I could wait until after dinner, but watching you paint is the most potent kind of aphrodisiac," he said, his eyes gleaming with heat. She glanced down and saw him lowering his pants.

# Twelve

When he withdrew his cock, she understood why he'd had to stretch the waistband so wide to free himself. He was huge and hard. Her clit twanged in arousal. When she saw the rigidness of his bold, handsome features, she immediately sunk to her knees. No handcuffs this time. No vibrator.

Just Ian's naked need . . . and her own.

His fingers furrowed in her hair when she angled his penis with one hand. She was stunned at the weight of it, the pulsing warmth . . . the teeming life. She used her other hand to touch a thigh, which felt iron hard and was dusted with crisp dark hair. She couldn't get enough of the sensation of him—so virile, so flagrantly male. He grunted when she brushed the flaring crown of his cock against her cheek and then her lips, experimenting with sensation. His testicles felt round and taut beneath her seeking fingers.

She sighed in pleasure and slipped him into her mouth, his girth stretching her lips.

He was letting her touch him for the first time, and she

luxuriated in the experience. She slid her tongue around the delineated crown of the head, loving the way his fingers tightened in her hair, sucking him into her mouth, pulling on him hungrily.

She closed her eyes and was lost in the voluptuous, eternal moment. Her entire world narrowed down to the sensation of Ian's hard, throbbing flesh—the very essence of him—thrusting between her sensitive, squeezing lips, the feeling of the thick staff sliding through her tight fist, his taste being pounded into her awareness until her craving for the distilled flavor of him overwhelmed her.

She took him into her throat, not because he wanted it but because she did. Her need was that absolute.

Distantly, she became aware of him saying her name, sounding desperate . . . a little lost. Her mouth and jaw hurt from squeezing him so hard, and her throat was being punished by his thrusts, but she sucked harder, wanting to alleviate his pain . . .

. . . if only for one bright, shattering moment.

Her eyes sprang wide, her thick, lust-induced spell shattered at the sensation of his cock swelling impossibly large in her mouth. He erupted while lodged deep, Francesca feeling both utterly at his mercy and completely in control, because she trusted him not to harm her. Sure enough, he withdrew with a guttural groan and continued to come on her tongue, his fingers fisted in her hair as he controlled the motions, moving her mouth back and forth over his length, stroking her shallowly. She sucked until the last sweet, musky drops of his semen spilled onto her tongue, his ragged pants echoing in her ears, his fingers loosening from a grip in her hair to a caress.

"Come here," she heard him say harshly a moment later.

She reluctantly slid his cock out of her mouth, preferring to stay there and milk the softening but still formidable flesh, play with him . . . learn him. He helped her to her feet and immediately swept down to seize her lips in one of his patentable forceful yet tender kisses.

"You're so sweet," he said a moment later, his breathing still choppy against her puffy sore lips. "Thank you."

"You're welcome," she said, smiling full out. Something about his honest need and her ability to answer it had pleased her greatly. His head bent over her, he touched his thumb to her smile.

"You make me lose control, Francesca."

Her smile faded slightly when she saw the shadow fall in his eyes. She had the distinct impression that he wasn't entirely pleased about his greediness for her.

"There's nothing wrong with that. Is there?"

He blinked, and the shadows dissipated.

"I suppose not. But we have a schedule," he murmured, leaning down to rain kisses on her cheek and then her ear. She shivered, her sex heating again. "God you smell good," he muttered, his warm lips now examining her neck.

"Ian? What schedule?" she managed with difficulty.

He lifted his head, and she wished she hadn't asked.

"We have reservations for dinner at eight thirty."

"We could be a little late, couldn't we?" she coaxed, furrowing her fingers through his short, thick hair, relishing in the sensation. He so rarely let her touch him. She hated the idea of stopping because of a *schedule*.

"Unfortunately, we can't be," he said regretfully, stepping

away from her and refastening his pants. She did the same with her own. He grabbed her hand and started to lead her out of the studio. "We're dining with the owner of a company that I've been maneuvering to buy. I have good reason to believe that tonight Xander LaGrange is going to stop playing his infuriating games of cat and mouse and sign on the dotted line. I think I've finally sweetened the deal sufficiently to something even that greedy prick can't refuse," he muttered under his breath as he led her down the silent plush hallways of his penthouse.

"Oh," Francesca said, practically running to keep up with his long-legged stride. She was surprised he'd asked her to such an important business meeting. *Was it entirely wise on his part*, she wondered, as the nerve butterflies started to flicker around in her belly. Her parents would certainly have said it was a terrible decision on Ian's part. "Where do we have reservations?"

"At Sixteen," he said, pulling her into his bedroom suite and shutting the door after them.

She blinked. "Ian, that's one of the nicest restaurants in the city," she said, panic starting to encroach. "I haven't got anything to wear to a dinner like that . . . in one hour!" she added, horrified by the realization. "Did you reserve another private room?"

"No." He waved at her in a follow-me gesture. He opened the door and flipped on a light. She entered, staring around in wonder at the rows of perfectly hung suits. She'd thought it was a closet, but it was a dressing room. It was bigger than her bedroom, long and narrow. The scent of Ian's aftershave clung in the air along with the smell of something pleasant and spicy. She noticed perfectly aligned cedar hangers and rows and rows of highly buffed shoes, and realized the hangers and cedar shoe trees were the origin of the scent.

Ian waved his hand in front of a rack, and she stared for a moment, not comprehending what she was seeing.

Why were there *dresses* in his closet? And women's shoes and accessories?

Her throat suddenly seemed to swell closed. She stared at him, aghast.

"I'm not wearing other women's clothes!" she said, stung to the core that he'd even suggest her putting on clothing that had once belonged to his former lovers.

He looked a little nonplussed by her reaction. "They aren't *other women's* clothes. They're yours."

"What are you talking about?"

"Margarite had them delivered yesterday. They're off-the-rack," he said almost apologetically, "but she had them tailored for you."

"Margarite," Francesca said slowly, as if pronouncing a foreign word for the first time. "Why would Margarite have done that?"

"Because I told her to, of course."

For a moment, they just stared at each other in his still dressing room.

"Ian, I told you specifically I didn't want clothing from you," she said, anger rising.

"And I told you that there would be occasions I wanted you to attend with me where you couldn't wear jeans, Francesca. Tonight is one of them. I also asked you to wear your new hairpins this evening," he said so briskly it drove her off course. "Where are they?"

"*Wha* . . . in my purse," she sputtered. "In the studio."

He nodded once. "I'll go and get them for you. In the meantime, you can shower and get ready. You'll find lingerie there," he said, nodding in the direction of a small antique chest of drawers near where the dresses hung. He started to walk out of the room.

"Ian—"

He turned around, his stare like a flicking whip. "I won't argue with you about this. Do you want to be with me tonight?" he asked quietly.

"I . . . *yes*, you know that I do."

"Then get ready and choose one of the dresses. You can't attend a dinner like this in jeans."

He left her standing there, her mouth hanging open, her nerves tingling with anger. She tried to think of a way around it but couldn't. It was true what he'd said. She couldn't be escorted by Ian Noble to the main dining room of one of the nicest, most luxurious restaurants in the city dressed like this.

Looking like *her*.

Her anger simmered at his heavy-handedness, though. For some reason, memories of her father's impatience and vague disgust with her appearance when she'd occasionally been in social situations with his peers rose up and bit her, aggravating the sting from Ian's imperious behavior.

*For God's sake, Francesca, if everything that spills out of that mouth of yours is going to be so stupid, why don't you just keep it shut! And not by stuffing your face any more than you already have tonight.*

She'd been twelve years old when her father had taken her aside in the kitchen and uttered those words. She re-experienced the flood of shame and insubordination she'd felt back then—a familiar brew of emotion. Francesca never gorged herself in public—it was just that her father's critical eye seemed to be on her every time she took a bite of food. It'd always been that way.

If her father thought she was an unsightly blemish on the earth, then she'd make sure that's precisely what she was.

Ian had willfully ignored her wishes about the clothing and gone right ahead with his own agenda. And all the while, Francesca had thought he'd understood her . . . sympathized with her, even.

She jerked open one of the dresser drawers and ran her fingers over exquisite silk panties, bras, and hosiery.

He'd said he wanted her to own her sexuality . . . feel empowered by it. Was this all part of his manipulations to get her to do so?

She withdrew a pair of sheer black thigh-high silk stockings. Well, if Ian wanted her to *flaunt* it, he better be prepared for the result.


He was in the process of tying a tie when she walked out of the bathroom fifty minutes later. Their eyes met in the reflection of the mirror he used, above a cherrywood dresser. His gaze slowly lowered over her, his body going rigid in abrupt male awareness.

She looked like she ought to be declared illegal, wearing a black V-neck bandage dress that hugged her willowy waist, the taut, lush curves of her hips and slender thighs like a lover. He realized, with a potent mixture of regret and possessive arousal, that her lush lips were still puffy from his forceful possession of her mouth earlier. Another experienced man would recognize the evidence for what it was, and he didn't care for the idea of putting Francesca on display in that manner before a man like Xander LaGrange. Her gleaming strawberry-blonde hair had been affixed to her head with what he suspected were the diamond pins he'd bought her. She wore simple pearl earrings. He couldn't take his eyes off the flawless ivory expanse of skin in the wide V-neck, revealing the majority of her chest and part of her alabaster shoulders. He couldn't believe it was an off-the-rack dress. It looked like it'd been tailor-made for her alone.

She was tightly packaged sexual elegance.

"Choose another dress, please," he said, forcing himself to look away from the shockingly alluring image of her to finish tying his tie.

"We're going to be late as it is," Francesca replied. He glanced back at her, wondering if she was avoiding his stare with those long-lashed nymph eyes of hers that always killed him. She checked the contents of the ebony lizard-skinned clutch in her hand. A flicker of suspicion went through him, even as he was once again captured by the vision of her.

She hadn't chosen that ridiculously sexy dress to make him pay for buying her clothing, had she? The four-inch heels and the sheer stockings she wore made a vivid fantasy pop into his brain of having those long, gorgeous legs wrapped around him while he was riding her furiously into submission . . .

. . . into screaming bliss.

He scowled and stalked into his dressing room. Xander LaGrange was a lecher. He couldn't stand the man, to be honest, and it'd been the worst kind of torture to cater to his ridiculous, narcissistic demands in order to make the final acquisition on Ian's terms. He'd specifically asked Francesca to the ceremonial dinner tonight to seal the deal because he was worried he'd say something rude or sharp to the oily LaGrange, ruining his chances to acquire the other man's company. With Francesca there, he'd be less focused on LaGrange's smug belief that he'd bettered Ian with the deal.

It'd be easier for him to control his temper while Francesca was there. Her freshness softened him.

But he hadn't expected to take a sex siren to a dinner where Xander LaGrange was present.

He returned to the bedroom, a lightweight cropped black sweater with a jeweled clasp in his hand. "If you must wear it, please put this on. It'll cover all that—" he paused, his gaze on her exposed chest in the wide V-neck. Her breasts were decently under wraps, even if a large expanse of skin at her chest and shoulders was bare. The way the dress molded and shaped her breasts, however, equated to visual sex candy. The black fabric made her skin look exceptionally white and smooth by contrast . . . very naked.

"Skin," he finished under his breath, willfully ignoring the eager lurch of his cock. "I'll speak to Margarite. I asked her for sexy-discreet, not jaw-dropping and eye-popping."

"I don't see your jaw dropping," she said lightly, turning so he could slip the cover-up over her shoulders. When he didn't immediately put the sleeves next to her hand, she glanced back, catching him staring at her luscious ass encased in the clinging fabric.

"It's dropping on the inside," he mumbled before he slipped the sleeves over her hands and she shrugged on the cover-up. He grasped her shoulders and turned her toward him, examining her. "You didn't wear this particular dress to make some sort of point, did you?"

"What point would that be?" she asked, her chin going up.

"A point of defiance."

"You asked me to wear one of the dresses, and I am."

"Take care, Francesca," he said in a quiet, ominous tone, brushing his fingertip across the soft skin of her jaw and feeling her shiver. Heat rushed through his cock. She really was going to kill him before this was through.

"Take care of what?" she asked.

"You know what I think of impulsiveness. You know the consequences for it," he added quietly, before he took her hand and led her out of the suite.


Sixteen was housed in the Trump International Hotel & Tower, the dining room dominated by the modern, clean lines of cherrywood-paneled walls and an enormous, stunning Swarovski-crystal chandelier. They dined next to thirty-foot tall floor-to-ceiling windows, looking down at magnificent views of the city, some of the buildings so close she felt like she could reach out and touch them.

Francesca initially thought that the best way to describe their dinner companion, Xander LaGrange, was *polished*, but she quickly altered the descriptor to *slick*. She learned that Ian and he knew each other through the University of Chicago and were old rivals—or at least from Xander's viewpoint.

"So you were in college together?" she clarified when Xander made a vague reference to how long he and Ian had known each other.

"I was a graduate student when Ian was a freshman at the University of Chicago," Xander explained. "Once he came along, myself and the rest of the computer-science department were constantly trying to find our ways out of his brilliant shadow. Ian and I shared an academic mentor. Professor Sharakoff asked me to grade his papers and Ian to write a book with him."

"Don't exaggerate, Xander," Ian said quietly.

"I thought I was downplaying things," LaGrange said with a swift smile that didn't quite reach his eyes.

LaGrange was in his mid-thirties, with short sandy-blond hair graying at the temples. He was handsome and charming enough, Francesca supposed, for a dinner companion. She immediately sensed the underlying conflict between Ian and him, however. By the time the waiter came to take their drink orders, she'd gauged that while Ian was the epitome of polite charm toward the other man, he despised him. She sensed his dislike from where he sat next to her, with his rigid posture and strained muscles.

Xander LaGrange, on the other hand, was full-out envious of Ian . . . possibly even aggressively so. She studied his white-toothed smiles, which reminded her more of a snarl, and wondered if LaGrange's jealousy wasn't at the bottom of his reluctance to Ian's terms for the acquisition of his company all this time.

"Would you like club soda?" Ian asked her when the waiter arrived.

"No. Champagne, I think," she said, returning LaGrange's smile of appreciation at her choice. She was feeling a little daring tonight . . . euphoric. Maybe it was the sexy dress, or the stunning view, or the appreciative gleam in LaGrange's eyes as he studied her from across the table—or Ian's quiet threat before they'd left his bedroom—but she was definitely feeling rebellious and . . .

. . . stirred up.

Was *this* the power that Ian wanted her to own?

"Where did you find this long-stemmed rose, Ian?" LaGrange mused, his eyes hot on Francesca, after Ian had placed an order for a bottle of champagne. Ian explained about her winning the commission to provide the painting for his lobby. "Gifted in addition to being beautiful," LaGrange complimented when Ian was finished. He gave Ian a glance that struck her as wolfish. "I can understand why you wanted to bring her tonight."

Her gaze immediately flew to Ian. Was LaGrange insinuating that Ian had brought her as a piece of arm candy to make final negotiations go more smoothly? She'd wondered herself why he'd asked her to the dinner. A shadow flickered across Ian's countenance and was gone.

"I brought Francesca because I've been so busy on this deal with you that I haven't had the opportunity to see her much."

"And it's greatly appreciated," LaGrange assured, his dark eyes flickering across Francesca's face and chest. The waiter uncorked their champagne, adding to Francesca's giddy mood. "There's no deal that a beautiful woman doesn't sweeten," he added, making her flush in embarrassment.

Did Ian stiffen next to her? She thought not, when he began to converse with LaGrange amiably enough about some final details of their deal. She gathered from their exchange that a major holdup in negotiations thus far had been that LaGrange wanted partial payment in stock from

Ian's company, while Ian insisted on a cash-only purchase. She could well imagine Ian refusing to give a hold—even a relatively minor one—to any other person over his company. Apparently, he'd finally offered LaGrange a cash amount that couldn't be walked away from.

"No sane man could refuse that offer, Ian," LaGrange finally conceded, raising his champagne flute for a toast. "So here's to your new company."

Ian's smile seemed a little strained as Francesca joined them in the toast. "Lin Soong delivered all the necessaries to my penthouse this evening. We can go there for a nightcap following dinner and take care of all the paperwork."

Talk turned to more mundane matters. LaGrange encouraged Francesca to talk about her artwork and school, which she did so more ebulliently than usual, likely due to the champagne. Ian gave her a gleaming sideways glance when the waiter poured her a third glass, but she determinedly ignored his subtle warning for propriety. Instead, she heartily agreed with LaGrange when he suggested they get another bottle.

Halfway through her delicious entrée of wild black bass, she felt an imperative need to attend the lady's room. She excused herself and started to push back her chair. Ian stood and pulled it back for her.

"Thank you," she murmured, meeting his eyes. He blinked when she started to remove the cover-up. "I'm a little warm," she explained breathlessly.

He really had no other choice but to help her remove it, but she noticed the stiffness of his jaw. She grabbed her clutch and headed in search of the lady's room, both embarrassed and thrilled by the number of heads that turned her way as she progressed across the dining room. She prayed Ian's eyes were on her as well. The attention she was getting was more intoxicating than the champagne.

Was *this* the type of thing that beautiful women experienced on a daily basis? *Incredible*, she thought, as she smiled at a man in his forties who was staring at her, and he tripped, ruffling his female companion when he grabbed for her arm to steady himself.

LaGrange looked highly amused when she returned to the table and Ian stood to seat her. "I expect you bring traffic to a halt on a regular basis, Francesca?" he murmured, holding her stare over the rim of his champagne glass.

"Never," she replied with sincere cheerfulness. "Except for once—I tripped in the middle of Michigan Avenue after running a mini-marathon and getting a bad cramp."

LaGrange laughed as if she were being delightfully coy. He wasn't so bad was he, really? Ian was being too harsh. She grinned back at him, glancing sideways at Ian. Her smile faded when she noticed that subdued flash in Ian's eyes that always reminded her of heat lightning—the signal of an approaching storm.

The rest of the dinner passed by in a sensual whirl of delicious food, Swarovski crystal, LaGrange's admiring glances and flirtations—Ian's dark, intense sexuality simmering next to her all the while . . . building . . . coiling tight. She laughed a good deal more than she should have, and did the same drinking champagne and taking pleasure in the admiring glances of Xander LaGrange and many of the other men in the restaurant. She was exquisitely attuned to Ian as the three of them chatted, and somehow knew he was just as aware of her. She relished in the knowledge that she held a man like Ian Noble fast on the hook of the intoxicating power of her sexuality.

When she backed up her chair a tad as they sipped coffee later, she realized the tight dress had ridden up on her thighs, revealing the lacy top of one of her thigh-highs. She saw Ian's hand pause as he reached for his coffee cup and felt his gaze on her lap.

Stunned by her daring, she slipped a finger beneath the lace of the thigh-high, stroking the soft skin in a slow, sensual, in-and-out fucking motion. Risking an innocent glance at Ian's face, she saw a barely contained inferno blazing in his blue eyes.

She swallowed thickly and lowered her dress, feeling scorched by his stare.

Ian was quiet where he sat next to her in the back of the limo on the return to the penthouse. She strained to keep up the conversation, hoping LaGrange didn't take Ian's silence for surliness. Hadn't Ian asked her to attend this business dinner to charm LaGrange, to soften him up a bit for the final negotiations? Well, she'd done it, hadn't she? LaGrange had appeared to have a wonderful time at dinner, and he seemed all too ready and willing to sign on the dotted line now.

LaGrange proved a little *too* ready and willing, however, as he shouldered Jacob aside and helped her out of the limo when they reached Ian's. His hand dropped to cup her hip as she alighted, then lowered to stroke her ass. Francesca started and immediately moved away, repelled by the man's touch. She recoiled internally when she glanced back and saw the icy gleam in Ian's eyes as he got out of the limo.

*Crap*. He'd noticed.

She was quiet on the elevator ride up to Ian's penthouse. The intoxicating effect of the champagne was waning, and she suddenly felt the full weight of her foolish behavior that evening. Ian was polite but quiet—perhaps furious with her, it was always hard to tell with his stoic expression—while LaGrange continued on with his pointless banter, apparently clueless as to Ian's thundercloud mood and Francesca's flattened, suddenly regretful one.

"I'll just leave you two to finish your business," Francesca said when they reached the entry to the penthouse. "It was a pleasure to meet you, Xander."

LaGrange took her hand and held it between both of his. "No, you must come with us for a nightcap. I *insist*."

"I insist I can't," she said, her manner friendly but equally firm. "I have a big day tomorrow at school. Good night," she said, edging in the direction of Ian's bedroom suite. She suddenly was wild to get out of this dress.

"But *no*, that's—"

"Wait for me," Ian said to her in his crisp British accent and authoritarian tone, cutting off LaGrange's protests with rapier precision.

Another stab of rebellion went through her when she saw the glint in his eyes. How dare he talk so imperiously to her in front of others? Her chin went up, but then she recalled how giddily she'd behaved at the restaurant. How foolishly. She glanced at an insulted-looking LaGrange. Was he offended for Francesca, or was he pricked by the way Ian had just cut him off? She nodded to Ian once and turned down the hallway, leaving them. A rush of trepidation went through her.

She'd wanted to tweak Ian for his heavy-handedness earlier, but perhaps she'd gone too far?

He likely was going to be furious at her silly, flirtatious behavior all night. *But hadn't he deserved it?* she thought as she nervously checked her messages on her phone once she reached Ian's suite. She couldn't have him constantly trying to mastermind her life.

She stood in Ian's bathroom a moment later and began to remove the beautiful diamond hairpins, trying to convince herself she'd been right to defy him in her subtle fashion. The way he'd ignored her input about the clothing purchase . . . taking her to dinner where he apparently expected her to charm and beguile his prey with her sexuality. How dare he objectify her in that way?

*Well, he'd know better than to use her in that way in the future,* she thought with anxious contempt as her hair spilled down her back and she reached to unzip the dress.

She froze when she heard a loud thumping sound in the far distance. What in the world had that been? She hesitated, unsure if she should go and check on Ian. It sounded like someone had just hit the floor very hard.

Her heart leapt into her throat a moment later, when she heard the door to Ian's suite open and close with a brisk bang, then the unmistakable sound of the lock clicking.

She glanced sideways and saw Ian through the open bathroom door.

"Leave the dress on," he said, his voice like frozen steel. She realized her hands were still at her back in preparation to unzip the dress. "Come here."

His jacket was unbuttoned, his muscles tense, his expression rigid. Her gaze dropped to the gleam of his belt buckle and the stark evidence of his virility beneath it. Her heart started to throb against her breastbone.

"Is Xander already gone?" she asked as she left the bathroom, her voice sounding tremulous to her own ears.

"Yes. For good."

She paused a few feet away from him. "What do you mean *for good?* You mean because he's sold you his company, you won't be seeing him anymore?"

"No. Because I told him to take his company and shove it up his ass."

She blinked, thinking for a second she'd misunderstood him saying something so crass in his crisp, accented voice. Her eyes widened when she noticed the feral gleam in his eyes.

"Ian . . . you *didn't* . . . but you wanted that software for your company so much, you've been working so hard on this deal." Dread sank in her belly like a weight. "Oh no. You didn't tell Xander LaGrange to shove it because of the way *I* acted tonight, did you?"

"I told Xander LaGrange to shove it and threw him face-first on the elevator just now because I can't *stand* that bloody bastard," Ian grated out through a clenched jaw as he approached her. She looked up and saw the fury and heat in his eyes. She almost backed up, he looked so fierce, but he stopped her with a hand on her wrist. "And also because he had the balls to ask for one additional item before he signed."

"What?"

"You." He ignored her shocked gasp. "He wasn't entirely selfish. He said I could watch while he sealed the deal in your pussy."

She gasped.

"*His words*, Francesca," he bit out. "Not mine."

She stared in disbelief and rising anxiety. She couldn't believe Xander LaGrange was such a loathsome slimeball. Yet . . . if she hadn't behaved so flirtatiously tonight, trying to defy Ian, Xander wouldn't have done what he'd done. Ian would have his deal. Tears smarted in her eyes.

*Oh, no.* She'd completely ruined things for him. He may have deserved a little tormenting for his relentlessly arrogant behavior, but she'd never intended *this*.

"Ian, I'm so sorry. I didn't mean . . . surely you don't *think* I meant—"

He placed his hand along the side of her head, holding her immobile, his scoring stare making her fall silent. "I know you didn't mean to ruin the deal. You're not that vindictive. Besides that, you're too foolish to even know what you're doing. Xander's utter stupidity in suggesting I share you with him was just icing on the cake. The second that asshole touched you, the deal was finished. I only brought him up to the penthouse to tell him so. Before I got the chance, he made his last demand for the buyout and ended up leaving a lot more . . . *abruptly* than he'd planned as a result."

"I can't believe it," she muttered, horrified.

"That's because you have no idea how a man like Xander LaGrange thinks. You were having your fun playing with fire. You've got the body and a face of a goddess and the mentality of a six-year-old with a pretty new toy."

Anger filtered through her misery. "I'm not a child, and I was just trying to prove to you that I won't be treated like one, Ian!"

"You're right," he said, tightening his grip on her wrist. He began to walk to the far side of his enormous suite, Francesca trailing after him clumsily in her high heels. "You want to play the games of a woman, you want to flick matches at me to see if I burn? Well, you better be willing to take the consequences, Francesca," he said, reaching into a drawer and drawing out some keys roughly.

Her chest felt so full of anxiety and regret and rising excitement, she couldn't draw breath. What was he doing unlocking that door? She followed after him when he pulled on her wrist and entered a room that was about twenty feet by fifteen. This space contained a whole bank of built-in cherrywood drawers and cabinets. He shut the door behind her, and she looked around. The entire far corner was lined with mirrors and a contraption of some sort with springs and harnesses and black nylon straps. She stared wide-eyed at the device, her heart starting to drum in her ears.

"Go stand in front of the couch and take off your dress."

She tore her eyes off the intimidating device and realized there was a plush sofa on the wall opposite from the shelves and mirror. An elegant chandelier strangely didn't look out of place on the ceiling. *So like Ian to pair crystal with kink.* There were also other things in the windowless room, like two hooks with straps spaced along the wall, an unusually curved tall stool sitting in front of a piece of wood affixed to the wall like a ballet bar, and a padded bench.

"Ian, what is this room?"

"It's the room where you'll receive your more serious punishments," he said before he walked over to the drawers and opened one. Her eyes widened when she saw several paddles and instruments with leather straps. Her mouth went dry when he grasped the handle of the familiar-looking black leather paddle and lifted it.

*Oh no.*

"I really didn't mean to ruin the deal for you tonight," she said in a rush.

"And I told you I knew that. I'm not punishing you because Xander LaGrange is a fucking tool. I'm going to punish you for tormenting me all night. Now didn't I ask you to remove your dress?" he asked, the slightest hint of amusement in his dark-angel eyes when he turned to regard her, paddle in hand. His mirth vanished when she didn't move.

"The door isn't locked, Francesca. You can go if you choose. But if you stay, you will do as I say."

She walked across the room, pausing in front of the couch, having trouble catching her breath. She noticed that her reflection in the mirrors across the way was pale as she reached to unzip her dress. Ian paused across the room in the action of opening another drawer as she peeled the tight garment off her skin.

*Bundage dress* indeed.

She hesitated when she'd removed the dress. "These too?" she asked shakily, referring to the bra, panties, and thigh-highs she wore, along with the black lizard-skin heels.

"Just take off the bra and panties," he said, grabbing some items from a drawer and stalking toward her. His body blocked her view, making it difficult to see what he set on the padded table in addition to the paddle as she removed the requested garments. She glimpsed only one thing before he blocked her view as he walked toward her—an item that was like a long cone-shaped tube made of black rubber, a ring affixed to the thicker end.

She focused on his hand, her clit twanging in excitement when she saw the jar of stimulant. He must have noticed where she stared—or perhaps he noticed her stiffening nipples—because a grim smile tilted his hard mouth.

"That's right. I'm weak when it comes to you. Pitifully so. I can't bear to think of you experiencing only discomfort," he said as he unscrewed the jar. He dipped a thick finger into the white emollient and met her stare. "Even for this—when you deserve a good, hard punishment."

She swallowed thickly. "I really am sorry, Ian," she said, not because of the intimidating black paddle over on the table, and not because of that strange black plug she'd glimpsed.

He frowned slightly and stepped toward her. She gasped loudly as he plunged his finger between her labia, rubbing the cream into her clit with a brisk precision that made her whimper.

"I spoil you," he said, withdrawing his hand, leaving her to burn.

"I'll have trouble believing that in a few minutes when my butt is on fire," she muttered.

His gaze skipped to her face. Her eyes widened when she saw his potent smile. Heat rushed between her thighs.

She watched him, anticipation rising, as he went back over to the table and removed his jacket, admiring the lean flex of muscle beneath his dress shirt. He rolled back his shirtsleeves. She caught a glimpse of strong forearms and his gold watch. Nervous excitement frothed in her belly at the sight.

*He meant business.*

When he returned, she immediately tried to see what was in his hand.

"Curious?" he murmured.

She nodded.

"Since I'm going to blindfold you in a moment, I'll tell you what I'm going to do," he said quietly. He held up the familiar handcuffs. "I'm going to restrain your wrists, blindfold you, and give you an over the knee spanking. Once your ass is nice and hot," he held up the black rubber plug with the circular end like a pacifier handle, as well as a bottle of clear gel, "I'm going to lube up this butt plug and ready your ass for my cock."

Her heart froze for a suspended few seconds.

"You're going to do *what*?"

"You heard me," he said as he set the lubricant and butt plug on the couch. He nodded at one of her wrists. "The front," he said, and she put her hands together before her mons, following his concise instructions without thought, her brain in stall mode. "Surely you knew men like to do that," he said, noticing her bewilderment.

"Even if women don't?"

"Some women do. A great deal."

She thought of Ian's huge penis and made her decision then and there. It would be a punishment to take it in her ass, pure and simple, no matter the clitoral stimulant that was beginning to make her prickle and burn in pleasure. He went to the table and came back holding a long black strip of silk—the blindfold. She frowned at him for good measure as he raised his hands to tie it around her eyes.

When he'd affixed the cloth and she was blindfolded, he led her to the couch. She thought she heard the soft sound of his large, solid body falling on the cushions. He guided her onto his lap. She came down awkwardly, her bound wrists causing her elbows to jab into his rock-solid thighs.

"I'm sorry," she mumbled.

"It's all right. Remember the position I taught you?" he murmured from somewhere above her. She nodded and slid her breasts over his outer thigh until the lower curves pressed against hard muscle, her bound hands were stretched out above her head, and her bare ass curved over his other leg. Her sex clenched tight when she clearly felt the outlines of his cock against her ribs and belly. A flare of panicked excitement bubbled up from her chest when she fully absorbed his dimensions and felt his throbbing warmth through the cloth of his pants.

"Ian, you'll never be able to put *that* inside my—"

He cracked her ass with his palm, and she jumped in his lap.

"I will, lovely," she heard him say. "And I'll love every second of it. Now keep that bottom still."

She bit her lip to keep from moaning as he began to slap her buttocks, and occasionally her thighs, with quick, stinging spanks. Her clit pinched in arousal. She decided she liked over-the-knee spankings more than the paddle. She liked Ian's personal touch, and how his hand grew as warm as her smarting ass, and how his cock leapt against her body when he landed those firm slaps on the lower curves of her buttocks. Her entire focus narrowed to the feeling of his stark arousal pressing against her body and the anticipation of his next spank.

She adored how he paused in her punishment and stroked her now-fiery bottom with his big hand, as if to soothe the sting. She moaned when he suddenly squeezed an entire buttock tautly and flexed his hips, grinding her body against his raging erection.

"Why do you have to torment me, lovely?" she heard him rasp.

"I wonder the same thing about you," she mumbled frantically, her face pressed into the couch, muffling her speech. He was still pressing her against his hard, aroused body, and her clit loved the pressure.

He grunted and released his hips.

"You're a constant thorn in my side," he said, sounding grim.

"I'm sorry," she mumbled, missing the pressure of his cock, and his hand on her ass. What was he doing? She wondered, twisting her chin around, trying to hear something that would answer her question. A cry leaked out of her throat when he matter-of-factly spread an ass cheek with a large hand and kept it pried back. Her muscles tensed in anxiety when she felt a cool, hard pressure against her anus.

"I don't really think you are sorry," she heard Ian say from behind her. The pressure increased, and the tip of the plug slipped into her ass. "I think you like to torment me as much as I love to punish you."

"Ian," she moaned uncontrollably when he pushed the plug farther into her, and then began to slide the rubber tube out and back in several inches, back and forth, fucking her ass using the handle at the end, the lubrication making for a smooth glide despite the pressure.

"Yes?" he asked, his voice sounding rough.

Her mouth hung open, her flaming cheek pressed to the velvet of the couch.

"It feels so . . . strange," she managed in a broken voice. She couldn't adequately put into words how it felt—anxiety-provoking to lay in his lap at his mercy, shameful to give him control over such a private, forbidden part of her body, arousing to feel nerve endings flicker to life at the stimulation, mounting the burn at her clit in a way she'd never before experienced . . .

. . . beyond thrilling to feel the tension level leap in Ian's muscles as he fucked her ass with the plug.

He sunk it deep, making her yelp in surprise.

"Does it hurt?" he asked, maintaining pressure with his fingers to keep the plug inserted.

She shook her head into the sofa, too overwhelmed to speak. The clit cream had gone into full effect. She tingled and simmered. As if Ian had sensed this, he reached beneath her and parted her labia, rubbing the erect piece of flesh. She shuddered in his lap.

"You begin to see why a woman might like this," he drew the plug out of her and slid it back into her ass again, "as much as a man?"

She moaned uncontrollably. Did she ever. Nerves all along her sacrum flared to life as he continued to plunge the plug in and out of her while he rubbed her slick clit. If he kept this up, she'd soon be quivering in orgasm.

Unfortunately, that wasn't Ian's plan. He removed his hand, and the plug slid out of her ass, making her groan at the sudden interruption. She felt his fingers moving on the handcuffs. He unfastened the buckles and then slid the blindfold off her head. She blinked, even the subtle illumination from the crystal chandelier seeming bright after the pitch black of the blindfold. He took her hand.

"Stand up. I'll help you," he said.

She appreciated his guiding hands as she tried to do what he'd demanded, still disoriented from the light and the abrupt cessation of pleasure. She stood before him, feeling flushed with arousal and flustered and unsteady in the high heels. He looked up at her, his eyes glowing with heat and arousal, his long legs spread slightly, his arousal flagrantly obvious.

"You liked that, didn't you?" he asked, his narrowed gaze studying her.

"No," she whispered, knowing her hot cheeks, flushed skin, and tight nipples betrayed her lie.

He just smiled and stood. She looked up at him, unable to disguise her longing, when he gently smoothed her loose hair away from her face. She gasped softly at the feeling of his hand on the small of her back, caressing her, and the cloth of his pants and shirt brushing against her sensitive skin.

"Mutinous even in the face of sure defeat? You never cease to amaze me, lovely," he murmured. "Come with me," he said, taking her hand. She walked beside him, halting suddenly when she saw her reflection in the mirror.

The sheer black thigh-highs made her skin look very pale in contrast, as did the red-gold thatch of hair between her thighs. Her hair tumbled in a wild mess all the way to her waist. Her nipples were stained a dark pink and beaded tight in arousal, the pale globes of her breasts rose and fell as she panted shallowly.

She stared, slain by the image of herself transformed by desire.

"You see it?" Ian asked, leaning down near her, his warm breath in her ear causing a spike of pleasure to go through her. "You see it, don't you?" he murmured as he spread his hand over her belly in a possessive gesture. "You see how beautiful you are?"

Her flushed lips parted, but no words came out.

"*Say it,*" he whispered roughly. "Say you see what I see when I look at you."

"I see it," she replied, her tone dazed . . . a little wondrous, as if she actually thought, for a few seconds, that he possessed magic mirrors.

"Yes. And that's not a power you play with, is it?"

It took her a moment to realize Ian's small smile didn't come from smugness or cockiness. No—he looked triumphant because of what she'd seen in the mirror . . . because of her admission. *Why did he care whether or not she thought she was beautiful?*

He led her over to the kinky-looking contraption that hung from the ceiling with the inexplicable harnesses and straps, her heart pounding uncomfortably fast. He pulled down on the main horizontal black bar, stretching a spring on the contraption so that three four-inch-wide padded-leather harnesses fell horizontally about four feet from the floor. *Wait a second* . . . those leather loops could be used to suspend a body in midair. If that circular pad of leather was to support the head, and that harness was for the chest area, and the lower one for the pelvis, then those other straps could be used to bind a person's hands and ankles.

They'd be completely restrained . . . helpless, Francesca realized. She looked at Ian as he held the swing. The light from the chandelier gleamed in his blue eyes. Her incredulous expression faded as a heavy pressure fell on her chest.

*Oh no.*

She already *was* completely helpless when it came to Ian Noble . . . and it had nothing to do with the restraining swing.

He put out his hand, beckoning her.

Her ass muscles clenched tight; liquid heat rushed at her sex.

She raised her hand and he grasped it, drawing her toward him.

"It's time you learned that when you play with fire, you're going to end up at its mercy," he said.

Ian's hands were gentle, his hold firm when he lifted her off the floor and slid her body, belly downward, through the loops of the swing. He arranged the padded straps below her hips, beneath her breasts, and under her forehead. She gave a shaky yelp when the harnesses dipped once he gave them her weight.

"*Shhhh,*" he soothed from above her, stroking her back. "The swing is hooked through a steel beam in the ceiling. It's extremely secure. Relax."

She exhaled after a moment, realizing that now that she'd settled, she did, indeed, feel steady. Strange and aroused and a little scared, but secure in the knowledge that Ian would keep her safe. His hand left her back. He touched her calves, and then her ankles. She peered sideways but couldn't see through the thick fall of her hair. She felt him slip first one foot through a nylon loop, then the other, and tightened them on her ankle. He'd bound her feet at a lower angle from her body, making her legs drop below her hips, as if she was in a bent-over position, but in midair. Once he'd secured her feet, he came around to the front of her and restrained her wrists in a similar fashion, letting her arms fall in a semi-straightened position beneath her chest.

His brisk, knowledgeable manipulation of the swing and her body let her know Ian had a lot of experience with it.

"Let me get you something for your hair."

For an anxious moment, she couldn't see him. Then his deft hands were sweeping her long hair away from her face, lifting the gathered mass. She turned her chin slightly and was able to see him in the mirror as he twirled his hand, twisting her hair and finally binding it on her head with a huge clip. She couldn't take her eyes off his powerful form in the mirror; couldn't take her eyes off herself, naked and suspended there in midair, vulnerable to anything and everything Ian wanted to do to her.

Perhaps he noticed her anxious studying of them in the mirror, because he brushed his long fingers beneath her chin and met her stare in the mirror.

"Don't be afraid," he said.

She blinked, seeing something in his eyes that gave her courage. Passion. Tenderness. A clear intent to possess, but not in a way she should fear or abhor. She nodded once, feeling breathless.

He walked over to the table, and when he returned, he carried the paddle. Her clit pinched in arousal at the sight of it gripped surely in his large hand. It suddenly struck her how vulnerable her bottom was, suspended there at hip height in midair. She held her breath when he came to a halt and raised the paddle, brushing the exquisitely soft fur over her still-tingling spanked ass.

He gripped the straps above the harness that held her hips, securing her in place. She watched wide-eyed in the mirror as he tossed the paddle in the air a few inches and flipped it expertly. When it landed, the leather side faced her ass.

"I will give you ten strokes," he said gruffly, placing the paddle against her ass. Her cheeks heated at the sensation . . . at the vision of the black leather pressing into the flesh of her pink buttocks.

He lifted the paddle and swung. She gasped at the impact, her body swinging forward ever so slightly in Ian's grip. "*Ow*," popped out of her throat when he paddled her again, stinging her nerves. He kept the paddle pressed to her ass cheeks.

"I said you'd be safe, and you always will be." In the mirror, she saw that he stared at her ass as he circled the paddle, massaging her. "But that doesn't mean there won't be some discomfort. This is a punishment, after all."

She whimpered when he landed another smack on her lower buttocks. He grunted, low and rough, and used the paddle to massage the smarting skin once again. "I love turning your ass red," he muttered and landed another smack. This blow was forceful enough to send her jerking forward in Ian's hold several inches. "You keep the count, Francesca," he said. "I'm losing my concentration."

She stared at his rigid features when he said that, her heart charging like a locomotive, the clit cream taunting her between her thighs. *Ian* lose concentration? He swung his arm back, and her eyes sprang wide in trepidation.

*Smack.*

"Five," she squeaked. She couldn't take her eyes off him in the mirror: the way his shirt stretched across his wide chest when he swung his arm back, the rigid focus on her as he landed the paddle, the absolute strength of his grip on the swing as he kept her ass in place for her punishment.

He landed several more smacks, and then cursed under his breath. He released his death grip on the hip harness. Francesca swayed forward and back six inches in each direction. She hardly noticed, she was too busy watching him in the mirror. He rapidly slipped a loop of leather at the end of the paddle around his wrist and began to unfasten his pants. The garments remained around his hips, but he drew his erection over the waistband of his white boxer briefs. He stroked the long, thick, naked shaft.

*"Ian,"* she moaned, heat rushing between her thighs at the vision of his stark, virile power. He slipped the paddle off his wrist and gripped it tight again.

"Yes?" he asked, his voice rough with arousal.

"You're killing me," she said uncontrollably, not sure what she meant. There was just so much pressure pent up inside her. It felt like she was about to combust and burn. Why did this suspended, helpless position arouse her so much?

"It's no more than what you do to me," he said grimly as he firmed his hold on the hip harness and swung the paddle.

"Eight," she yelped. Her ass was burning now, but still most of her attention was on the sensation of Ian's cock leaping up in the air as he landed the blow, the velvety soft, firm crown batting her hip.

By the time "ten" popped out of her throat, things were soaked between her thighs, she was panting raggedly, and her ass was on fire. Ian ran the fur over her stinging ass cheeks and released his hold on the harness. She bit off a whimper when he grabbed one of her flaming buttocks and massaged it greedily with his palm.

"You're ass is going to be so good, lovely. So hot. You're going to melt my cock," he said, a wry smile tilting his hard mouth.

"Will it hurt?" she asked shakily.

He paused in his lascivious caress, still gripping her ass, and met her eyes in the mirror.

"A little at first, perhaps. But my intent is to punish you for your impulsiveness, not to torture you."

"And . . . and putting your cock . . . *there* is part of my punishment?"

He released her bottom and turned, walking over to the table. She tried to see what he was doing over there in the reflection, but his body, and her own, partially blocked her view. When he returned, he carried a glistening black rubber plug. Her eyes widened. It was larger than the one he'd put into her before. Between that intimidating-looking sex toy and Ian's flagrant erection standing out lewdly from his body, Francesca didn't know where to land her anxious gaze.

"I don't consider ass-fucking to be anything but a pleasure," he said as he approached her. "Whether you consider it a punishment or a mutual exchange of pleasure is yet to be determined."

Having said that, he looped his left forearm around the straps of the hip harness, holding her steady. He used the side of his hand to pry back her ass cheeks and touched the tip of the plug to her anus.

"Reach with your hands and rub your clit," he ordered tensely.

She swung her bound hands toward her pelvis, bending her elbows. Her clit was nestled against the padded strap.

She sent a finger beneath the restraint and burrowed it between her labia. She was soaked. The second she rubbed her eager clit, pleasure spiked through her.

Then . . . there was a sharp pain that was quickly gone.

She gasped, realizing Ian had pushed the thick head of the plug into her ass. She rubbed with increased vigor. The building pressure was unbearable. Her body was on fire. *Oh* . . . she was about to come . . .

Ian grabbed her wrists and pulled down her arms. She squawked a choked protest.

She saw his amused expression in the mirror.

"I think we have our definitive answer as to whether this will be a punishment or a pleasure for you, no?"

She bit her lip, her gaze flickering nervously to her ass in the mirror. He'd fully inserted the rubber plug while she lost herself to pleasure. The flat base of the sex toy pressed tight against her ass cheeks.

She was about to explode as she hovered there helplessly in the air, a tight bundle of burning nerves and quivering flesh. She froze at what she saw in the mirror. *Ian was undressing.* He removed his shoes and socks. He stripped off his shirt. She gawked at the sight of his lean waist, ridged abdomen, and wide, powerful chest. Her breath burned in her lungs in anticipation.

*Yes.*

He drew his pants and underwear down his long legs. She finally saw his fully exposed naked body.

She clenched her eyes shut. He was so beautiful, such the epitome of male power, it hurt her to look at him a little, as hyperaroused as she was. A cry fell past her lips when she was suddenly spinning. Her eyes sprang wide, the room zooming past her. She came to a relative halt and lifted her forehead from the harness. Ian stood just inches from her face, his grip shifting to the chest harness, keeping her steady before him. She looked up at him.

"That's the beauty of the swing," he said, obviously noticing her stunned expression. "I can put you in any position I want you, in the blink of an eye." He grasped his cock from below and lifted it to her mouth, making his intention clear. The crown of his cock slid between her lips, stretching them. She looked up at him as she bathed the head, then batted at it with a firm tongue. A snarl pulled at his mouth as he watched her.

How was it possible for her to feel so helpless and masterfully in control at once?

He used his hand to swing her body several inches forward, several inches back. His cock slid in and out of her mouth. He continued this for a moment, fucking her face, totally controlling her, but never taking advantage, only sliding several inches along her tongue, back and forth, until his cock swelled huge between her clamping lips.

"That's good," he muttered, stepping back, his cock popping out of her mouth. "Too good, in fact," he added under his breath. "Hold steady."

Suddenly she was spinning again in the opposite direction. She stared at him in the mirror, bewildered. He slid the hip harness lower so that it trailed down her thighs.

"Oh!" she squeaked when he suddenly lifted her by the waist, taking her body weight as though he lifted a feather pillow. He gently kept the butt plug inserted with one hand.

"Loop your feet the other way through the lower strap, so that you're in a sitting position. She did her best to follow his instructions, but it was his expert maneuvering that got her into the position he desired. When she'd settled again and he'd secured her, the lack of tension in the head harness had caused it to fall away. The upper-body harness had lowered to her ribs, and she sat in the lower leather harness, her knees bent, her bound wrists in her lap. Once she was secure against the upper restraint, he slid the butt harness lower, down to the top of her thighs.

She was dizzy with excitement and Ian's masterful handling of the swing. She felt like she was taking part in some kind of triple-X-rated version of Cirque du Soleil.

He slid the lubricated black rubber plug out of her ass, making her gasp. He dropped it to the floor. She stared, panting, mesmerized as she watched him lubricate his cock until it glistened. He stepped behind her. He grabbed first the straps to the lower harness, then the ones to the upper one, flexing his biceps until they bulged, pulling her body toward him.

She was in a sort of suspended sitting position in front of Ian, her back to him, her upper body slanted forward at an angle . . . her ass fully exposed as it draped in the loop of the harness like an offering.

She couldn't breathe. She felt the slick, hard head of his cock brush against her tingling ass, then press against the entrance of her anus.

"*Ian,*" she grated out between clenched teeth.

"It's time for you to burn, lovely," he said in a low growl.

He lowered his grip on the straps and grabbed the edge of the padded leather beneath her thighs. She had nowhere to go but onto his cock. He thrust his hips and pulled her toward him at once. She cried out as his cock slid into her ass several inches and sharp pain spiked through her. He paused, his large body a coiled spring.

She gaped at his reflection in the mirror. It looked like he'd just undergone a strenuous workout. Every bulging muscle in his body was delineated and tense. Perspiration gleamed on his ridged abdomen and heaving rib cage. His powerful ass and thigh muscles were flexed tight as he held himself on the edge. He was awesome to behold in that moment—a sexual storm on the threshold of breaking. The part of his cock that wasn't sunk into her ass looked intimidatingly huge. He throbbed in the narrow channel. She swore she could feel his pulse in the sensitive flesh. It stunned her, this feeling of their flesh being so close, so melded.

"Are you all right?" he asked tautly.

"Yes," she said, realizing she meant it. The initial sharp pain had faded, leaving only a compelling, forbidden pressure. Her cheeks and lips were stained dark pink. Her clit sizzled.

"Good, because your ass is on fire," he muttered at the same time he thrust and pulled her body closer. A ragged shout tore from his throat. He began to swing her back and forth on his thrusting cock. "Ah God, it's good to be inside you raw."

Francesca whimpered in awe at the new erotic sensation . . . at the vision of Ian losing himself in desire. There was no pain, but an intense, unbearably exciting pressure built in her. The nerves in her ass were so sensitive she could feel every nuance of his cock. Her thigh muscles squeezed tight, putting pressure on her clit. Orgasm loomed. She stared in openmouthed wonder at the mirror as his cock disappeared farther and farther into her body with each new thrust. Finally, his pelvis bumped against her ass cheeks.

He held her to him and growled gutturally. The moment was too full for her. Too incendiary. She began to shudder as orgasm slammed into her, the force of it all the more powerful because it had been held at abeyance for so long.

Distantly, she heard Ian's harsh curse. He fucked her as she came, serving her ass to his cock in a forceful, greedy possession, his hips thumping rapidly against her tingling, sore bottom as he maneuvered the swing—and her body— taking his pleasure to the fullest. It was too much, really. She couldn't have taken the pressure for long. She was utterly at his mercy, her ass tightening around his driving cock as she climaxed thunderously.

He drove into her one last time, his groan striking her as helpless somehow, even though he was the master in this situation. He wrapped his forearm around her waist, pulling her to him in a desperate hold. She cried out brokenly when she felt his cock swell impossibly large. A roar erupted from his throat. He bent his head, grimacing, and pressed his mouth against her back. She bit her lip and clenched her eyes as she felt him explode deep inside her.

He groaned and thrust in and out of her shallowly as he continued to ejaculate, his breath falling hot and ragged against the skin of her back. Her eyes stung. Her tears weren't from pain but from the powerful feeling burning in her chest.

*Had she fallen in love with this man?*

How else could she explain her total and absolute trust in him, her willingness to surrender completely to him?

What else could this euphoric feeling be as she watched

him there in the mirror, abandoning himself completely to bliss? Either she was falling in love or she was going mad.

Either way, he'd been right before. She was completely at his mercy.

# Part Seven

## Because I Need To

# Thirteen

Ian unbound her, then gently helped her out of the harnesses, still raw from shattering climax and a brew of emotion he couldn't quite identify. When her feet touched the floor, he immediately took her into his arms, wincing in pleasure at the sensation of her silky naked skin pressed against his.

He placed his hand on her jaw and tilted her face up to his. He kissed her deeply, wondering how he could feel so much driving, almost harsh, desire for her and this swelling tenderness all at once. Had he been too hard on her? She was so soft, so feminine, so exquisite, he thought dazedly as he caressed her firm, taut curves. He'd been gauging his reaction from hers. When she'd squeezed his cock rhythmically as she whimpered in orgasm minutes ago, he'd hardly thought of her as delicate.

She was a mystery to him—a compelling, tormenting, sweet one that he couldn't resist.

He lifted his head a moment later and grabbed her hand.

He shut the door behind them as they left the room, and then led her to the bathroom. Without speaking, he opened the glass door to the steam shower and twisted the handle. When the temperature was comfortable, he stepped aside and nodded for her to get in. He followed her, shutting the door behind them.

She seemed to have caught his subdued mood, because she said nothing as he meticulously washed her beautiful body in the minutes that followed. He felt her gaze on him, though, as his lathered hands whisked over satiny skin. Steam curled around his knuckles as he washed . . . worshipped. A small part of him still wanted to withdraw like he had in Paris, when he'd been so overwhelmed by her sweetness and generous response.

The experience tonight had choked his defenses, though, making it impossible for him to maintain his sanity and resist her.

He washed himself in a much more cursory, if thorough, fashion and shut off the water. After drying them both with a towel, he again took her hand and led her to his bed. He whipped back the duvet and turned to her, releasing the clip on her hair. The heavy weight of it fell, tumbling around her shoulders and back. His fingers immediately furrowed into the silky, unbound glory.

Her large dark eyes made something clench tight inside his gut.

"Get into the bed," he murmured.

She lay down, curling onto her side, her front facing him. He came down next to her, his belly brushing against hers, and whipped the sheet and cover over them. He stroked the silky length of her hip as the heavy, pregnant silence settled upon them. Neither of them spoke for a moment or two, even though he sensed her alert attention on him.

Then she touched his mouth with soft fingertips. He closed his eyes, trying and failing to shelter himself from a rising tide of unwanted but unstoppable feeling.

He rarely allowed a woman to touch him so intimately, but he let Francesca. Her eager, searching fingertips tormented him for the next several minutes as she charted his face, neck, shoulders, chest, and belly. When she gently scraped a nipple with her nails, he hissed in a burst of sublime pleasure. He held her stare as she wrapped her hand around his cock a moment later.

Her touch was so gentle. Why did it feel like she ripped a bandage off a wound deep inside him when she began to move her arm, pumping him?

Unable to take anymore of her sweet torture, he twisted around and located a condom in the bedside drawer, longing for the day when Francesca had been on the pill long enough, when he could be inside her naked.

A moment later, he lay on top of her, their bellies heaving against each other in tandem, his cock fully sheathed in her warm, clasping pussy. He opened his clenched eyelids and saw her staring up at him.

"Do I wrong you, Francesca?" he demanded toughly.

She didn't answer for a moment, but he knew from the somber expression in her eyes that she understood he'd meant not just tonight but everything—his inability to resist this vibrant, talented, beautiful woman despite the fact that he'd inevitably taint her brilliance with his darkness . . . eventually make her turn away in hurt.

The thought of seeing rejection of him on her beautiful face sliced at him deep.

"Does it matter?"

A spasm clenched his facial muscles at her soft reply. He began to move, fucking her with long, thorough strokes, shuddering at the distilled blast of pleasure.

*No.* It didn't matter.

He couldn't stay away from her, no matter the consequence to her . . . or to himself.


After they made love again, he held her and they talked like lovers—or at least that's what Francesca suspected lovers talked like, not having any experience herself. It was a heady experience, listening to him talk about his childhood growing up at Belford Hall, his grandfather's estate in East Sussex. She wanted to ask him about what his experience had been like with his mother in northern France—surely it had been a night-and-day experience in comparison with the luxury and privilege of an earl's grandson—but she couldn't muster the courage.

She anxiously brought up the topic of Xander LaGrange again. Ian was adamant, however, that her behavior hadn't been the primary issue with the business deal going sour.

"It was just the final straw," Ian said. "I hated having to court him in order to get that software. I've always despised him, ever since I was seventeen years old. It grated, having to smarm up to him. I've been avoiding meeting with him in person for weeks now." He blinked as if in memory. "Actually, I was supposed to meet with him that first night we met, the night of your cocktail party at Fusion. I asked Lin to cancel."

Her heart jumped at that. "I thought you looked annoyed when Lin approached you at Fusion because you didn't want to have to waste time with meeting me."

He nudged her chin softly as she looked up at him. "Why would you think that?"

"I don't know. I just imagined you had a lot better things to do than meet me."

His low chuckle warmed her. He pressed gently on her head, and she contentedly rested it back on his chest.

"I don't say things I don't mean, Francesca. I had been looking forward to meeting you ever since I saw your entry painting and recognized you as the artist who painted *Cat*," he said, shortening the name of the painting that hung in his library . . . the painting she'd inadvertently done of him. She pressed her mouth to his skin and kissed him, thrilled to the core by this little revealed truth. His fingers tightened in her hair.

"But what will you do about the software you need for your start-up company?" she asked after a moment.

"I'll do what I should have done to begin with," he said briskly, his fingertips massaging her scalp, making her shiver in delicious pleasure. "I'll design my own. It'll be an effort, and it'll take extra time, but I should have gone that route to begin with instead of bothering with that ass. It's never good business to deal with a man like LaGrange. I'd been kidding myself."

Later, she told him about when she first began to understand she was an artist, during a camp for overweight children when she was eight years old.

"I didn't lose a pound at that camp, much to my parents' dismay, but I learned that I was an ace at sketching and painting," she murmured, lying still with her head on his chest and feeling content and drowsy as Ian stroked her hair.

"Your parents seemed obsessed with your weight," he commented, his deep voice vibrating up through his hard chest and tickling her ear. She stroked his biceps with curious fingertips, wondering at how dense and hard the muscle was.

"They were obsessed with controlling me. My weight was one of the few things they couldn't manipulate."

Did his muscles tense when she said that?

"Your body became a battleground," Ian said.

"That's what all those psychologists used to say."

"I can just imagine what those same psychologists would say about you becoming involved with me."

She lifted her head from his chest and met his stare. The lighting was at a dim setting in his bedroom suite. She couldn't quite make out his expression.

"You mean because you're so controlling?" she asked.

He nodded once. "I told you that I practically drove my former wife over the edge."

Francesca's pulse began to throb as she stared at his stark male beauty. She knew how rare it was for him to speak of his past. "Did you . . . did you care about her so much that you were always worried about her well-being?"

"No."

She blinked at his rapid, absolute response. He winced slightly and glanced away. "I wasn't in love with her or anything, if that's what you're asking. I was twenty-one years old, still in college, and a fool for having gotten involved with her. I'd had an argument with my grandparents at around that time. A big one. We hadn't spoken for months. I suppose I was a little vulnerable for the possibility of being blinded by a woman like Elizabeth. I met her at a fundraiser at the University of Chicago—one that my grandmother happened to attend while trying to mend fences with me. Elizabeth was a gifted ballet dancer who came from an affluent American family. She was taught to crave the type of status my grandmother represents."

"And you," Francesca said softly.

"That's what Elizabeth thought at first—before we married and she actually got to know me, and she came to realize what a mistake she'd made. She wanted a prince charming and got stuck with a bastard devil," he said, a small, mirthless smile twisting his mouth. "Elizabeth may have been a virgin, but she was far from innocent in the art of getting what she wanted. She designed to snare me in her trap, and I was stupid enough to let her."

"She . . . she got pregnant on purpose?"

Ian nodded, his gaze flickering over her face. "I know a lot of men say that, but in our case, it was a proven truth. After she became pregnant and we married, I discovered her old pill packs in the bathroom. She appeared to be taking them very irregularly. When I confronted her about it, she admitted that she'd stopped taking the pill once we began seeing each other. She claimed it was because she wanted to have my child, but I didn't believe her. Or I should say, she did want to become pregnant in order to marry, but I don't believe she truly wanted the experience of motherhood."

She experienced a sinking feeling. "Aren't you worried

about the possibility of me doing the same thing? With the birth control, I mean?"

"No."

"Why are you so certain?" Francesca asked, although warmth flooded her at his quick, confident reply.

"Because I'm a much better reader of character at thirty than I was at twenty-one," he stated dryly.

"Thank you," she whispered. "So what happened after you confronted Elizabeth?"

"I was convinced she would do something to harm the child once I discovered how she'd manipulated me. The pregnancy had served its purpose. We were married. She was very beautiful, physically anyway, and a dedicated dancer. Despite her need for a pregnancy, I think she despised the idea of what it would do to her body . . . how it would change her life. She was hardly the maternal type. I thought she might do something to end the pregnancy. I wouldn't have put it past her, anyway." He met her stare steadily. "It wasn't Elizabeth I was so worried about protecting. It was the child she carried. So yes, I did become overly controlling. You know how I can be."

"But you said once that she tried to blame *you* for the loss of the child," she recalled.

He nodded. "She said it was because I rode her so hard about taking care of herself, because I was so controlling about her daily activities and schedule. She felt I restricted her freedom . . . made her a prisoner to my anxiety. She was undoubtedly right about that. It's what I do when I care about someone, and I cared about that child."

"Even so, that doesn't sound like a viable reason for someone to lose a child. One out of five women miscarry, right?

Why couldn't it have just been a natural thing versus something *you* did?" Francesca asked, puzzled and little annoyed with this Elizabeth. She sounded like a manipulative wimp.

"We'll never really know for certain. It doesn't matter anyway," he said.

Francesca thought it *did* matter—very much. It related to why he considered himself so tainted when it came to relationships, so broken.

"Why did you *marry* her if you didn't really love her?" she couldn't resist asking.

He gave a small shrug, and she couldn't help but touch a muscular shoulder. She wanted to soothe him. She couldn't keep her hands off him. Who knew when he'd let her touch him so freely again?

"I would never allow a child of mine to be a bastard," he said.

Her caressing fingers stilled at that. It was only the second time he'd ever mentioned his illegitimacy to her. She recalled that he'd called himself a bastard the first night they'd met, at the cocktail party in her honor.

"Your father," she whispered, noticing the gleam in his blue eyes. Was that a warning glint, a silent message for her to tread carefully? She continued despite the potential risk. "Do you know who he is?"

He shook his head. She definitely felt the tension in his muscles now, but he stayed put in the bed. She decided to take courage that he didn't excuse himself and walk away, as she suspected he might have before tonight.

"Were you curious about who he is? *Are* you?"

"Only insofar as I'd like the knowledge in order to kill the bloody bastard."

Her mouth fell open in shock. She hadn't expected his focused, intense aggression. "*Why?*"

He closed his eyes briefly, and she wondered if she'd gone too far. Would he retreat now?

"Whoever he was, he must have taken advantage of my mother. I don't know if that means out-and-out rape or the seduction of a very vulnerable, sick woman, but whatever the case, I definitely carry the genes of a fucking degenerate."

"Oh, Ian," she whispered, her heart swelling with compassion. What a nightmare for a young boy to live with. What a nightmare for an adult man. "And you never saw him, he never came around?"

He shook his head, his eyelids still closed.

"And your mother, she never—"

He opened his eyes and met her stare. "She grew anxious every time I brought it up as a kid, started doing some of her repetitive, ritualistic behaviors. After a while, I avoided the topic of my father's identity like the plague. But inside, I grew to hate him. *He'd* done that to her, made her that scared and nervous. Somehow I just knew it."

"But she already was ill . . . schizophrenic . . ."

"Yes, but there was something about the mention of him that never failed to send her into a bad period . . . a dark one."

She couldn't stand that expression on his face. It pierced her from the inside out. She hugged him tight. "Ian, I'm so sorry."

He grunted at her energetic embrace, and then chuckled softly. He resumed stroking her hair. "Do you think squeezing me like a python is going to make it all better, lovely?"

"No," she muttered, her mouth moving next to his bare chest. "But it couldn't hurt."

He encircled her in his arms and laid her on her back, coming down over her. "That it couldn't," he murmured, before he leaned down and kissed her in that masterful Ian-like way that made her forget everything for a period of time . . . even his suffering.


Francesca knew she'd remember that night spent in Ian's arms, and in his bed, forever. It'd been sublime to have him open up to her . . . even a little. In the past, he'd told her that their relationship would be a purely sexual one, and there could be little doubt that their attraction—their obsession—with each other sexually was powerful stuff.

But that night, their exchange had been more than about sex. Or so Francesca had thought . . .

She woke up to brilliant golden sunlight filtering around the lush drapery. She blinked sleepily, noticing she was alone in the luxurious mussed bed where she'd spent so many erotic, intimate hours with Ian last night.

"Ian?" she called, her voice still rough from sleep.

He came walking out of the bathroom, looking amazing in a pair of dark blue trousers, a stark white button-down shirt, a black silk tie with pale blue stripes, and that belt buckle that always distracted her so much riding low on his lean hips. Had she really seen him completely naked last night, truly seen his awesome reflection in those mirrors, all of those lean, bulging muscles flexed tight as he fucked her?

Had it been a dream, having him hold and make love to her all night?

"Good morning," he said, walking toward the bed and fastening a cuff link with deft fingers.

"Good morning," she said groggily, smiling up at him, feeling content in the warm sunshine, sublime at the sight of him.

"I'm afraid I have to leave town for a while. I'm not sure when I'll be back."

Her giddy grin faded. His words echoed around her skull like a ricocheting gunshot.

"I've spoken to Jacob, and he's going to give you a lesson on motorcycles. I'd like you to get that license at the same time he takes you to get your vehicle license. Lin is sending you the 'Rules of the Road' for motorcycles. I'm leaving you my tablet to use for studying," he said, pointing to the table in the sitting area of his bedroom suite. His brisk no-nonsense manner only furthered her stunned disbelief.

"Excuse me, Ian? I'm still sort of stuck on 'I'm leaving town, and I'm not sure when I'll be back,'" she said, sitting up partially in bed, propping her upper body on her elbow.

"I received a call this morning." Was he avoiding her eyes? "I have an emergency to attend to."

"Ian, *don't*."

He paused at her sharp tone, his hand still at his shirt cuff. His eyes flashed.

"Don't *what*?" he asked.

"Don't leave," burst out of her throat.

For an anxious, awful moment, silence reigned.

"I know you probably feel vulnerable about last night, but don't run away," she pleaded, a little shocked at herself. Had she secretly feared this very thing all night as they talked and made love and truly shared of themselves? Had she been worried all along he would abandon her in the aftermath of intimacy?

"I'm not sure what you're talking about," he said, dropping his arms. "I have no choice but to leave, Francesca. Surely you understand I have business that takes me away at times."

"Oh, I see," she said, emotion bubbling in her breast. "You're flying away right now has nothing to do with what happened last night."

"No. It doesn't," he said sharply. "Where is all this coming from?"

She stared down at the bedsheet, not wanting him to see the tears that stung her eyes. She wanted to spit in anger . . . in hurt. "Yes. Where's it coming from?" she mused bitterly. "Stupid, naïve Francesca. Why didn't I remember this was just a sexual thing, a matter of convenience for you? Oh, and your cock, of course. Let's not forget that crucial player in the game."

"You're acting foolishly. I got a phone call. I *must* leave. That's all there is too it."

"Why?" she demanded. "What's the emergency? Tell me."

He blinked, obviously taken aback by her blunt demand. She noticed the corners of his mouth had gone pale in anger. "Because I *need* to. There are certain things that are unavoidable, and this is one of them. I'm not leaving for any other cause than that. It should be reason enough for you. Besides, your sullen behavior hardly makes me want to confide in you," he added under his breath, striding away. Fury rose in her. It was too much, having him dismiss her in this way yet again, especially after she'd laid herself open to him last night . . . after she'd thought he'd done the same to her.

"If you leave right now, I won't be waiting for you. It'll be finished."

He spun around, his nostrils flared in anger. "Are you *daring* me, Francesca? Are you throwing down the gauntlet? Are you truly so vindictive?"

"How can you ask me that when you're the one who is running away because of what's happening between us?" she exclaimed, sitting up in bed, holding the sheet over her breasts.

"The only thing that's happening between us is that you're acting like a selfish brat. I have an emergency to attend to."

"Then tell me what it is. At least give me that courtesy, Ian. Or do you think that given the rules of this godforsaken relationship, because of my supposed *submissive* nature, that I don't even have the right to ask that?" she seethed.

He reached for the jacket he'd placed on the back of an armchair. Belatedly, she noticed his packed leather suitcase next to his briefcase. He really *was* leaving. She felt blindsided all over again. He shrugged on his suit jacket and regarded her with a glacial stare.

"As I said, I have no desire to explain myself to you when you're behaving this way." He picked up his luggage. "I'll call you this evening. Maybe you'll feel better about things by then."

"Don't bother. I won't feel *better*. I can guarantee that," she said with as much dignity . . . as much coldness as she could muster.

The color seemed to rush out of his face. She had a wild urge to take back what she'd said, but her stubbornness—her pride—wouldn't let her. He nodded once, his mouth set in a hard line, and stalked out of his bedroom, shutting the door behind him with a brisk click that sounded horribly final in her ringing ears.

Francesca clamped her eyelids shut as misery settled upon her like a weight.

Three days later, she sat in the Department of Motor Vehicles office in Deerfield, Illinois, studying the motorcycle "Rules of the Road" on Ian's tablet. Yes, she still planned never to see Ian again on any sexual basis, and no, he'd definitely believed what she'd told him on that sunny Friday morning, because he hadn't tried to contact her since he'd left. She kept trying to tell herself she was glad he wasn't calling her, but somehow, her self-convincing didn't feel all that persuasive.

What was that expression that had shadowed his face when she'd told him not to call her? Why is it that both in that situation three days ago and also on that occasion when he'd freaked out upon finding she was a virgin that *he'd* been the one who looked abandoned, not the other way around? The thoughts made it feel as if her heart was being squeezed by a giant invisible hand.

No, she wouldn't dwell on such things. It was impossible to pierce the dark, complex inner workings of Ian's soul. It was folly to even try.

It surprised her a little that she'd continued on with her driving lessons with Jacob, given her and Ian's break. But she'd become strangely fixated on the idea of getting her license. Maybe part of her believed what Ian had told her. It was an important milestone of development that she'd passed up because of her emotional issues as a child and teenager. Her compulsion to drive somehow related to her wanting to take full control of her life for the first time.

School was going well. Her painting for Ian would soon be finished.

For the first time in her life, she really did feel like she was starting to gain control . . . not just fumbling along, surviving from day to day. She wanted to be in the driver's seat of Francesca Arno's life, just like Ian had suggested. If it was destined to be a train wreck, well . . . at least she could say who was responsible.

Her eyes burned from all her studying on the tablet. She'd already passed the regular driver's test, but the motorcycle test remained.

"Feeling confident?" Jacob asked from where he sat next to her, reading a newspaper. The DMV was packed. They'd been waiting for almost two hours now to be called so that Francesca could take her test.

"For the written part anyway," she said. "Maybe we should have practiced for more than one day on Ian's motorcycle?"

"You'll do fine," Jacob assured. "You're actually more of a natural on a motorcycle than you are behind the wheel of a car, and you passed that test with flying colors."

She gave him a wry glance. "I barely passed the driver's portion. The first thing I did when I pulled onto the road was cut off another driver."

"But that was the only mistake," Jacob reminded her. *Sweet man.*

Someone called her name.

"Wish me luck," she said anxiously to Jacob as she stood.

"Luck isn't necessary. You can do this," he said with far more confidence than was warranted, in her opinion.

She took the driving portion of the motorcycle test on

Ian's motorcycle: a sleek, badass European bike. Jacob had told her over the past few days that Ian had a long-term love of motorcycles.

"I think he told me he used to fix motorcycles when he was a kid. He's got a scary natural talent for it. Guess it all goes with that math, computer brain he's got. All I know is, he can fix a car in twice the time I can, and I'm nearly twice his age," Jacob had told her a few days ago, a hint of pride in his tone.

She also learned from Jacob that Ian was part owner in an increasingly popular, innovative French company that made superexpensive high-tech bikes and scooters.

The only reason she'd agreed to Jacob's motorcycle training is that she suspected Ian recalled what she'd said about those motor scooters in Paris. And in truth, one of those scooters fitted with her limited budget, her transportation and parking needs in a busy city, not to mention her burgeoning sense of independence and desire to better run her life. Her plan was to buy an inexpensive scooter after she got her license, and screw it if she'd taken advantage of what Ian offered after he'd abandoned her.

She'd accept the hundred thousand dollars she'd earned on the commission. She'd take everything he'd offered and walk away from him, just as he'd walked away from her.

That's what she told herself anyway. It comforted her to imagine she was as callous about Ian as he'd been about her.

*Bloody bastard. Up and leaving town after she'd bared herself to him . . . after he'd seemingly done so to her.*

"Well?" Jacob asked, standing when she approached him in the waiting room after taking her motorcycle test, her expression somber. He studied her face anxiously, his eyes springing wide. "Don't worry. We'll take it again as soon as you've practiced more."

Francesca grinned. "I was ribbing you. I passed. With true flying colors this time."

He gave her a quick hug and congratulations, Francesca laughing, ebullient with relief. She'd done it! Better late than never.

Jacob excused himself to secure Ian's motorcycle in the back of the limo—she'd been shocked at how much room was in the cab of the luxurious car once Jacob broke down and stored the table between the couch seats. Francesca sat in the waiting room, held up again until she was called to get her photo for her license. The DMV was a synonym for waiting. After a few minutes of growing impatient and bored, she opened up Ian's tablet, glad to be able to look at whatever she wanted to pass the time instead of having to study the rules of the road. She clicked for a search and several items came up on the drop-down menu . . . obviously sites Ian visited regularly. Feeling a little guilty, she studied the history. Where did Ian surf on the Internet? Most of the topics made sense— businesses and people he was doing background searches on.

One of them didn't. She clicked it on it, glancing warily to the side to ensure Jacob wasn't there to observe her nosing into Ian's business.

The Genomics Research and Treatment Institute—a highly respected research and treatment facility located southeast of London in a lovely wooded landscape. Francesca studied the sylvan scenery and large ultramodern building. It took her a moment of reading to understand that the facility was a world leader in the research and treatment of schizophrenia.

She thought of Ian's mother and her heart sank. Did he keep up on the research for cures for the cruel, debilitating illness in memory of Helen Noble? Did he, perhaps, fund some of the research?

"Jacob? What's the Genomics Research and Treatment Institute?" she asked the driver in a false casual tone when he came and sat down next to her a few minutes later.

"No idea. Why?"

"You don't know? It's a sort of research facility and hospital. You've never heard of it in association with Ian?"

Jacob shook his head. "Never. Where's it at?"

"Southeast of London."

"That explains it then," Jacob said matter-of-factly as he folded his newspaper. "If it's one of Ian's British companies, I wouldn't know much about it."

"Why's that?"

"He never has me drive in London. He keeps his own car at his apartment in the city."

"Oh," Francesca said lightly, hoping she was hiding her rabid curiosity adequately. "And is there any other place where he keeps a car and doesn't take you?"

Jacob considered for a moment. "No, not really, now that I think about it. I go everywhere but London. But that's not too surprising. Ian's a Brit, isn't he? It'd make sense he doesn't need a driver in London. That's why I'm not driving him right now."

"Right," Francesca agreed, nodding, her pulse racing at this unexpected news. Ian was in London. Ian hadn't told her, of course, and Mrs. Hanson either didn't know his

location or was keeping mum about it on orders from Ian. It
was odd. Ian Noble was at home anywhere. He could
maneuver around any city. He didn't *need* a driver. He just
wanted one for convenience. He was the cat who walked
alone, after all. All places were alike to him. She recalled
how she'd captured that aspect of his character in her
painting so many years ago, and compared it to the Rudyard
Kipling story. She knew from experience that everywhere he
went, he was confident, sure, utterly the master of his
environment . . . determinedly alone.

So why was London different? Why did he leave his
trusted driver, Jacob, behind?

Her head swung around when her name was called.

"This is it," she said, barely restraining her excitement at
getting her license—not to mention hardly stopping herself
from pressing Jacob with more questions about Ian and
London.

"You're driving home," Jacob said.

"You better believe I am," she said, smirking.

The next afternoon, she sat on a bench alone in the Noble
Enterprises lobby. The entry managed to convey a sense of
sleek, modern efficiency, luxury, and warmth—thanks to the
beige-pink marble floors, rich woods, and tan walls. The
security guard at the circular desk in the center of the lobby
kept glancing her way with increasing suspicion. She'd been
there for almost two hours, studying the light on the large
swath of wall where her painting would hang, occasionally
taking photos with her cell phone.

She wanted to make sure she was taking into account the

lighting in the painting's soon-to-be home.

The security guard finally decided she was up to no good and left his circular booth. Francesca stood, stowing her phone in her back pocket.

She didn't really feel like explaining herself. "I'm going," she assured the youngish man who had a face like a boulder and huge hands. His eyes were alert and not unkind, however.

"Is there some way I can help you, miss?" the guard pursued.

"No," she hedged, walking backward. When he took a step toward her as if to follow, she sighed. "I'm the artist doing the painting that's going to go right there," she said, pointing at the large expanse of wall overhanging the guard's desk. "I was watching the light change in the lobby."

When the guard gave her a skeptical, incredulous look, she glanced sideways and noticed the restaurant Fusion. "Er . . . excuse me. I'm just going to dash into Fusion and say hello to Lucien."

For a second, she thought the security guard would follow her when she ducked into the restaurant, but when she glanced around after approaching the elegant bar, the glass doors remained closed and the guard was nowhere to be seen. She gave a sigh of relief.

"Francesca!"

She recognized Lucien's French-accented voice.

"Hi, Lucien. Zoe! Hi, how are you?" Francesca greeted the pair, happy to see the beautiful young woman who had tried to make her feel at home at the cocktail party in her honor. Zoe and Lucien stood side by side. It was three o'clock in the afternoon on a Tuesday and the bar was empty except for the three of them. She paused uncertainly when she saw Lucien's arm fall away from Zoe's waist and the slightly guilty cast to both of their expressions. Why should they be self-conscious about touching each other?

"Really good," Zoe said, shaking her hand. "How is the painting going?"

"As good as can be expected. I'm having some trouble with the lighting. I was sitting out in the lobby studying what the light would be like on the painting throughout the day, and the security guard sort of ran me off," she said, giving them a sheepish smile. "I ducked in here hoping to escape him."

Lucien chuckled. "Would you like something to drink?" he asked, moving toward the entrance to the large walnut bar. "Club soda with lime, right?"

"Yes," Francesca said, pleasantly surprised that he'd recalled. Zoe sat next to her on one of the stools, asking her a few more questions about the painting. She noticed Lucien didn't ask Zoe for her drink order, just automatically placed a bottle of ginger ale in front of her.

"So are you guys going out?" Francesca asked a few minutes later, taking a grateful sip of her soda. She blinked when she saw Lucien's and Zoe's startled expressions. "I mean . . . I just thought it looked like . . . never mind," she said, taking another gulp and setting her glass back on the counter. "Just ignore me. I'm always saying stupid things."

Lucien broke into laughter. Zoe gave a faltering smile. "It's not that. Yes. Zoe and I *are* going out. We're just trying to fly under the radar about it, that's all."

"Radar?" Francesca asked, confused.

"Ian, in a word," Lucien said, still smiling.

"Ian? Why are you trying to avoid Ian?" Francesca asked.

"It's frowned upon for Noble Enterprises employees to date, especially a manager and non-manager," Lucien said.

"I keep telling Lucien that I'm an *assistant* manager," Zoe spoke up heatedly, glaring at Lucien. Obviously this was a much-talked-about, incendiary topic between the couple. "I don't think we're breaking any rules. We're in two completely different industries for the company. Surely Ian wouldn't mind."

"Who cares if Ian minds?" Francesca blurted out, leaning forward on the bar and frowning. "Why does everyone have to defer to him like he's the king of the realm or something? You two have the right to live your life based on what *you* want, not Ian Noble's whims."

A thick silence followed her outburst. It took Francesca a moment to realize that Lucien was staring behind her and that Zoe was turning slowly in her stool, her expression frozen.

Francesca shut her eyes and inhaled through constricted lungs. "Ian's behind me, isn't he?" she whispered to Lucien. Lucien's flattened expression was her answer.

She twirled around on her stool, anxiety rising in her. He stood between the entrance of the restaurant and the portion of the bar where Zoe and she sat. The sight of him ripped a jagged, deep crack in her defenses. Longing welled up in her, so strong it stole her breath. He wore an impeccable black suit that highlighted the masculine lines of his long body to perfection, one of the crisp white dress shirts he favored, and a pale silver tie. His face was liked carved marble: beautiful, cold, impassive. His eyes gleamed with heat, however, as he studied her—and her alone—from the shadows of the dimly lit restaurant bar.

"When did you get back?" Francesca asked, her mouth dry.

"Just now," he replied. "Mrs. Hanson said that you mentioned your plan to stop by the lobby. When I didn't see you, I was headed to my office, and Pete—the security guard—told me about his encounter with a young woman who sat in the lobby all afternoon staring into space, occasionally taking pictures of nothing and who told him she was studying the light." Did his full lips twitch slightly in amusement at that? "I got the feeling he wasn't sure if you were a potential threat to security or a fairy."

"Oh . . . I see," Francesca said, feeling strangely as if he'd just reached out and caressed her with his last comment. She glanced uncomfortably at Zoe. Had her big mouth just gotten Lucien and Zoe in trouble?

"Taking a break, Ms. Charon?" Ian asked with brisk kindness.

Zoe slid down from her stool and smoothed her skirt, her cheeks taking on a rosy hue. "I was taking a break, but it's time that I got back to the office."

Ian nodded, glancing from her flustered appearance to Lucien. "Yes. It's always best to be discreet in these matters," he said, meeting Lucien's stare.

Lucien nodded once. Francesca realized, dazedly, Ian had just told the couple he was okay with their relationship as long as they didn't flaunt it.

"May I speak with you for a moment? There's something I want to show you," Ian said to Francesca. Zoe swept past them, clearly intent on making her escape while the going was good.

"I . . . okay," Francesca said, feeling a little trapped by the situation, not to mention by Ian's compelling eyes and her upsurge of raw longing. Had she really believed she could expunge him from her mind and soul so easily because of anger? What was fury to the swelling, inexplicable feelings she had for him?

She said goodbye to Lucien, giving him an apologetic glance in the process. Lucien smiled in reassurance.

"Where are we going?" Francesca asked Ian when she trailed him out of Fusion and they walked toward the exit of the lobby versus the elevators. She'd thought he'd take her to his office, but instead he led her through the turnabout to the sidewalk.

"Back to the penthouse. There's something I want to show you there."

She came to an abrupt halt, her gaze leaping to meet his. Something flickered across his stoic features, and she wondered if he'd also recalled how he'd said a similar thing to her weeks ago . . . the night when she'd first met him right here at Noble Enterprises.

"I don't want to go to the penthouse with you," she said stiffly. Had it sounded like a lie to him? It certainly had to her. Part of her very much wanted to go to the penthouse with him. Why did she have to find him so irresistible? He was like a drug in her system, but it was worse than that kind of addiction. Worse because her soul was involved. Worse because she couldn't help but see a part of Ian's soul as well . . . couldn't help but be haunted by it.

"I'd hoped you'd changed your mind about what you said before I left," he said quietly, stepping toward her. Clouds had prevailed over the struggling sunshine. His eyes looked especially brilliant with the dark, low-lying clouds as their backdrop. They stood on a crowded sidewalk as people bustled past, but it was like she was sealed in a bubble with him.

"It wasn't a matter of me throwing a temper tantrum like you made it out to be last week, Ian," she said. "You walked out on me."

"I came back. I told you I would."

"And I said I wouldn't be available to you when you did." Something flashed in his eyes at that. Somehow, she knew Ian wouldn't like her saying that particular thing.

*I like to know that you're available to me.*

Her body stirred at the memory. She broke his mesmerizing stare and gazed blindly in the direction of the river. "The painting is coming along."

"I know. I went and looked at your progress when I returned home this afternoon. It's spectacular."

"Thanks," she said, still avoiding his eyes.

"Jacob informs me that you passed both of your driving tests. He was very proud of you."

She couldn't help but smile a little at that. It'd been a proud moment for her, too—profound in many ways. She owed Ian for that.

"I did. Thank you for encouraging me to do it." She studied her shoes. "Did you have a good trip to London?"

When he didn't immediately respond, she looked up at him.

"I hadn't realized I'd told you where I was going," he said.

"You didn't. I guessed. Why do you always go by yourself to London?" she asked impulsively. "Jacob told me you never take him."

She noticed his expression darken. "Don't blame Jacob. He didn't know where you were, either. I was asking him questions about it and he happened to mention he never drives you in London. I figured you must be there, since Jacob was here in Chicago."

"Why were you so curious?"

She blinked at that. Why indeed, if she was professing not being interested in him anymore?

"What did you want to show me at the penthouse?"

His bland look told her he was very aware she was avoiding answering his question. He put out his hand, prompting her to walk next to him. "It's something that has to be shown, not described."

She hesitated for a few seconds. Was she really considering forgiving him for walking out so abruptly Friday without explanation of his errand?

She sighed and fell into step beside him.

She wasn't conceding defeat, but just like that first night, it was a grueling effort to resist him. Maybe it was because of the lonely days of his absence, or his sudden appearance had caught her off guard, or perhaps it was because of the dizzying rush of warmth and happiness she experienced upon seeing him again.

Whatever the reason, this afternoon her resources for resistance were running very thin when it came to Ian Noble.

# Fourteen

∽

She stepped off the elevator, the entryway to Ian's foyer striking her as strange, even though she'd grown quite familiar with it in the past weeks. So much had changed since she'd first peered into his world. Yet that feeling of anxious excitement as she entered the hushed penthouse with Ian just behind her was all too familiar.

"This way," he said, his hoarse, quiet voice like gentle knuckles caressing the back of her neck. Her anticipation and curiosity grew as she followed him to the room she now knew was the library-office where *The Cat That Walks By Himself* hung.

When he opened the door and she first entered the room, the first thing that struck her was the other man turned in profile to her as he attended to his task.

"Davie?" she exclaimed, full-out shocked to see her friend in this unexpected environment.

Davie looked over his shoulder and grinned. He set down the painting he'd been arranging and turned toward her.

Her gaze volleyed back and forth between the surprising vision of her friend and the painting he'd been perching on a long table against the wall.

"Oh my God! Where did you get it?" she gasped in disbelief, staring at a cityscape painting she'd done of the Wrigley Building, the Union and Carbide Building, and the Gothic-rocket masterpiece, 75 East Wacker. She'd done the painting when she was twenty years old and sold it for two hundred dollars to a suburban gallery. She'd hated parting with it, but she'd had no choice.

Before Davie could respond, she started to spin on her feet, her mouth hanging open in shock. She couldn't breathe.

Her paintings encircled the entire library. Davie had placed them all about the room, sixteen or seventeen of them—lost lovers—all of them fanning out from the mantel and *The Cat That Walks By Himself,* which hung above them all. She'd never seen so many of her own pieces together. She'd had to part with them one by one, a piece of her soul splintering away every time she did. Part of her always hated herself for not being able to keep the cherished pieces of her creativity close . . . sacred.

And now here they all were in one room.

She quaked with emotion.

"'Cesca," Davie said, his voice sounding strained. He stepped toward her, his happy smile a thing of the past.

"You did this?" she asked shrilly.

"I did it under request," Davie said. She followed his significant glance.

Ian stood just inside the entrance to the library, watching her with a hooded gaze that morphed to concern—and something else, something darker . . . sadder—as he studied her face.

*Oh, no.* She could protect herself against his arrogance. His controlling manner. His imperiousness.

But *not* against that anxious, vaguely lost expression on his bold, handsome face. It was too much. The weight of her emotions surged like a storm rushing a beach.

She hurried out of the room.


"Let me," Davie said when Ian turned to follow Francesca, his gut wrenching at the shadow of anguish on her lovely face. Ian abhorred feeling helpless. He'd fashioned his entire life to avoid the unpleasant sensation. And yet he had to accept that hateful emotion as he stilled his feet with great effort and watched Davie pass him in pursuit of Francesca.


"How in the world did you ever do it, Davie?" she asked when her friend entered the studio a minute later. She was glad to see it was him and not Ian. Ian had bulldozed her remaining fragile defenses by doing what he'd done. How had he known that giving her back pieces of her past would decimate her walls when it came to him?

Davie shrugged and walked over to the table where she kept her art supplies. He tore off a piece of paper towel and handed it to her.

"Ian gave me carte blanche in order to locate and purchase as many of them as I could. When you have those kinds of resources, it's not as hard as you might think."

"That kind of money, you mean," Francesca said, wiping tears off her cheek with the paper towel.

Davie gave her a soulful glance. "I know you told me last

week that this thing between you and Ian was over, but we'd started the ball rolling a while back . . . before you went to Paris, even. Are you mad at me?"

"For going into league with Ian?" she sniffed, smiling mirthlessly.

"I wouldn't have done it for a lesser cause. You know I've been trying to get ahold of some of your older works for ages now. It's because I think you're such a talented artist that I wanted to do that, 'Cesca. That was my main motivation for agreeing to help Ian collect the pieces. Not his money." His attention was diverted. He went to stand before the painting. "You've outdone yourself," he said in a hushed tone. "This is the best work you've ever done."

"You really think so?" she asked, walking over to stand next to him.

Davie nodded solemnly, his gaze traveling over the large painting. He met her gaze. "I know you said that your . . . affair with him was over, 'Ces, but I can't help but notice that Ian Noble is crazy about you. Granted, I've expressed my doubts about your involvement with him in the past. But this wasn't just about him throwing his money around. You wouldn't believe the effort and thought he's put into acquiring your work."

She was unsure of how she was supposed to feel. Two tears spilled out of her eyes. "He does it because he *can*, Davie."

"What's wrong with that?" Davie asked, looking confused. "What is it about Ian Noble that intimidates you so much? I can tell that you're attracted to him, but torn about it, too. What's he done to you?" Davie demanded, his bewilderment morphing to worry as he studied her face.

"Oh, Davie," she mumbled miserably. She'd never told him about the sexual aspect of her and Ian's relationship . . . about Ian being a sexual dominant and insisting she was a submissive. She suddenly blurted it all out, her explanation coming in uncomfortable fits and starts as she tried to give Davie a PG version and found it nearly impossible to do so.

"Francesca," Davie said, looking vaguely uncomfortable. "Having kinky sex *isn't* a terrible thing. I know you haven't had much experience—"

"*Any* . . . before Ian," she reminded him.

"Right. But people have all sorts of kinks in the bedroom. As long as it's consensual and no one is getting hurt . . ." He paled as he faded off. "Ian's not hurting you, is he?"

"No . . . no, it's not that," she exclaimed. "I mean . . . I like . . . *love* the way he makes love to me," she said, blushing hotly. She'd never had this graphic of a conversation with Davie before . . . with anyone, for that matter. "It's just that he's a control freak *all* the time. Look at how he went behind my back and did this whole thing with you! He knew it'd make me want to forgive him for walking out on me last week without an explanation after we'd started to grow close."

Davie sighed. "I told you. Ian asked me to locate your paintings a while back. He couldn't have known you guys were going to have a fight back then and suggested this to make up for it. Look, I've spent time dealing with him over the past few weeks as I located your paintings and we negotiated purchase prices. I know he's domineering, but he's also thoughtful. Yeah, he's stubborn, and it's his way or the highway, but it's been hard to argue with him about that when he clearly wanted to do this to please you."

She just stared at her friend . . . *wanting* to believe him . . .

"I only know one other person who's as stubborn as him," Davie said in a wry, challenging tone. Francesca laughed. She knew who that other person was.

"If you made it clear to him that his dominance over you could happen solely within the boundaries of sex and the bedroom, would that help?" Davie asked.

"But he shares so little of himself. He can shut me off like a light."

Davie nodded in understanding. "Well, it's your decision, of course. I wouldn't be too sure about his ability to shut you out, though. He's unreadable most of the time, no doubt about it, but that doesn't equate to a lack of caring. It just means he's good at hiding it. Anyway, I wanted you to know how focused and generous he's been in collecting your paintings. He's been a man on a mission." He checked his watch. "I have to get going. I'm closing the gallery this evening."

"Thank you, Davie," she said, giving him a big hug. "Both for getting the paintings and for talking to me about Ian."

"Anytime," he told her with a significant glance. "We'll talk more later, if you want."

She nodded, watching him walk out of the room, leaving her to stew in her doubts and hopes.

Ten minutes later, she knocked softly on the door to Ian's bedroom suite. She entered when she heard his distant "Come in." He sat on the couch in the sitting area, his suit coat unbuttoned, his long legs bent before him, paging through his messages on his cell phone, his gaze steady on her as she approached.

"I was just looking at the paintings again," she said. "I'm sorry for running off like that."

"Are you all right?" he asked, setting down his phone on the couch.

She nodded. "I was . . . overwhelmed."

A strained silence ensued as he studied her.

"I thought they would make you happy. The paintings."

Her eyes burned and she stared at the Oriental carpet. Damn. She'd thought she'd gotten rid of all the onerous tears.

"They *do* make me happy. More happy than I can say." She dared to meet his gaze. "How did you know they would?"

"I see how much pride you take in your work," he said, standing. "I can only imagine how hard it was for you to part with them."

"Like giving a piece of myself away each time," she said, attempting a smile, twisting her hands nervously. Her gaze flickered across his face as he stepped toward her, and she was snagged by his stare. "I don't know how I can ever repay you. I mean . . . I know the paintings are yours. You bought them. But for me to see them all together again is so special. But don't you think it's all too much?"

"Why would it be too much? Do you think I'm doing it to get you back in bed?"

"No, but—"

"I did it because you're singularly talented. You know how much I appreciate art. It would please me to see your work valued as it should be. My patronage would mean nothing if you weren't so talented, Francesca."

She exhaled slowly. How could she argue in the face of what appeared to be genuine sincerity. "Thank you. Thank you so much for thinking about me, Ian."

"I think about you more than you know."

She swallowed thickly, recalling what Davie had said earlier . . . "*He's good at hiding it.*"

"I'm sorry that I upset you last week. I really did have an important emergency to attend to. I wasn't trying to avoid you," he said. "My feelings about our relationship remain the same. I wish you'd reconsider what you said the other day. I can't stop thinking about you, Francesca," he said, his tone at the last making her gaze leap to his.

"If . . . if we do continue in the way we were, Ian . . . would you promise to only try and control me . . . dominate me in the bedroom?" she asked breathlessly. It'd cost her more than she'd been prepared for to say that. When he didn't immediately answer, her heart dipped in her chest. His expression was impassive, but his eyes gleamed with emotion.

"Do you mean during sex? Because I can't guarantee that I'll only want you that way within the confines of a bedroom. As you know from Paris, the urge could arise anywhere."

"Oh . . . well, yes. That's what I meant. I admit that I like it when you . . . dominate me during sex, but I don't want my *life* controlled."

"You mean like I tried to control Elizabeth's?"

"You admitted that you trust me more than you did Elizabeth."

She sensed him considering and felt the need to better explain herself.

"I actually want to thank you for encouraging me to gain better control of my life," she said, not wanting him to think she was clueless as to the changes he'd already wrought in her during their relatively brief relationship. "I appreciate you doing that. But *I* want to be the one to be in the true driver's seat, Ian. Outside of sex, I mean," she added under her breath.

His mouth pressed into a hard line. "I can't guarantee I won't tread where you don't want me."

"But will you try?"

His gaze ran over her face before he glanced away and exhaled.

"Yes. I'll try."

Her heart bounced. She rushed him and gave him a huge hug, squeezing his waist until he grunted. He looked amused when she looked up at him a moment later. He must be noticing the rush of happiness that had gone through her at his words. *I'll try.*

"I have an idea," she said. "Let me take you for a ride on your motorcycle."

"I can't," he said regretfully, stroking her cheek.

"But Jacob says I'm a really good driver—better than I am in a car."

He smiled full out, and she blinked at the impact. "That's not what I meant. I have to get into the office. I'm way behind with work."

"Oh," she said, crestfallen. She recovered quickly, though. She understood that he had massive responsibilities:

"But now that you mention it, I did bring home a surprise for you from London," he said, a grin still ghosting his typically stern mouth.

"What?"

He dropped his hands and walked around her to the closet. When he returned, he held a black motorcycle helmet in one hand, a pair of black leather gloves tucked into the opening, and a hanger with a sleek, superhip black leather jacket suspended from it.

"Oh my God, I *love* it," she breathed out, immediately going for the jacket. It was hip-length, with a silver diagonal zipper and buttons. She could tell it would fit her tight. Her fingers ran over the supple leather appreciatively. "Should I try it on?" she asked Ian, brimming over with excitement.

"No protests over the gift?" he asked humorously as she rapidly removed the jacket from the hanger.

She flushed at that. "I should protest . . . it's just . . . they both look like they were made for me," she said, eyeing the helmet excitedly.

"That's because they were," he murmured. She gave him a smile over her shoulder as she hurried into the bathroom, wanting to see her reflection wearing the jacket. How did he always know the perfect gift? She wished she could do the same for him in return. She heard Ian's phone ring in the distance as she zipped the coat and turned from side to side. It fit her perfectly—tight, sleek, and sexy.

She walked back into the bedroom suite, beaming. He sat on the couch again, talking on the phone. His eyebrows went up in subdued admiration as she modeled the jacket for him, his blue eyes running over her from head to toe.

"Let's look into a bond issuance," he was saying to whomever was on the other line. She walked toward him, feeling ridiculously happy after her conversation with Ian.

Had she made a mistake in reneging on her dare to be finished with him?

But he'd said he'd *try* to not be so controlling. That'd meant a lot to her. She knew people couldn't change their stripes overnight, and in Ian's case, his desire to control and monitor those around him went all the way back to his childhood, when he'd been forced to look out for his mother versus the other way around.

Maybe that was what was partially behind her willingness to accept his gift. If he was going to try and bend a little, she should, too. Of course, the darling jacket and helmet were definitely easy gifts to accept, she acknowledged to herself, her hands running over the sleek lines of the jacket. Something sparked in Ian's eyes when she caressed the leather just beneath her breasts.

Something flashed in her blood, as well. She took another step toward him. He watched her fixedly, his nostrils flaring slightly. The absence from each other—her deep down fear that she'd never touch him again—suddenly flared bright in her awareness.

"Let's see the interest on the bonds and the filing costs, and we'll compare that to a bank loan," Ian said into the phone.

A strange brew of daring, gratitude, and desire stirred inside her chest. He'd given her the incalculable gift of her paintings. He'd given her back her past.

She wanted to give him something in return.

His expression flattened when she came before him and gently nudged apart his knees. His eyes widened when she knelt between them. He caught her hand when she reached for his silver belt buckle. She met his stare, imploring silently, and his grip on her slackened.

She unbuckled his belt and unfastened his pants with fleet fingers.

"But the bond issuance would give us more flexibility for future acquisitions where we want to use bank loans," Ian was saying into the phone. Her knuckles brushed across his brief-covered balls as she tried to lower the waistband of his pants. He grunted and then cleared his throat to cover it. She glanced up at him thankfully when he lifted his hips slightly, assisting her in getting his pants and briefs down to his thighs.

She held his cock in her hand a moment later, studying it with fascination. He was as soft as she'd ever seen him. A wave of tenderness and lust swept through her at the vision of him, at the sensation . . . at his male scent filtering into her nose. Within seconds, she felt him stiffen, saw him lengthen and thicken.

Amazing.

She closed her eyes and slid him into her mouth, wanting to feel him grow harder there. *Oh, I like this*, she thought as a haze of desire surrounded her. When she took him into her mouth before he was fully erect, she could swallow more of him. Her head bobbed in his lap as she became more enthusiastic. His cock swelled, stretching her squeezing lips wide. She thrilled as his fingers ran through her hair, and then spread across her skull. In the distance, she heard him say, "Uh . . . what was that, Michael? Yes, just price out the two scenarios."

He was fully tumescent now, filling her mouth . . . overfilling it, his hand on the back of her head gripping into her hair, using his hold to gently guide the rhythm. She began to use her hand in tandem with her mouth, stroking the thick stalk upward as she slid him out of her mouth, fisting it strenuously in a downward motion as she sunk down again over his cock.

He made a muted choking sound and coughed.

"Uh . . . yes, do me a favor Michael, and just get me the price scenarios for a ten-year bond issuance and a twenty. I'll make a decision when I see all the data. Yes, that's all for now, thank you."

She was vaguely aware of his phone dropping to the couch cushion. She looked up at him, his cock embedded at half-staff in her mouth.

"Don't give me that innocent look," he murmured, using his hold on her hair to move her up and down on the staff of his cock, controlling her. "You knew exactly what you were doing, didn't you? Didn't you?" he asked more firmly even as he encouraged her to move faster. She nodded and hummed an affirmation. He hissed. "You make it your goal to torture me, Francesca."

She sucked with all her might and shook her head slightly. He gasped.

"No need to deny the obvious, lovely," he said, his voice growing rough.

She moaned feverishly, losing herself in the magic of giving him pleasure.

She took him into her throat. He hissed in pleasure and then pulled up on her hair, demanding she suck him fast and shallow. She pumped with her fist, avid to please him, wild to feel him succumb, desperate to taste him. He pushed her head down on him, and she took him into her throat again, her nostrils flaring for air. His hips lifted slightly off the couch, and he gasped. His restrained moan became a growl as he began to come. She felt him swell huge, her eyes going wide as he began to ejaculate, bypassing her gag reflex by coming directly in her throat.

He backed out after only a second or two, plunging back and forth between her clamping lips, emptying himself onto her tongue.

After a moment, his tight grip on her hair loosened as he massaged her scalp. His big, solid body slumped into the couch cushions. She slid him out of her mouth with a wet popping noise.

"You deserve a pink ass for that," he said, watching her with a narrow-eyed gaze as she licked her lips of his residue. She saw his small smile and returned it. He hardly looked angry. More like a well-pleased, utterly satiated male.

"Are you going to give me one?" she asked, a shiver of excitement going through her.

"Without a doubt. You're going to get a good paddling. I can't have you distracting me while I do business, Francesca," he murmured, his actions belying his words as he stroked her hair with one hand and caressed her cheek with the other, his manner tender. Cherishing. She couldn't help but feel that he'd quite enjoyed being distracted.

"Go into the bathroom and put on a robe," he said.

She stood and followed his instructions, her pulse fluttering at her throat. When she reentered the suite a few minutes later, she paused at the sight of Ian waiting for her, wearing only a pair of pants, his muscular, ridged torso bare.

"Follow me," he said, taking her hand. Her eyes widened when she saw him extricate the keys from his briefcase.

"What I did wasn't that bad, was it?" she asked anxiously

as he unlocked the room where he said she'd receive her more severe punishments.

"You compromised my ability to think rationally while I was making a business decision," he mused as he led her into the inner chamber and closed the door behind them, locking it.

He led her over to the tall stool she'd noticed on her first night in the room, the one that was situated before the balletlike bar on the wall and was curved unusually at the back. The front of it was normal enough, like a half circle. But the rear of it dipped inward, as if a crescent of the circle had been cut out. Ian left her and went over to the cherry cabinet, opening a drawer. She studied the stool, puzzled and increasingly excited. When she saw that Ian carried the jar of clitoral stimulant and the black leather paddle, her sex clenched tight.

He watched her face intently a moment later as he rubbed the cream on her clit.

"I'm going to give you fifteen good whacks. You deserve more for what you did."

Her cheeks heated with defiance and arousal. "You were hardly complaining."

His stern mouth twitched at that.

"Sit down on the stool, your face toward the wall," he commanded. She did so, staying forward on the chair in order to avoid the crescent cutout at the back of the stool. "Scoot back so that your bottom falls over the edge. Lean forward and put your hands on the bar. That's right."

A rush of realization went through her as she leaned over and gave the bar her upper body weight and her ass fell over the edge of the chair into the cutout. The cream started to make her clit burn as she watched in the mirror as Ian moved behind her, the black leather paddle gripped in his large hand.

Oh, no. Her bottom was utterly exposed and vulnerable . . . and right at the perfect location for his swinging arm.

*Whack.*

A whimper popped out of her throat at the quick sting and the lingering burn.

"*Shhh,*" Ian soothed, turning the paddle and rubbing her ass with the fur. "Too much?"

"I can take it," she said breathlessly.

He caught her gaze in the mirror and smiled.

He swung his arm back and landed another smack, and then another. This time, he used his hand to soothe her bottom, caressing her and gently squeezing each buttock in his palm.

"It's too bad you have such a gorgeous ass," he muttered as he watched himself stroke her.

"Why?"

"Perhaps if you didn't, I wouldn't have to punish it so much."

Her snort altered to a moan when he swung again, stinging the lower curve of her buttocks. She saw his cock leap against the fabric of his pants. He hissed and grabbed at it through the material.

"I thought I was being punished for distracting you while you worked," she said, watching wide-eyed as he stroked his cock while he swung the paddle again. "Ouch," she said in a beleaguered tone a second later when he paddled her in the same smarting area—the lower curve of her buttocks. He really did like spanking her there. Despite the quick sting, her clit pinched tight in arousal.

"Sorry," he muttered, now landing the paddle higher up on her cheeks. "You *are* being paddled for distracting me. I'm just saying . . . such a gorgeous ass is destined to be punished often," he said, a small smile pulling at his mouth. She suppressed a moan when he landed another blow. She could see that her ass was starting to blush pink in the mirror to her right.

She couldn't suppress a moan of pure arousal when he unzipped his trousers and shoved them and his briefs beneath his balls and his erection.

"Ian," she groaned upon seeing his exposed cock.

"You see what I mean?" he asked, paddling her again and making air pop out of her lungs. He stroked his cock and smacked her again. She couldn't keep her gaze off his hand moving up and down on the delineated shaft of his rigid penis. "I hadn't planned to fuck you, just punish you. But your sweet ass has made me change my mind."

"*Ooh,*" erupted out of her throat when he paddled her ass again. Her bottom was starting to burn. She gritted her teeth when she saw him swing his arm back.

"How many more?" she asked, whimpering when he smacked her again.

"I don't know. You've distracted me again," he said grimly, landing another blow. She saw him stroke his now fully erect cock faster, wincing as he did so. He paddled her on the lower curve of her bottom again, making the flesh bounce upward with the stringent blow. He cursed hotly and tossed the paddle onto the couch, surprising her.

"My punishment is done?" she asked, put off by the abruptness of his action.

"No," he said, walking rapidly over to the cabinet and extracting a condom. "But my cock is just about," he said tensely. She watched in breathless anticipation as he removed his clothing hastily and came toward her, rolling the condom on his enormous erection as he did so.

"Stand up," he said, walking up behind her.

Her clit simmered between her thighs as she did his bidding. Her bottom burned. She resisted an urge to rub it to soothe the sting.

"Hold on to the bar and bend over," he said, his touch on her hip gentle. She followed his order. Almost as soon as she'd firmed her upper body by holding on to the bar, he parted her buttocks and drove his cock into her.

"So wet. So willing," he grated out, staring down at her ass.

"*Ahhhhh,*" she moaned, her eyes springing wide at his sudden, total possession.

"I told you," he muttered darkly, firming his hold on her hips and starting to pump in and out of her pussy. "You do this to me, Francesca. You have to accept the consequences. I will take you for my pleasure alone."

She felt like he rattled her entire universe for the next several minutes as he fucked her. She watched him in the mirror, her mouth sagging open, as he crashed into her again and again, every muscle in his beautiful body rigid, his cock a well-lubricated piston driving into her drenched pussy at a relentless pace.

He wasn't concerned for her pleasure, but watching him take his own, the delicious pressure his cock built in her, the clit cream . . . it was all too much. She broke in climax, shuddering around him, moaning uncontrollably. He cursed and slapped her bottom before he firmed his grip on her, holding her ass against him as he roared in orgasm.

They remained joined like that for what felt like minutes, although she suspected later she was wrong about that. Ian was typically so careful of spilling from the condom after sex. He certainly *did* stroke her back, hips, and ass tenderly for what seemed like a delicious eternity, though. Their breathing slowed.

Finally he withdrew, a harsh groan ripping at his throat as he did so. He helped her to stand, turning her in his arms.

His mouth closed over hers. Francesca shut her eyelids, giving herself as fully to his kiss as she had his lovemaking.

"Do you know what I want to do with you now?" he asked gruffly against her lips a moment later.

She licked his taste off her lips and looked up at him with a heavy-lidded gaze.

"What?" she asked throatily.

Something flashed in his blue eyes and she wondered if the flame in him hadn't been completely extinguished. He shook his head once, as if to clear it, and grabbed her hand. They left the inner chamber, and he locked it behind him.

"Get dressed and wait for me," he said. She watched, her expression one of mixed puzzlement at his behavior and admiration for the sight of his god-awful-sexy, taut bare ass—a sight she hadn't been treated to as much as she would have liked. When he stepped out of the room a moment later, she was fully dressed. She stared at him in pleasant surprise.

He was wearing a pair of extremely well-fitted jeans that

rode low on his lean hips, one of the tight white T-shirts he wore beneath his fencing gear, a leather jacket slung in the crook of his arm. Her breath caught at the sight of his lean, muscular body displayed to such stunning effect. She'd never grow tired of looking at him.

"What are you doing?" she asked incredulously.

"I changed my mind."

"About what?"

"About going into work. Let's go riding. I want to see you in action."

Her mouth dropped open, a bark of laughter popping out of her throat. She couldn't believe it. He was going to do something so spur of the moment . . . so spontaneous? *Ian?*

She put on her sleek jacket, excitement mounting in her, and went to pick up her new helmet and gloves.

"You're in for quite a ride," she told him before striding to the door.

"You think you're telling me something I don't know?" she heard him say wryly from behind her, causing her grin to widen.

*How was it possible for this day to have started out so dull and dreary and end up so ecstatic?* she wondered as she stood across the elevator from Ian a moment later. He looked drop-dead sexy in his jeans and jacket, his helmet cradled in the crook of his arm. He noticed her stare and smiled, slow, delicious . . . a little devilish. The elevator door dinged open in the garage basement, breaking her mesmerized stare on his gorgeous mouth.

She headed into the parking garage, familiar with it from her lessons with Jacob. A whole area of the garage was cordoned off for Ian's vehicles. Jacob kept an office of sorts down there, along with all the tools and electronics he used for mechanical maintenance and keeping the vehicles clean.

She paused a moment later when Ian straddled his black motorbike with confident ease.

"Well? Climb on," he said softly, noticing her staring at the motorcycle next to his. It was slightly smaller than Ian's bike, but fierce-looking in its own right, featuring glittering chrome and a shiny black cowling with red racing stripes.

"Where did that come from?" she asked, dazed.

He shrugged, planting his booted feet on the ground and tilting up the bike between powerful thighs. How could he look as natural on a badass bike as he did wearing an impeccable suit ensconced in the lap of luxury? The sight of his hands covered by tight black leather made her inexplicably shiver.

"It's yours," he said, referring to the bike.

"No! I mean . . ." She paused, regretting her outburst. She looked at him, silently pleading. The afternoon had gone *so* well. The paintings. Ian's agreement to try and not control her outside the bedroom, his gift of the jacket and helmet, and her returned, heartfelt one of pleasure, his forceful possession . . . her loving it. She didn't want to ruin it by arguing, but a *motorcycle*. It was too much, wasn't it? Especially after the paintings and her new biking gear.

Before she could word her protest, however, Ian superseded her.

"Okay, it's *mine*. I have several bikes. I'm loaning this one to you for the time being," he said, giving her a dry glance. "Can you accept that, Francesca?"

She grinned and stepped over to the bike, excitement

frothing in her chest as she straddled the leather seat and gloated over the sweetness of Ian's sleek machine.

*Oh yes.* This she could accept.

Jacob had told him that Francesca was a natural on a motorcycle when he'd consulted with him on the type of bike to buy her. He was glad to see just how correct Jacob had been. Watching her race down city streets, take tight turns, and zoom through country landscapes was a true pleasure. When he realized that the feeling he had watching was pride, he mentally laughed at himself. Why should it matter that he'd introduced her to something she loved? The important thing was that she'd *found* it . . . that she'd delved into another layer of what was undoubtedly a deep, rich vein of her many talents and glories.

He glanced sideways and saw Francesca at his side as they reentered the city on Lake Shore Drive that evening. She gave him a thumbs-up and he could just picture her grin behind the black visor of her helmet. Something about a motorcycle highlighted her natural physical strength, her fresh, vital energy . . .

. . . a jean-encased ass that made him want to drag her back to the penthouse every time he looked at it, which was pretty much constantly.

He signaled and called for her to pull over at a parking garage near Millennium Park. A few minutes later, they strolled out of the garage onto Monroe Street, between the Art Institute and Millennium Park. The clouds had scattered, and it was turning into a pleasant, crisp fall night.

"Where are we going?" she asked him, grinning from ear

to ear, a tendril of rose-gold hair brushing her cheek. He pushed it off her face and took her hand.

"I thought I'd take you to dinner."

"Excellent." Her enthusiasm made her sound adorably breathless. He yanked his gaze off the windswept, glowing vision of her with effort.

"You're a fantastic rider," she said. "You look so natural on a bike. How old were you when you first rode?"

"Eleven, I think," Ian said, his eyelids narrowing as he tried to recall.

"So young!"

He nodded. "When I first came to England from France, I had a tough time making the transition—a whole new world. A whole new way of life. My mother gone," he said, his lips pressed into a grim line. "It was hard to acclimate. I have a cousin who is older, so I always called him uncle. Uncle Gerard figured out one day that I loved engines. When I discovered an old broken-down motorcycle in the garage at his estate, which was nearby my grandfather's home, I begged him to let me rebuild it. My fascination with motorcycles began. My grandfather joined in, and I began to bond with both Uncle Gerard and him."

"And you started to come out of your shell?" Francesca asked, studying him as they walked along.

"Yes. A bit."

Some strains of music resounded in the crisp, clear air when they reached Michigan Avenue. Ian noticed a crowd on the sidewalk.

"*Oh*, Naked Thieves are playing in Millennium Park tonight. Caden and Justin are in that crowd somewhere," Francesca said.

"Naked Thieves?"

She did a double take. "The rock band? Naked Thieves?"

He shrugged, feeling a little foolish, although he knew he didn't show it. From the expression on her youthful face, he definitely was supposed to know who Naked Thieves were. His gaze fixed on her curving pink lips, and he forgot his fleeting embarrassment.

"How can you not know who Naked Thieves are? You're an icon among young people, but it's like . . ." She shook her head. Her laugh seemed both sad and incredulous. "It's like you came out of the womb in a suit, briefcase in hand."

That stung a little. He, of all people, would have loved a childhood—a true youth—summer afternoons that stretched on forever without a care in the world, teenage rebellion against helicopter parents whom he supposedly couldn't stand, and in reality, loved like crazy and knew would always be there for him . . . escaping to a rock concert in the park with a gorgeous girl like Francesca.

"What are you doing?" Francesca asked when he pulled his cell phone from his jacket pocket.

"Calling Lin. Since you want to go to the concert, she'll be able to procure us last-minute tickets for the seated section."

"Ian, the seated section has been sold out forever. Trust me, Caden and I tried to get tickets."

"We'll get some," he said, locating Lin's number.

He paused and looked up when Francesca put her hand on his forearm. The setting sun and the reflection from her hair gave her cheeks and lips an extra-rosy hue. Her dark eyes shone with just the hint of a challenge.

"Let's just go sit on the lawn."

"The lawn," he repeated dryly.

"Yeah, you can't see much, but you can hear pretty well. And anybody can go," she said, grabbing his hand and urging him toward the park.

"That's the problem, isn't it?"

"Oh stop being so *British.*"

A sharp retort flew to his throat—a knee-jerk reaction. He really wasn't used to having people speak to him in the way that Francesca did without a blink of an eye. He saw the excited sparkle in those nymph eyes of hers, however, and exhaled his protest. He could get used to being teased and subtly reprimanded—very easily—*if* it was her doing it.

"I really do spoil you," he said as they walked toward the writhing mass of youth ahead of them. "I wouldn't do this for anyone else. I want you to know that."

He came to an abrupt halt when she spun around, went up on her toes, and kissed him on the mouth. He caught her scent and taste, and his surprise faded. Her soft moan when he deepened the kiss was as delicious as the rest of her. Her face struck him as sublime as she looked up at him with a heavy-lidded gaze a moment later.

"That's the sweetest thing you've ever said to me," she breathed.

*Maybe because you're the sweetest thing that's ever happened to me.*

The flash of regret he experienced as they entered the packed park a minute later surprised him.

He should have said the words out loud.

He wasn't at all sure that he *could* have been so unguarded and honest, however, and that truth bothered him more than it ever had in his life.

"Best. Day. Ever," she emphasized, brimming over in enthusiasm as they entered Ian's bedroom suite later. "First my paintings—thank you again for that, Ian. I'm still stunned. Then that motorcycle ride—what an awesome bike-and then Naked Thieves in the park!"

"We could hardly hear anything at the concert. It sounded like someone screaming bloody murder to static," Ian murmured amusedly as he held up his hands in an expectant gesture. She turned so he could remove her jacket. Despite his dry comment, she'd noticed his small smile and knew he wasn't as unimpressed by the experience as he let on.

"That's just because you don't know the songs," she said, refusing to be anything but happy

"Is that what they call that noise?" he asked mildly as he laid her jacket on the back of a chair and Francesca turned to face him.

"You seemed to have a nice enough time."

He caught her challenging expression and shook his head. She laughed. She referred to the fact that they'd spent a majority of the concert making out, both of them getting so steamy and aroused that Ian had abruptly declared it was time to leave unless they wanted to get arrested for public indecency.

He'd surprised her when they'd first entered the park and found a rare open patch of earth. "Hold on for a few seconds," he'd said. "Don't sit yet."

She'd watched, curious and amazed, as he'd approached a particularly well-stocked group of picnicking young people who were sitting twenty or so feet away. He spoke to them and pointed to a few items. Money had changed hands. A moment later, Ian had walked away, leaving the people looking bemused and very pleased. He obviously hadn't given them a small amount of money for his prize—two blankets, a couple bottles of chilled water, and a napkin-covered paper plate that she'd discovered later contained four pieces of delectable fried chicken.

"I'm thinking you *liked* your first rock concert ever," she teased, recalling a truth he'd told her as they lay cozily beneath one of the blankets, the wild crowd just feet away seemingly miles from their insulated, private world.

"I liked touching you," he replied simply, making her cheeks heat in pleasure. His gaze dropped over her. "Why don't you go and get ready for bed?"

She shivered at the sound of his low voice and the heated gleam in his stare. She headed toward the bathroom.

"And Francesca?"

She turned to face him. Her brows pulled together in puzzlement when he didn't speak for several seconds.

"It was for me, too," he finally said.

Her bewilderment deepened.

"The best day ever."

She stood there watching as he disappeared into his dressing room, her heart throbbing in disbelief and something much more profound at his unexpected honesty. From the dark, fear-shrouded recesses of her brain, a memory rose to taunt her. She hated the dread that tainted the wondrous feeling she'd experienced at Ian's words.

*I offer you pleasure and the experience. Nothing else. I have nothing else to offer.*

How long could something so amazing endure given that

she shared the experience with a man who so reluctantly shared himself . . .

. . . given that she'd risked her heart to an enigma like Ian Noble?

The next several weeks passed in a blur, everything cast in the glow of Francesca's deepening feelings for Ian. She grew used to his moods, understanding that often when he appeared distant, he was in fact processing massive amounts of information, planning for his various companies on multiple levels, making decisions in a startlingly concise and rapid manner. He continued her lessons in the bedroom, Francesca flourishing under his tutelage. Ian was as demanding and intense as ever—perhaps even more so—but as she gained comfort with sexual submission and her trust in him grew, their exchanges altered, somehow becoming sweeter, a true give-and-take of power, caring, and pleasure. She suspected that the deepening level of intimacy in their exchange was responsible for the richer experience, and wondered if Ian felt it too.

He taught her lessons outside the bedroom as well, coaching her on fencing, which she took to with pleasure. They spent several Sundays poring over the basics of investing, Ian challenging her to come up with a feasible plan for her money given what she'd learned from her lessons. She'd showed him two options on two separate occasions. Ian's polite queries and slight frowns had made her go back to the drawing board both times. On her last investment-planning presentation, she'd earned a small, proud smile and knew she'd finally learned something valuable about how to handle her own finances. Thus, Ian taught her not only about passion and love but some basic lessons of life.

He wasn't the only one who taught, either. With Francesca's encouragement, he continued to be spontaneous once in a while, to live in the moment . . . to experience life like a thirty-year-old instead of a jaded, weary man several decades his senior.

The problem was, he never really came out and told her in so many words how he was feeling about her—about them—and she was too shy and afraid to tell him she'd fallen in love with him. Wasn't that precisely the opposite of what he'd said their relationship would be about? Would he think her a naïve fool for mistaking lust and infatuation for something much deeper?

The thought haunted her. She pushed it back repeatedly when she spent time with him, not wanting to ruin the moments she had, worried she'd waste them by ruminating about anxieties that weren't for now, but the future. It was a little like doing a high-wire act, always striving to keep her balance on the narrow edge of their passionate affair, constantly worried she'd find herself falling away from Ian . . . or him flying away from her.

One cool late fall evening, that jarring moment came.

Francesca worked in the studio at the penthouse, anguishing over the last final detail of the painting. She pulled her hand back from the canvas, her breath sticking in her lungs as she studied the tiny black figure—a man in an opened black trench coat, walking along the river, head lowered against the cold Lake Michigan wind.

Would Ian notice she'd inserted him again into one of her paintings? It made sense to her somehow, she thought as she wiped off her brush. He'd twined himself indelibly into almost every thread of her life.

Her heart swelled as she studied the painting.

*Finished.*

By tradition, once the word hit her brain with a note of finality, she would never put paint to that particular canvas again. Feeling ebullient with her accomplishment, she hurried out of the studio in search of Ian. It was a Sunday, and he'd opted to work in the library rather than go into the office.

She was about to round the corner of the hallway that would lead to the library when she heard a door open and low, tense voices—a man and a woman talking.

". . . all the more reason for me to act quickly, Julia," Ian said.

"I want to emphasize again that there are no guarantees, Ian. Just because it's a particularly good period doesn't mean lasting results, but we at the Institute are hopeful . . ."

The woman's British-accented voice faded as she and Ian proceeded down the hallway toward the elevator, but not before Francesca caught a glimpse of her. It was the attractive woman Ian had breakfasted with in Paris, the one he'd called a friend of the family. Her heart sank as she once again registered the thick tension in the exchange, similar to what she'd felt in the hotel lobby. Like that other time, she retreated, scurrying back to her studio.

She didn't know how she knew, but she just *knew* Ian wouldn't want her observing him right now . . . asking him questions . . . trying to care for him.

Even though she wanted to do just that more than anything else in the world.

She spent more time than was necessary cleaning up her work space in the studio, trying to give him time to recover. Eventually, she again went in search for him, but came up empty-handed.

She found Mrs. Hanson in the kitchen scrubbing the kitchen counters.

"I was looking for Ian," she said. "I've finished the painting."

"Oh, that's wonderful news!" Mrs. Hanson's excited expression fell. "But I'm afraid Ian's not here. He had to leave Chicago for a while. An emergency came up."

Francesca felt as if an invisible force had pummeled her in the chest. "But . . . I don't understand. He was just here. I saw him with that woman . . ."

"Dr. Epstein? You saw her arrive?" Mrs. Hanson asked, looking surprised.

*Dr. Julia Epstein. So. That was her name.* "I saw her leave. What was the emergency? Is Ian all right?"

"Oh dear yes. Don't alarm yourself over that."

"Where did he go?" she demanded, her hurt and incredulity over the fact that Ian had left and hadn't even bothered to come into the studio and tell her goodbye was still vibrating unpleasantly in her flesh.

Mrs. Hanson avoided her gaze and resumed her scrubbing. "I can't say for certain—"

"Do you truly not know, or are you saying that because Ian told you to?"

The housekeeper glanced at her, startled. Francesca fiercely held her gaze. "I truly don't know, Francesca. I'm sorry. There's a tiny part of Ian's life that he's always kept to himself, even from me, who knows his every habit and idiosyncrasy."

Francesca patted the older woman's arm. "I understand," she said.

And she did. If Mrs. Hanson didn't know where Ian had gone, it could only mean one thing.

He'd gone to London—the location of that secret corner of his universe, the place that Jacob had never been invited, nor Mrs. Hanson . . . and certainly not Francesca. That Dr. Epstein, though . . . *she* almost certainly knew about that part of Ian's life. She kept hearing Ian's tense tone ringing in her head, saw his lost expression as he stood in the lobby of the hotel.

The woman was a *doctor?* What if Ian wasn't well? No, it couldn't be that. He was the ideal specimen of male health and vibrancy. If she couldn't tell that just by looking at him, he'd presented her with proof when he'd handed her the results of his latest physical a while back in order to prove to her he was clean for sex.

"Do you know Dr. Epstein well?" Francesca mused.

"No. I've only met her briefly a time or two when she's visited here at the penthouse. I got the impression she practices somewhere in London, but I'm not certain what sort of a doctor she is, come to think of it. Francesca? Is everything all right?" Mrs. Hanson asked anxiously, making her wonder what the housekeeper had seen on her face.

"Yes, I'm fine," she squeezed Mrs. Hanson's forearm in reassurance and let go, starting to back out of the kitchen. *Just how much would a ticket from Chicago to London cost?* "But I think I might have to leave town for a few days as well."

# Part Eight

## Because I Am Yours

# Fifteen

Davie offered to come with her to London, but Francesca flatly refused. When she'd told Davie about her plans, she'd been purposefully vague and misleading, saying that she'd learned from Mrs. Hanson that Ian was having a family crisis in London and she'd decided to go there to offer support.

In truth, she didn't want Davie to realize she'd undertaken such a foolish plan without having a clue as to what she was going to do when she alighted from the plane at Heathrow. The only thing she knew is that whatever Ian was doing in London, it caused him anguish, and that he'd chosen to protect others in his life from that pain.

He would be furious at her, if, by some miracle, she ever actually located him. Yet she couldn't stand the idea of him suffering alone in any way, and she had become utterly convinced that these "emergency" visits to London related to the spiritual demons that plagued him.

Besides, if what was in London was destined to destroy

whatever they might have together in the future, wasn't it best just to find out now instead of delaying the inevitable?

Ian had called her during the flight from O'Hare to Heathrow, she noticed as she deplaned. This had been what she'd hoped for, considering she really had no plan of action once she arrived in London. However, when she tried to return his call, she got his voice mail.

Discouraged, she lingered in the airport, exchanging currency, picking up her luggage, hoping for some kind of miracle revelation as to the location of Ian's apartment or his whereabouts. When nothing came to her, and she still hadn't successfully made contact with Ian, she got into a taxi and told the driver the only place she'd ever connected to Ian and his London trips.

"The Genomics Research and Treatment Institute," she told the driver, referring to the hospital and research facility for schizophrenia that she'd read about on Ian's tablet. She recalled how Dr. Epstein had mentioned "the Institute." Could she be referring to the Genomics Research and Treatment Institute? What other clues did she have to his possible location?

Forty minutes later, the cabdriver pulled up to the ultramodern glass-enclosed entrance to the facility, which was housed on beautifully landscaped grounds within a wooded park. In the far distance, she glimpsed several pairs of people walking in a lush green meadow, one of the pair always wearing white. Were they nurses or attendants with patients?

Uncertainty hit her like a blow now that she sat there in the back of the cab. What in the world was she doing? What madness had made her jump on a plane and come to a hospital in a remote part of London, where she knew no one and had no reason to be present?

The driver was giving her a questioning look.

"Would you mind waiting for me?" she asked him nervously as she handed him payment.

"I can wait ten minutes, tops," he said brusquely.

"Thank you," she said. If this trip ended up being a dead end, she'd know soon enough.

She blinked when she entered the lobby a moment later. It wasn't precisely like the Noble Enterprises lobby in Chicago, but there were similarities—the elegant, warm woods, pink-beige marble, and neutral-toned furnishings.

"May I help you?" a young woman sitting behind a circular desk asked her when she approached.

For a few seconds, Francesca just stood there speechless. Then something hit her brain, and she said the thought before she'd fully processed it.

"Yes. I'd like to see Dr. Epstein, please."

Her heart seized in her chest for a split second that stretched surreally long as she stared at the woman's blank expression.

"Certainly. Who shall I tell Dr. Epstein is visiting?"

She exhaled in a burst of relief and immediately experienced a subsequent wave of anxiety. "Francesca Arno. I'm a friend of Ian Noble's."

The woman's eyes widened at that.

"Right away Ms. Arno," she said, picking up the phone.

She waited on pins and needles as the receptionist spoke to several people, the last Dr. Epstein herself. What could the doctor be thinking, being told that a complete stranger who said she was a friend of Ian Noble had shown up at the

Institute asking for her? Unfortunately, Francesca couldn't glean much from the one-sided conversation she overheard. The receptionist set down the phone.

"Dr. Epstein says she'll come to the lobby to get you herself. May I offer you any refreshment while you wait?"

"No, thank you," Francesca said. She didn't think anything would stay in her stomach, it was frothing so much. She pointed at a comfortable seating area just behind her. "I'll just sit and wait."

The receptionist nodded once cordially and returned to her paperwork. It was five minutes before Dr. Epstein appeared in the lobby—five long, tortuous minutes. Francesca shot up from her chair like she was on springs when she recognized the doctor, now wearing a white lab coat over a sophisticated dark green dress. An elegant woman walked next to her, her clothing casual but obviously of the highest quality and taste. Francesca got a fleeting impression that although Dr. Epstein's companion was older—in her seventies, perhaps—she was brimming with vibrant health.

"Francesca Arno?" Dr. Epstein queried as she approached. She extended her hand, and Francesca took it.

"Yes, I'm sorry to pounce on you unexpectedly like this, but—"

"Any friend of Ian's is welcome." The doctor's tone was warm, but was that curiosity or puzzlement she saw shadow her features as she studied Francesca? "I understand you haven't yet met Ian's grandmother? Francesca Arno, the Countess Stratham, Anne Noble."

Francesca glanced in shock at the attractive elderly woman. For a horrified moment, she wondered if she was supposed to bow or something to a countess? Surely there was some etiquette that she didn't know, and her gauche Americanness would be showcased right from the start?

Thank goodness the countess noticed her discomfort before she began to stutter like a fool.

"Please, call me Anne," Ian's grandmother said warmly, extending her hand. Francesca looked into eyes that immediately called Ian to mind—cobalt blue, sharp, and incisive.

"I guess I did come to the right place," Francesca muttered as she shook Anne's soft hand.

"You weren't sure?" Anne asked.

"No, not entirely. I was . . . looking for Ian."

"Of course you were," Anne said matter-of-factly, ratcheting up Francesca's anxiety and confusion. "He mentioned your name to me, although I didn't realize you'd be coming to London. Ian is out for a walk on the grounds at present, so I came to greet you in his stead."

"So Ian *is* here?" Francesca asked, her voice ringing with shock.

Anne and Dr. Epstein exchanged a glance.

"You didn't *know* he was?" Anne asked.

Francesca experienced a sinking sensation as she shook her head to the negative.

"But you must have known about my daughter being here, at the very least?"

"Your . . . daughter?" Francesca asked, her head spinning. The glass-enclosed entrance suddenly seemed too bright, casting a surreal brilliance onto everything. Hadn't Mrs. Hanson said that Ian's grandparents had only one child?

"Yes, my daughter, Helen. Ian's mother. Ian is taking a walk with her right now. Thanks to Julia's and the Institute's hard work," Anne gave a warm sideways glance to the doctor, "Helen is having an amazingly lucid period. James, Ian, and I couldn't be more thrilled."

"We must take things one day at a time . . . one hour," Dr. Epstein cautioned.

Both women glanced at Francesca. Anne reached out and touched her elbow. "You're very pale, dear. I think it would be best if we let this young lady sit down somewhere comfortable, don't you Dr. Epstein?"

"Absolutely. We'll take her to my office. I have some orange juice there; perhaps you're blood sugar is a bit low? Should I send for food?"

"No . . . no, I'm all right. Ian's mother is still *alive?*" Francesca croaked, her brain fixated on that single piece of news.

A shadow passed across Anne's face. "Yes. Today she is."

"But Mrs. Hanson . . . she told me Ian's mother had died years ago."

Anne sighed. "Yes, that is what Eleanor believes." It took Francesca a few seconds due to her bewilderment to realize Eleanor was Mrs. Hanson's given name. "James and I made the decision once Helen was returned home to England that it would be perhaps . . . best? Easiest?" Anne mused, her expression heartbreakingly sad as she tried to find the right words for a decision made decades ago, during a time of stress and anxiety. "For those who had known and loved Helen before she became ill to remember her like she was rather than to see how this cursed disease had ravaged her, taking away her identity . . . her very soul. Perhaps it was wrong of us to do. Perhaps it wasn't. Ian certainly didn't agree with our decision."

"Well . . . he was only ten years old when Helen was returned to England, isn't that right?" Francesca asked.

"Nearly," Anne replied. "But we didn't tell Ian his mother was alive and being cared for in an institution in East Sussex until he was twenty—old enough to comprehend why we'd made the decision in order to protect him. Ian, like almost everyone else, thought his mother had died."

The silence rang in Francesca's ears.

"Ian must have been furious when he found out," she said before she could edit herself.

"Oh, he was," Anne said dryly, not taken aback in the slightest by Francesca's bluntness. "It was not a good time for Ian, James, and me. Ian barely spoke to us for almost a year while he was in school in the states. But we did eventually come to terms, and our relationship was mended." She waved her hand in a vague sense around the elegant entryway. "And then Ian had this facility built, and the three of us worked together to develop it, finding some common ground. The Institute has been a place of healing for our relationship with our grandson as well as for Helen," she said, giving Dr. Epstein a grateful smile, even though her eyes remained sad.

Anne seemed to rally and tightened her hold on Francesca's elbow, urging her to walk alongside her. "I can see that you're shocked by this news. I think it'd be best if Ian was the one to talk with you further about the matter, given the . . . unusual circumstances."

"Ian and Helen will arrive at the morning room following their walk," Dr. Epstein mentioned to Anne.

"We'll go there, then," Anne told Francesca, suddenly brisk and purposeful, as they walked to a bank of elevators.

"James is already there. I'll be able to introduce you to Ian's grandfather."

Too stunned to argue, Francesca followed along, her brain seemingly vibrating with the news that Helen Noble was still alive and apparently being treated at this facility, her heart squeezing in anguish for Ian.

They took the elevator to a lower level. When the door opened, Dr. Epstein bid them goodbye, saying she must return to her lab.

"She's a brilliant scientist," Anne told Francesca confidentially as they made their way down a hallway that ended in a light-filled, many-windowed room. A few patients shuffled past them, casting curious glances at Francesca. "Now that the human genome has been decoded, Dr. Epstein and her colleagues have been using the information to come up with better medications for schizophrenia. Ian funds all of her work. It's truly been groundbreaking. A medication that Dr. Epstein developed has been recently approved by the European Medicines Agency, and she recommended Helen be put on it. There have been some ups and downs with the treatment so far, but just this week, there have been some dramatic improvements. Ian is so happy. Helen often didn't recognize Ian, her father, and me, her psychosis was so severe, but *now* . . . what a difference. She's even been allowed a pass to go out onto the grounds, something that hasn't been possible ever since she first arrived here six years ago."

"That's wonderful," Francesca said, glancing around as they entered what Dr. Epstein had called the morning room. Many large windows overlooked a lovely wooded area and meadow. Patients, attendants, and perhaps family members were scattered across the comfortable room, some playing board games, others talking and enjoying the view. Francesca supposed the patients here were some of the luckier ones whose symptoms were more controlled. They appeared to be very high functioning and moved in and out of the room of their own volition, without attendants escorting them.

A robust-looking older man stood when they approached him. His tall, fit form reminded her of Ian.

"Francesca Arno, I'd like you to meet my husband, James," Anne said.

"A pleasure to meet you," James said, taking her hand. "Ian mentioned your name to us yesterday—something we took note of, as it's a rarity for him to mention a woman, much to Anne's and my disappointment," James said, a twinkle in his brown eyes. "We were with Dr. Epstein when she got the call that you were here. We didn't realize you would be coming to England."

"That's because I came on the spur of the moment."

"Ian doesn't know you're here?" James asked, looking politely confused.

"No," Francesca said. Perhaps James noticed her anxiety over that fact, because he patted her shoulder kindly, his gaze transferring to the windows overlooking the meadow. "Well, he'll know soon enough. I see Helen and him approaching. *Dear God*—"

James's fingers tightened momentarily on her shoulder. Francesca had glanced out the window when he'd spoken, following James's gaze. She started as well at what she saw. Ian was walking next to a fragile-looking woman wearing a blue dress that hung loosely on her painfully thin figure. As James had been speaking, the woman had abruptly swung around, her fist striking Ian in the abdomen. She'd stumbled and started to fall, but Ian had caught her against him. His attempts to stabilize his mother were interrupted, however, by Helen's struggling as if she suddenly feared for her own life at Ian's hands.

"Call Dr. Epstein," James said sharply to one of the attendants who had also noticed what was happening out the window. James and three other attendants started for the door that led to the meadow in order to assist Ian.

"Oh no. Not again," Anne said in a strangled voice as she and Francesca watched, horrified. Helen flailed wildly as Ian tried to subdue her. Her opened hand struck him on the jaw. Francesca's heart seemed to spasm in her chest when she saw the stark, distilled anguish on his handsome face as he received the blow. How many times had Ian seen his mother behave in this way? How many times had this loving, kind woman disappeared only to be replaced by this violent, frightening stranger? A piercing wail could now be heard in the morning room—the sound of Helen Noble's fear and her returned madness.

"Wait," Anne said in a thick voice, grabbing Francesca's elbow, halting her when she started toward Ian, unable to stand still while he was at his most vulnerable. "They have her now."

She and Anne stood side by side, watching miserably as the three attendants expertly lifted and restrained the struggling psychotic woman and began to carry her writhing form toward the facility. When they passed Francesca and Anne in the morning room, moving rapidly toward the hallway, she caught her first glimpse of Helen's face—her teeth bared in a grimace, spittle running down her chin, her blue eyes huge and glazed, seeming to focus on some terrifying nightmare that only she could see.

*No*, Francesca thought. That wasn't Helen Noble. Not really.

A nurse ran down the hallway toward the attendants, Dr. Epstein trailing behind her at a rapid pace. The attendants carefully laid the shrieking woman on the floor, and the nurse gave her an injection.

Anne began to cry silently as she watched them carry her daughter away. Francesca put her arm around the older woman's shoulder, at a loss for what to say, still in a state of shock herself.

"Ian," she exclaimed when she glanced around and saw him and his grandfather walking in their direction. She'd never seen him so pale. His facial muscles were rigid.

His glance at her was glacial.

"How dare you come here," he said as he approached her, his lips barely moving, his mouth and jaw were drawn so tight. Her heart seemed to stop in her chest. She'd never seen him this way . . . so anguished, so furious . . . so exposed. She couldn't think of what to say. He'd *never* forgive her for coming here uninvited, for seeing him at what was perhaps one of the most vulnerable moments of his life.

"*Ian—*"

But he cut her off by merely walking past her in the direction where they'd taken his mother. James gave his wife a sad glance and followed his grandson.

Anne took her hand and led her to a chair. She sat down next to her, all the vibrancy Francesca had noticed upon first meeting her seeming to have drained away.

"Don't blame Ian," Anne said hollowly. "Helen and he had been sharing a wonderful morning and now . . . all ripped away again. He's upset, obviously."

"I can understand why," Francesca replied. "I shouldn't have come. I had no idea—"

Anne patted her forearm distractedly. "It's a ravaging disease. Brutal. It's been hard on all of us, but the hardest by far for Ian. From an early age, he had no choice but to be Helen's sole caretaker. He told me after he'd lived with us for a while and started to open up, that he had to constantly monitor her, for fear her madness would be exposed to the townspeople in too flagrant of a fashion, and they'd take her away to the hospital and send him to an orphanage. He lived in daily, hourly fear of her harming herself or of being separated from her. He barely attended school like the other children, because he needed to look out for Helen. The town where Helen ended up—we, to this day, don't know how or why she ended up there—was very remote and a bit backward. I have little doubt some kind of child protection agency would have been contacted about Ian's poor school attendance if it'd been more centrally located. As it was, he managed to keep Helen's illness a good secret, learning where she kept her reserve of money and managing it frugally, taking up odd jobs around the village, running errands, and once it was learned that he had a genius for fixing electronic things, repairing small appliances. He did all their shopping and housekeeping, cooking for them, making their little cottage as neat as he was able and securing it with various safety measures, given Helen's odd behaviors and occasional violence during her psychotic episodes . . . such as the one you just witnessed," Anne mused wearily.

She gave a heavy sigh. "All that, and when we finally discovered Helen and him, Ian hadn't yet passed his tenth birthday."

Francesca shuddered with silent emotion. No wonder he was so controlling. *Oh God, that poor little boy.* How lonely he must have been. How brutal for him to experience moments of love and connection during his mother's lucid periods, only to have them vanish from him when psychosis hit . . . just as it had today. Suddenly, she recalled that expression he wore once in a while that tore at her so deeply and bewildered her so much, the look of someone who not only had been abandoned and lost but who knew with certainty he would eventually be rejected again.

"I'm so sorry, Anne," Francesca said, feeling the inadequacy—the shabby *thinness*—of her words.

"Dr. Epstein warned us not to be overly optimistic. But it's so hard not to hope, and Helen was making such progress. We *saw* her, ever so briefly, talked to her—*her*, our Helen. Dear, sweet Helen." She sighed heavily. "Well. There are other treatments that are still in the works. Perhaps . . . some day . . ."

Francesca couldn't help but feel, however, given the barren quality of Anne's tone and the slight grayish cast to her skin, that she was very close to giving up hope of ever seeing her daughter happy and well. She wondered how many times the Nobles had seen some improvement in Helen, only to have their hopes dashed again and again as madness reared its head.

Francesca stood up shakily several minutes later when Ian reentered the morning room. "She's asleep," Ian told his grandmother, his gaze ominously avoiding Francesca. "Julia has pulled the medication. Mom will go back on the regime she took before. At least it kept her stable."

"If stable means sedated, I suppose you're right," Anne said.

Ian's mouth twisted slightly at that. "We have no other choice. At least she wasn't harming herself." He looked at Francesca. She cringed inwardly when she saw the ice glittering in his eyes. "We're leaving," he said. "I've called my pilot, and he's getting the plane ready for departure to Chicago."

"All right," Francesca said. She'd be able to try and explain why she'd come once they were aboard the plane. She'd apologize for horning in where she wasn't wanted. Maybe she could make him understand . . .

. . . although every time she thought of how vulnerable he'd been . . . how raw, she quailed, dreading he could never forgive her.

He hardly spoke to her in the car ride to the airport, just stared straight ahead as he drove, his knuckles white as he gripped the leather-bound wheel. When she tried to break the silence with an apology, he cut her off briskly.

"How did you know where I was?"

"I've seen you several times with Dr. Epstein . . . once in Paris and another time at the penthouse. I heard her mention 'the Institute,' and Mrs. Hanson told me that she was a doctor."

He flashed a glance in her direction. "That's not an explanation, Francesca."

She shrank in the passenger seat. "I . . . I noticed that

you'd visited the Genomics Research and Treatment Institute Web site several times while I was borrowing your tablet to study for the driver's test." Guilt made her wilt further when she noticed his outraged glance.

"You checked my history?"

"Yes," she admitted miserably. "I'm sorry. I was curious . . . especially about where you'd run off to so abruptly. Then Jacob told me you never took him to London, and I started connecting the dots."

"Well, I could never accuse you of being stupid," he grated out, his hands tightening on the wheel. "You must be so proud of your detective skills."

"I'm not. I'm miserable. I'm so sorry, Ian."

He said nothing, but his mouth was strained and his skin looked especially pale next to the contrast of his dark hair. His silence effectively stopped her from any more communications until they boarded the plane.

The pilot's voice came through the intercom, saying they had clearance to take off.

"Sit down and buckle up for takeoff," he said tersely, nodding toward the lounger where she usually sat. "But once we're airborne, I want you in the bedroom."

Her mouth fell open at that. Something in his tone told her exactly why he wanted her in the bedroom. She buckled her seat belt with trembling fingers. "Ian, it's not going to make you feel better to try and control me because you feel so . . ."

She trailed off when she saw his eyes flash in barely subdued fury. "You're wrong. It's going to make me feel fantastic to turn your ass red and ride you hard. You've been on the pill long enough now. I'm going to fuck you raw and come so deep in you, I'll be spilling out of you for days."

She flinched, not because of his crudeness—under different circumstances, his raunchy talk would have aroused her. But it *wasn't* another circumstance. He'd said what he'd said to intentionally hurt her for having the temerity to see him at his weakest.

"You wanted to gape into my private world, fine. Just remember that you might not like what you see," he said quietly.

"Nothing I saw today made me think less of you," she declared hotly. "If anything, it made me understand you about a hundred times better . . . it made me love you about a thousand times more."

His expression flattened. The small remaining vestiges of color drained from his face. Her heart throbbed in her ears in the strained silence that followed. Why didn't he speak? She barely noticed when the plane left the ground. She couldn't believe she'd just blurted out the truth she'd been trying to hide from him.

The silence stretched for an eternity, seemingly made worse by the pressure on her ears as they gained altitude.

"You are such a child," he finally said, tight-lipped. "I told you from the very beginning this was purely a sexual relationship."

"Yes, but I thought . . . over the past few weeks, it seemed as if things had been changing," she said weakly. Her heart plummeted when he shook his head slowly, his stare never leaving her face. He unbuckled his seat belt. "I want to possess you, Francesca. Dominate you. See that stubborn streak in you submit to pleasure . . . to me. That's what I offered you. You insisted upon interfering in my world, so now you can stop deluding yourself with a girl's fantasies. That's *all* I can offer you," he said, pointing in the direction of the bedroom. "Now go in there, take off all of your clothes, and wait for me."

For several seconds, she just stared at him, still reeling from the wound his words had inflicted. She was about to refuse when she thought of the stark, concentrated pain on his face when his mother had begun to randomly attack him. His wounds were so much deeper than hers. Perhaps it would help him, to feel in control after experiencing so much helplessness and pain? Didn't people act out their anguish all the time during sex, using the intense physical act to ground themselves in the midst of chaotic emotion?

Yes. She could be there for Ian in that way. She understood that his anger stemmed from his pain at being so exposed . . . so vulnerable.

She unbuckled her seat belt slowly.

"All right. But I'm only doing it because I really have fallen in love with you. And I'm not a naïve little girl. I think you love me in return and are just too proud and stubborn—and hurt about what happened with your mother today—to have recognized it."

A spasm of pain flickered across his rugged features ever so fleetingly, and was gone. He said nothing as she stood and headed to the bedroom.

# Sixteen

Ian entered the bedroom ten minutes later. His body immediately tightened with lust when he saw her sitting nude at the corner of the bed. She'd piled her hair onto her head and fastened the rich glory of it somehow. Her pink nipples were mouthwateringly erect, and not, he suspected, from arousal, but from chill. He'd known there was no robe in the bathroom. It'd been wrong of him to make her wait while she was exposed. Nevertheless, something about her pale, naked body struck him as potently vulnerable and almost painfully arousing.

"Stand up," he said briskly, refusing to soften at the exquisite vision of her. Would he ever meet a more beautiful woman?

Would he ever be *affected* by another female the way he had been by Francesca? A volcanic brew of emotion had begun boiling in him when she'd blurted out those incendiary words.

*"It made me love you about a thousand times more."*

It'd been too much for him. He'd already been slain by the news James had given him just after the attendants had carried away his raving mother, that Francesca was in the morning room . . .

. . . that Francesca had witnessed everything that had happened.

He experienced an untenable need to punish her for seeing not only his mother when she was so vulnerable, but himself. He'd spent a good portion of his life guarding Helen from prying, horrified gazes. Somehow, knowing Francesca had witnessed the full extent of his mother's madness felt exponentially more painful than a stranger's observance of it.

He went over to the bureau and unlocked a cabinet. A jolt of excitement went though him when he saw her eyes widen as she stared at what he carried a moment later. "Yes. I keep only a few items here on the plane, and not the ones you're used to. We'll start with your punishment and then move onto other ways to make you squirm."

Her cheeks turned pink at that, but he couldn't tell if her reaction was from arousal or anger at his words. But he *did* want to see her squirm, he thought as he picked up the black elastic flesh plumper. He wanted to see Francesca squirming in regret and undiluted lust; he wanted her to beg him through those pink lips that haunted his dreams . . .

. . . he wanted to hear her say she loved him again.

The thought was banished almost as quickly as he had it. He maneuvered a padded chest that sat at the end of the bed toward the center of the room.

"Step into this," he told her a few seconds later, approaching her, holding the elastic restraining strap. Standing this close, he could the smell clean, fruity fragrance of her shampoo. "Hold on to my shoulders to steady yourself."

"What is it?" He tried to ignore how soft but sure her grip felt through his dress shirt.

"It's a band that will bind your legs while I punish you, restricting you. It might be a little uncomfortable, but it will give me great pleasure."

"I don't see how," she said, her face grimacing as he stretched the black, five-inch-wide, circular elastic band, pulling it up until it rested just below her buttocks, binding her thighs tight and plumping her ass over the edge, displaying firm flesh for his hand and paddle. He reached out and molded a buttock in his palm. His cock jerked.

"Now do you see?" he asked her pointedly, reluctantly letting go of her plumped ass. The elastic binder achieved the equivalent of what a bustier did for breasts, fully showcasing her ass, even as it bound her.

"Ian!" she exclaimed in surprise when he suddenly lifted her into the air, carrying her toward the padded bench.

"I have to carry you, with your legs bound," he said, lowering her knees onto the cushion. "Stay on your knees for a moment. Don't move." When he returned, he carried a pair of handcuffs. Unlike the soft leather ones he typically used with her, given her sensitive skin, these were metal. "Wrists at your lower back," he said. He frowned after he'd fastened her hands at her back. "I don't want you struggling against those cuffs, Francesca. You might bruise yourself."

"O . . . Okay," he heard her say. He met her stare, looking into dark, velvety orbs. A wild surge of something went through him—lust, raw need, anger—when he recognized what shone in her eyes.

"Why do you look at me with so much trust?" he bit out.

"Because I do trust you."

"You're a fool." He touched her elbow, guiding her. "Stay on your knees. Bend over. Expose your ass. Rest your breasts against your knees. Press your forehead to the cushion and keep it there throughout your punishment. Do *not* look at me, or I will punish you harder." She truly was a nymph; her eyes possessed some kind of magic over him. If he looked into them enough, he'd soon start to believe in what he saw there shining like a steady, unwavering beacon.

He went and got the paddle. He knew why her eyes had gone wide upon seeing it a moment ago. It was made of varnished wood, long and narrow—only three inches wide. It was a more serious tool for corporal punishment than the black leather paddle he preferred for her delicate skin.

But he was determined to make her pay for her impulsive decision to follow him to London. He was determined to make her pay for igniting this storm of feeling inside him.

He barely restrained a groan as he approached and took in the vision of her. The elastic binder displayed her shapely ass to cock jerking effect. He caressed one cheek, then the other, lifting the buttocks fully out of the restraint so that he might touch and punish every precious bit of the firm, fulsome flesh.

She started when he landed the paddle on the sweet lower curve of her ass, but he sensed that she held back her cry. Her restraint pleased him.

Just as everything about her did . . .

. . . *everything but her impulsiveness; everything but her foolishness and innocence in believing she loves me.*

*Everything about her . . .* especially *her impulsiveness, and an innocent wisdom that should be cherished, not scorned.*

He paddled her three times in quick succession, obliterating the confusing thoughts from his brain. His cock lurched in the increasingly confining material of his pants. Yes, this is what he needed. Lust would guide him through the bewildering brew of emotion he experienced.

Lust always did.

She couldn't suppress her cry this time, and he paused, soothing the satiny heating ass cheeks with his fingertips.

"I can't believe you came to London," he said, his voice vibrating with anger.

"I'd have gone farther to find you."

He paused, his expression stiffening when he heard the quiver in her voice.

"Are you crying?" he asked sharply, studying the back of her head.

"No."

"Are you in undue pain?"

"No."

He tightened his hold on the paddle and swatted her ass twice. "This is the first time I've punished you without the clitoral stimulant. Perhaps the discomfort is trumping the pleasure," he said, swinging the paddle back and landing it, snarling at the erotic sight of the blow reverberating through her firm, plump flesh. He grabbed his aching cock through his pants, wincing.

"No, it's not that," he heard her say in a muffled voice. She jumped slightly in her kneeling position when he paddled her again.

Curious as to what she meant, he pushed his fingers into the tight crevice of her thighs just above the binding restraint. Warm wetness coated his forefinger. Without making a remark, he withdrew his hand and whacked her ass several more times.

He would *never* truly control her, because she slayed him every time he tried.

Her ass was red and hot to the touch by the time he'd finished with her. She panted softly, and her cheeks were stained pink when he lifted her from the chest and placed her on her feet. He knelt before her, peeling the black elastic binder off her thighs and then down over her feet.

He unfastened the cuffs. She made a sound of surprise when he looped the elastic binder around her neck and began to work the wide strap down over her breasts. It wasn't easy, but by the time he'd finished, her beautiful flushed breasts were plumped and displayed just as erotically over the top of the thick binder as her ass had been. He grunted in approval and cuffed her wrists again at her back.

"What are you going to do?" she asked him uncertainly when he picked up a black leather flogger. It was a supple one, meant more to enliven and sting the flesh than whip and cause pain. He understood the flicker of fear in her tone. He'd never used a flogger on her before.

"Your punishment isn't finished yet. This is a flogger." He held it up for her to examine the thin, foot-long, supple straps attached to a leather-bound handle. "Don't look so fearful . . . it looks more ominous than it is. It's safe enough, in my hand. It will cause a nice sting and awaken your nerves."

Her eyes went huge when he lifted it, but she didn't protest when he brought the leather straps down on the side of a pale breast. "There. Is that too much?" he asked gruffly, pausing to caress and gently squeeze the firm globe. When she didn't answer, he looked into her face. Her expression was a little helpless, but her eyes glowed with arousal. She shook her head, apparently speechless.

He hid his grim smile and brought down the flogger on her other breast, then back to the other, watching in fascination as the pale globes deepened in color to a pale pink and the nipples grew tight and hard, making his mouth water.

"Do they sting?" he asked her a moment later after he set down the flogger and massaged her breasts in his hands.

"Yes," she whispered.

"Good. You deserve it," he murmured. He pinched gently at both of her nipples and she shuddered in pleasure. "If I weren't so careful of you, I'd be giving you much worse right now for what you dared."

"For falling in love with you?"

He paused in his lewd squeezing of her breasts and met her stare. She was panting heavier now, causing her flesh to rise and fall subtly in his molding palms.

"No. For nosing into my business and prying into my life."

*For seeing my mother at her most vulnerable . . . for seeing my pain.*

"I told you I was sorry, Ian," she said through flushed pink lips.

"I don't think you are," he said, suddenly furious again. He leaned over and seized her lush mouth in a ravaging kiss. All he could think about was burying his cock in her tight, wet pussy and losing himself to the forgetfulness of pure, slamming pleasure. Her breath was warm and sweet as she panted against his lips a moment later.

"You aren't going to change my mind," she whispered.

He closed his eyes as if to prevent the rush of feeling that went through him. His desperation mounted.

"We'll see," he said, turning her so that he could unfasten her cuffs, his gaze lingering on her still-red ass. He'd paddled her harder than he ever had before, he realized with a stab of regret, but she hadn't complained, even when he'd given her the chance. And the abundant moisture he'd felt between her thighs had told him loud and clear her arousal was greater than her discomfort.

"Turn around and bend over at the end of the bed. Put your hands on the footboard to brace yourself."

She followed his instructions without hesitation, leaning over the bed, bent over while standing. She didn't look around when he approached her from behind, although he sensed her focused curiosity and anxiety.

*Sweet, trusting Francesca.*

"Don't be afraid," he murmured. "This time I will see you submit to pleasure, not pain."

He turned on the Rabbit vibrator to a low setting, peeled back her buttocks, exposing the entrance to her pussy. His cock jumped, throbbing furiously when he saw how slick the tiny hole was, how glistening her sex lips and entire perineum were from her arousal.

He pushed the vibrator into her vagina all the way. She gasped, and then jumped when he turned on the rabbit ears and they wiggled energetically over her clitoris.

"Oh!"

"Nice?" he asked as he drew the vibrator out of her slit and pushed it back in. Her pussy clung around the silicone like a little sucking mouth. God, he couldn't wait to get into her . . .

. . . but he would wait. He'd see Francesca submit first . . . beg him. Why he needed that like he did his next breath of air remained a puzzle to him, but he couldn't dampen the potent desire.

He manipulated her with the vibrator, stroking her pussy, letting the rabbit ears do their work on her clit, listening all the while to the sound of her gasps and whimpers and cries . . . gauging. When her breathing became ragged, he turned off the clitoral vibrators and just pleasured her pussy lips and vagina with the sex toy.

"Oh, please," she moaned after a moment. He knew she'd been about to climax before, and that while the vibrator in her pussy was pleasurable, she wanted the rabbit ears on her clit.

"Your clit is too sensitive. You'll make things end too quickly."

"Please, Ian," she repeated, sounding mindless as she firmed her hold on the footboard and began to pump her hips, riding the vibrator.

He smacked her bottom hard enough to sting. She paused in the frantic grinding of her hips.

"Who is in charge here?" he asked quietly.

"You," she whispered after a pregnant pause.

"Then hold your ass still," he ordered, before he began to slide the vibrator in and out of her again, letting the rotating beads and ribbed shaft do their work. Her moan a moment later sounded harsh and desperate. He relented and turned the motor to a higher vibration.

"*Ohhhh,*" she mewled. "Oh, Ian . . . let me move."

"Stay still," he ordered, plunging the vibrator deep into her until he felt her heat and moisture against the ridge of his forefinger where he held the handle. His vision narrowed to the intensely erotic image of the silicone shaft sliding in and out of her tight slit. Her moans and aroused, frustrated whimpers filled his ears. He tormented her, keeping her right on the edge, relishing in his power.

"Please . . . let me come," she begged, her plea bursting out of her throat. He paused in his thrusting motion when he heard the strain in her breaking voice. He yearned to deny her. He longed to give her everything she ever asked for . . . and more.

The conflict warring inside him was too much. He removed the vibrator and tossed it onto the bed.

"Stand," he said, arousal making him sound harsher than he intended. The color in her cheeks had deepened when he spun her toward him. A sheen of perspiration shone on her brow and upper lip. She was beyond beautiful. He burrowed the ridge of his forefinger into the drenched crevice between her labia. She gasped, but he kept his hand motionless.

"If you want to come, show me," he demanded.

She looked up at him, her eyes glazed with intense arousal, but he saw her confusion.

"You may come against my hand, but you have to show me you want it. I'm not moving."

She bit at a trembling lower lip, and he almost gave in. Almost.

"Go on," he prompted.

She shut her eyes, as if to protect herself from his gaze, and began to thrust her hips against his finger. A moan fell past her lips. He watched, enthralled, keeping his hand, . finger, and arm firm, but not stroking her, making her work for it.

"That's right. Show me that you have no shame. Show me that you can submit to desire," he rasped. She bobbed her hips more stringently, hopping up and down against his hand . . . so desperate for her pleasure. When a small, frustrated cry popped from her throat, he almost relented.

Almost.

"Open your eyes, Francesca. Look at me," he demanded, his voice breaking through her wild quest for relief.

She opened her eyelids sluggishly as she continued to ride his stationary hand. He saw her desperation, her utter helplessness, her fear that her need was greater than even her pride.

"Don't be afraid," he murmured. "You're more beautiful to me right now than you've ever been. Now come against my hand."

He flexed his biceps, applying pressure, giving her the relief she so desperately needed and deserved. He shut his eyes briefly at the delicious sensation of her warm juices anointing his fingers as she climaxed.

A moment later, he spun her and managed to get out a couple words from his lust-dazed brain, telling her to bend over and brace herself against the footboard again. When he finally drove his cock into her clinging liquid heat, his eyes sprang wide. It was like entering a woman his first time— no, immeasurably better—a whole new arena of life, a fresh, intimidatingly powerful experience.

He lost himself in her, everything seeming to go black for a period of time as pleasure and need swamped him, pummeling at his consciousness. He bucked against her like a wild man, his lungs burning, cock aching, muscles clenching . . . soul tearing.

"Francesca," he grated out, sounding angry, even though he wasn't anymore. He opened his hands around her delicate ribcage and pulled her up so that she stood before him, her upper body slightly bent forward. He continued to fuck her, feeling her heart beating rapidly in his hands, the shudders quaking her flesh as she climaxed, the muscular walls of her pussy clamping and convulsing around his pillaging cock.

Without thinking, he pushed her upper body down again, his hands falling to her hips, fucking her with short, hard thrusts, his teeth bared in a rictus of blinding pleasure. He jerked her against him, his muscles clenching so tight he lifted her feet off the floor.

Orgasm ripped through him with the power of a lightning strike. He groaned in agonized bliss as he began to come at Francesca's farthest reaches. A sharp, primal need overwhelmed him, even in the midst of his crisis—a need to mark her, to utterly posses her . . . make her his.

He jerked his steaming, glistening cock out of the heaven of her pussy and pumped, ejaculating on her ass and her back, until his essence pooled on her skin.

He just stood there for a full minute after the cyclonic storm had passed, his cock gripped tight in his hand, gasping for air, and staring down at the powerful image of her nude body dripping with his semen. He thought of how ruthlessly he'd punished her, of how he'd forced her to swallow her pride and bring herself off on his hand, of how he'd fucked her like a madman.

Regret flickered into his awareness. Then it roared.

He helped her to stand, then went to the bathroom to retrieve a towel. He gently dried her, then unbuttoned his dress shirt and draped it over her nakedness. It'd been wrong of him to expose her so greatly.

He met her solemn stare with supreme effort as he buttoned up the shirt, covering soft skin that he wanted to linger over . . . to cherish. He opened his mouth to speak, but what could he say? His actions had been harsh and selfish and probably unforgivable.

He'd intended to prove her foolishness for believing she'd fallen in love, but now that he'd likely succeeded, he felt nothing but a bone-deep regret.

Unable to stand her dark-eyed gaze a moment longer, he turned and walked out of the bedroom.

Ten days later, Davie stood in her closet wearing a tuxedo and whisking hangers along the rack while Francesca looked on listlessly from where she sat at the edge of her bed.

"What about this?" Davie asked, coming out of the closet holding a dress.

She blinked when she saw that he held the boho dress she'd so foolishly worn to her celebratory dinner at Fusion several months ago—the night she'd first met Ian. It seemed impossible that her life had changed so drastically in such a short span of time. It seemed unlikely that she'd fallen so profoundly in love, and then lost at it with Francesca-like expertise. But then when she considered everything, it made depressing sense.

Davie noticed her less-than-enthusiastic appraisal of the dress. He held it up and examined it. "What? It's cute."

"I'm not going, Davie," she said, her voice sounding hoarse from not being used.

"Yes, you are," Davie said, giving her an uncharacteristic fierce glance. "You're not going to hole up in your room for your entire Thanksgiving vacation."

"Why not? It's my vacation," she said dully, picking up a decorative pillow and picking at the tassel. "I haven't bailed on anything I was supposed to do. Don't I get a chance to veg out in my room, if I want to?"

"So . . . the truth finally comes out. Francesca Arno is the very type of girl that she used to despise, who sulked and refused to eat after breaking up with a guy."

"Ian and I didn't break up. We just haven't spoken in a week a half." *And we're likely never going to speak again.* She thought of the way he'd looked before he'd left her standing in the plane's bedroom suite—his regret, his bewilderment . . . his hopelessness. She believed he had something to offer her beyond sex, but *he* didn't. And wasn't it a two-way venture? What did it matter if she had all the faith in the world, yet he doubted? "Besides," she continued, "breaking up implies that we were together to begin with, and we weren't. Not in any traditional sense of the word."

"Have you even tried to contact him?" Davie said, hanging the dress in her bathroom.

"No. I can still feel his fury. It's like it's emanating all the way from the Chicago River to our house."

"It's not fury," she thought she heard her friend mutter under his breath.

"*What?*" she asked, puzzled.

"It's your *imagination,* 'Ces. Why don't you call him?"

"No. It wouldn't matter."

Davie sighed. "Both of you are so stubborn. You can't engage in a standoff forever."

"I'm not in a standoff."

"Oh, I see. You've given up entirely, then."

For the first time in days, anger flickered into her hope-lessness at Davie's words. She shot him an irritated glance and he grinned, holding out his hand.

"Come on. Justin and Caden are waiting. Plus, we have a surprise for you."

She exhaled in frustration, but stood. "I don't want to be cheered up. And even if I did want to be, why would you guys drag me to a stupid singles meet-up—a black-tie event, no less—in order to do it? You knew I didn't have anything good to wear. I hate these events. You used to, as well."

"I've changed my mind. This is for a good cause," he said as she passed him on the way to the bathroom.

"What, saving my ravaged heart?"

"I'd settle for getting you out of this house," Davie replied, unaffected by her dripping sarcasm.


The singles black-tie event was at a new, trendy club on North Wabash, downtown. Caden and Justin were in rare form in the car on the way to it, Friday-night buoyant and brashly handsome in their newly purchased tuxes. Francesca, on the other hand, was already ready to leave, and they hadn't even gotten there yet. Horrible, wonderful memories had started to barrage her when she put on the boho dress and recalled in vivid detail the last time she'd worn it.

*The woman wears the clothes, Francesca. Not the other way around. That's the first lesson I'll teach you.*

She shivered at the memory of Ian's rough, quiet voice. How she missed him. It was like an open wound deep inside her, a place she couldn't reach in order to soothe.

Davie was having trouble finding parking near their destination, and they'd been circling around for a while now. She looked out of the car window as they crossed the Chicago River and saw the Noble Enterprises building towering a few blocks away.

Was she really the same naïve young woman who had attended her celebratory cocktail party there, she who'd been so brittle, so uncertain . . . so defiant lest anyone would notice? And was it really she who had first entered Ian's penthouse, her enthrallment associated more with the enigmatic man who stood beside her than the sight of his magnificent penthouse and display of art . . . the stunning view.

*"They're alive, the buildings . . . some more than others. I mean they seem like it. I've always thought so. Each one of them has a soul. At night, especially . . . I can feel it."*

*"I know you can. That's why I chose your painting."*

*"Not because of perfectly straight lines and precise reproductions?"*

*"No. Not because of that."*

Her eyes burned at the potent memory. He had seen her so well, even then, seen things in her she hadn't. He'd cherished those things, cultivated her strengths until . . .

. . . no. The answer was no. She was no longer that same young woman.

Davie parked in a paid garage on Wacker Drive, south of the river, farther east than their desired destination. Francesca shivered uncontrollably when the river wind sliced straight through her thin wool coat as they crossed the bridge. Davie noticed and took her under his arm. Justin got into the spirit and put his arm around her from the other side, hunkering around her, their bodies helping to protect. Caden, too, had to join in on the gallantry, much to her amusement, hooking arms with Justin to help block her from the brutal, east lake wind. They'd bundled her so close between them that as they guided her down the sidewalk once they cleared the river and bridge, Francesca stumbled.

"You guys, I can't see!"

"But you're warm, aren't you?" Justin asked jovially.

"Yes, but . . ."

Suddenly Justin and Caden were pushing her into a revolving glass door. Her eyes sprang wide when she realized where they'd maneuvered her. She balked, but Justin was pushing from behind her and she had no choice but to go forward into the Noble Enterprises lobby.

She stared around, aghast to find herself in Ian's territory so suddenly . . . so *undesirably.*

Several dozen faces looked around at her ungraceful arrival. She saw Lin's familiar, smiling face, and Lucien's and Zoe's . . . and—she gasped—Anne and James Noble beamed at her from a distance. That elegant man with the salt-and-pepper hair that held up his champagne glass to her in a silent salute, wasn't that Monsieur Garrond, the curator of the Musée de St. Germain whom Ian had introduced her to in Paris? No. It couldn't be.

Her eyes widened in sheer disbelief when she recognized her parents standing awkwardly next to a fern, her father tight-lipped, but her mother doing her best to attempt a warm smile.

"Why is everyone looking at me?" she whispered to Justin when he stepped up next to her. A panic rose in her chest at the surreal scene before her. Justin kissed her warmly on the cheek.

"It's a surprise. *Look*, Francesca. It's all for you. Congratulations." She gaped at where he pointed, the once-empty swath of wall that dominated the lobby. Her painting had been framed and mounted. It looked awesome . . . perfect . . .

Justin gently tilted her jaw when she couldn't stop gawping at the centerpiece, urging her to see what else was in the room. The entire lobby had been filled with her paintings, each displayed on easels, all of them professionally mounted and framed. People were strolling around in black-tie attire, sipping champagne, and seemingly admiring her work. A small string quartet played Bach's Brandenburg Concerto No. 2.

She glanced from Justin to Davie, slain. Davie gave her a reassuring smile. "Ian planned it," he said quietly. "Some of the most affluent collectors, renowned art experts and critics, museum curators and gallery owners from around the globe are here tonight. This party is in your honor, Francesca . . . a chance for the world to see just how talented you really are."

She cringed inwardly. *Oh my God. All those people looking at my work? But no one appeared to be laughing or snidely incredulous, at least*, she thought as she checked several faces anxiously.

"I don't understand. Did Ian plan this before London?" she asked.

"No. He contacted me a day or two after your return from London and asked me to help him arrange things. I had all of the paintings mounted and framed. We've even managed to acquire four more of your paintings to add to the collection. Ian can't wait to show them to you."

A sudden prescience struck her, and she looked into the crowd.

Ian stood next to his grandparents, looking somber, regal, and devastatingly gorgeous in a classic black tux with bow tie. His gaze was alight as it pinned her . . . soulful. Only Francesca, who had grown to know him so well, saw the shadow of anxiety ghosting features that would have looked cold and impassive to other eyes.

She thought she'd had a heart attack. She clasped her chest.

"Why's he done this?" she asked Davie under her breath.

"I think it's his way of saying he's sorry. Some men send flowers, Ian—"

"Sends the world," Francesca whispered through numb lips. Ian started toward her, and she followed in kind in his direction, moving like a sleepwalker toward the man she couldn't take her eyes off of, and whom she craved more than anything she had in her life.

"Hello," he said quietly when they met.

"Hi. This is quite a surprise," Francesca managed, her heart seemingly crowding out everything else in her rib cage, squeezing her lungs. She realized distantly that probably dozens of stares were on them, but she only could focus on the warmth—the wary hope—in Ian's.

"Did I have it hung to your satisfaction?" he asked, and she knew he meant the painting.

"Yes. It's perfect."

Her heart did its usual jump when he smiled. He held up his hands. Recognizing the familiar gesture, she unbuttoned her coat and turned. When he slid her coat off her arms she spun toward him, chin high, spine straight—yes, even in the boho dress. His gaze ran over her fleetingly and she saw he recognized the dress. His smile reached all the way to his eyes. He took two glasses of champagne from a waiter who was passing and murmured a request before handing the man her coat.

A moment later, he handed her a flute and stepped closer. Francesca had the impression that the other party participants tried to focus their attention back on their own conversations, giving them a little privacy. Ian touched his flute to hers.

"To you, Francesca. May you have everything you deserve in life, because there is no one so deserving."

"Thank you," she murmured, taking a reluctant sip, unsure as to how she should be feeling in these bewildering circumstances.

"Will you spend this evening with me, both now," he glanced around the crowded lobby, "and later? There are some things I'd like to tell you in private. I hope you'll listen."

Her throat tightened when she guessed at what some of those 'things' might be. She suddenly doubted she could endure the next few hours, wondering what he'd say. A tiny part of her said she should refuse, the part that wanted to keep her heart safe. But then she looked into his eyes, and her decision was made.

"Yes. I'll listen."

He smiled, took her hand and escorted her into the crowd.

It was past midnight by the time Ian opened the door to his suite for her and she walked into the subtly lit, elegant room.

"I thought maybe I'd never be in this bedroom again," she said breathlessly, glancing around, cherishing little details of Ian's private sanctuary as she never had before. They'd been together all night, Ian never leaving her side, Francesca highly aware of him as he introduced her to movers and shakers from the art world or showed her the last four of her paintings that had been recovered, or they conversed with friends and family. All the while, she wondered what he was thinking . . . what he would say to her when they were alone in private.

She'd been courted by three renowned galleries for future collections and asked to do a showing at the Barcelona Museum of Contemporary Art. She'd looked to Ian for that, since he was the owner of her current paintings, and he'd told her point-blank it was up to her to decide. Four collectors had made bids on her paintings, although Ian had refused to sell, point-blank. To top it all off, one of the offers had been made in the company of her father, whose incredulity at the price mentioned had made her father turn pale. In general, Ian's effect on both of her parents had been quite marked. They'd been so tongue-tied and eager to please in his presence that she was quite sure Ian must have thought her a liar about all she'd told him about them. Francesca was a little annoyed by this unexpected servile bent in their character, but mostly just relieved they behaved quite pleasantly all evening.

Ian shut the door of his bedroom suite and leaned against it. She faced him.

"Thank you, Ian," she said breathlessly. "I felt like the belle of the ball tonight."

"I'm just glad that you came."

"I doubt I would have if Davie and the others hadn't tricked me. I didn't think you would want to see me after London . . . after it all. You were so angry."

"I was, yes. I haven't been for a while, though."

"No?" she asked in a hushed tone.

He shook his head, never breaking her stare. His mouth tightened. "No. But I also couldn't quite figure out just what the hell I *was*. It didn't take me long to know, but then I had to find a way to tell you in a situation where you couldn't run away from me too easily. I apologize for the subterfuge tonight." His mouth twisted into a bitter expression. "I'm sorry, in general."

She started in surprise at his harsh declaration. "For which part?"

"For all of it. From the first thing I said to you that was unappreciative and callous to the last selfish thing I've done. I'm sorry, Francesca."

She swallowed thickly, unable to meet his stare for some reason. Even though she knew exchanges like this were necessary, given everything that had happened between them, it still seemed so secondary compared to what she'd seen in London.

"How is your mother?" she asked quietly.

"Stabilized," he said, still leaning against the door. He exhaled after a few seconds and took a step toward her. She couldn't look away as he removed his tuxedo jacket and laid it on the back of a chair, mesmerized by his male beauty. "There isn't much hope that she'll improve on this particular medication regime, but she won't get worse. That's something, at least."

"Yes. It is. I know you don't want my pity, Ian. I understand that. I didn't go to London to offer you sympathy."

"Then why did you?" he said, his quiet voice lending to the subdued, full moment.

"To offer you my support. I knew that whatever was in London pained you, even though I had no idea what I'd find there. I just wanted to be there for you. That's all."

He gave a small smile. "You make it seem like that's such a small throwaway thing. No . . . *I* made it seem that way. I took your act of caring and kindness and threw it in your face," he said bluntly, his jaw rigid.

"I know it made you feel exposed. I'm sorry."

"I've had to protect her for a long time," he said suddenly, following a long pause.

"I know. Anne told me," understanding he referred to his mother.

He frowned. "It was grandmother who told me I was being a selfish, stubborn ass. She wouldn't speak to me for a week when I confessed some of the things I'd said to you for showing up at the Institute. She's never done that before," he said, his brow furrowed as if he still wasn't one hundred percent sure what to make of his loving, very elegant grandmother calling him an ass.

Her heart stuttered in grateful surprise at the news of Anne's support. "I wasn't there to judge. Even if I were, there would have been nothing to put on trial but a very sick woman and a son who loves her and hopes for her, despite everything."

He jerked his chin, staring at the far wall.

"I treated you unfairly . . . wrongly. I like to punish you for sexual excitement, but I never truly want to hurt you. But that day on the plane—I did. Not completely, but *part* of me wanted to—"

"Make me hurt like *you* were hurting?"

His gaze flashed guiltily to her face. "Yes."

"I understood, Ian," she said softly. "It wasn't what happened in the plane's bedroom suite that upset me. You didn't hurt me, and you must know I took pleasure in it. It was that you walked away from me afterward."

She sensed his rising tension.

"I was ashamed. Of her. Of you seeing her. Of myself for still having that damn feeling rise up in me of not wanting others to see her. *Why should it matter now?*" he bit out.

The bitter words seemed to hang in the air between them, an expelled toxin, secret words that he'd carried deep inside his spirit since he was a child, perhaps the most crucial, powerful words he'd ever said to her . . . to anyone.

Francesca walked over to him and put her arms around his waist, resting her cheek on his white shirt. Inhaling his unique male scent, she hugged tight. She clenched her eyelids shut as emotion washed over her. She understood how difficult this was for him to say these things, a man who ritualistically guarded against vulnerability, who remained stoic and strong because he believed he had no other choice.

"I love you," she said.

He captured her chin with his fingers and lifted her face to his. He brushed his finger over her jaw. She noticed his frown as he studied her.

"What's wrong?" she whispered.

"I didn't give myself permission to fall in love with you."

She laughed softly when she absorbed his starkly spoken words. So like him, to say something like that. Love swelled in her breast, so great and so pure, it verged on pain. "You can't control everything, Ian, least of all this. Does that mean that you do? Love me?" she asked hesitantly.

"I think I might have loved you even before we met, since I first realized it was you who captured me on canvas . . . you who treated my pain with such a knowing hand. It shamed me, what you saw, but I couldn't help but want you to see more of me. You're too good for me," he declared roughly. "And I'm sure I don't deserve you. But you're mine, Francesca. And for what it's worth . . . I'm yours. For as long as you'll have me."

The words rattled and rocked her world, setting her off balance. But then his mouth settled on hers, and she found her center.

Don't miss this sneak peek of the new
erotic serial romance from Beth Kery

# When I'm With You

*Available now from Headline*

It was past midnight when Lucien opened the rear entrance
to his restaurant and immediately went on high alert, hush-
ing his movements. An intruder had breached his restaurant's
security. In the distance, he heard the sound of a low male
voice. Although Fusion was frequently bustling with the
chic, late-night dinner and nightclub crowd, it was closed on
Sundays and Mondays. There definitely shouldn't be anyone
inside. Quietly, he closed the rear door, his fist tightening
around the polo mallet he carried. He'd been planning on
replacing this cracked mallet with an intact one from his
storage closet at Fusion. He had different plans for it now.

For the most part, Lucien maintained the vaguely
amused, cynical stance of an experienced, world-weary
libertine, a man who claimed no family, no country, no
creed, and few of the worldly possessions to which he was
entitled by law, which were many. But what he *did* claim, he
fought for. Always. He just hadn't realized that the restaurant
he'd recently bought had gotten so deeply into his bones
until that very moment, when he was ready to do battle
for it.

He eased down the dim hallway, following the glow of a
light shining around a partially closed door that led to the

large bar area of the restaurant. He turned his head, his hearing pitched. A tingle went down his spine at the sound of female laughter. A man's low chuckle twined with it—rough and intimate. He heard the unmistakable sound of glassware clinking, as if in a toast.

Lucien approached the door and leaned his head into the crack.

"Why do you play games with me?" he heard a man ask.

"Play games?"

Lucien's escalated heartbeat seemed to hesitate for a moment at the woman's voice. Strange. She was from the country of his birth. The female's tone was amused, melodious and light, her French accent laced with a British tinge. Perhaps he recognized it because it was very similar to his own.

"You *are* taunting me," the man said roughly. "You have been all night. Not just me. There wasn't a man in that restaurant tonight who wasn't bewitched by you."

"I'm actually being very cautious. We are going to work together, after all," the woman replied, her tone suddenly brisker, cooler. Lucien got the definite impression she was sending up red flags.

"I want more than just to work with you. I want to help you. I want you in my house . . . my bed," the man said, ignoring the warning.

Lucien went from high alert to irritated in a second flat when he recognized the man speaking. He hadn't interrupted a burglary on his premises.

He'd walked in on a seduction.

Disgusted, he pushed open the door and strode into the dimly lit, luxurious restaurant. The couple stood next to the

her features. She must have
harms didn't work on Lucien. "
ecause you don't like me!"
atever I please. This is my place." H
t expression tighten her features, t
re when she'd been a fourteen-year-old
er that a stallion in his father's stables
dangerous for her to control.
"
e's no *but* about it," Lucien said, forcing
usual calm cadence and volume. He would *no*
nce of Elise set him off balance. She had a
g just that—of whipping the usually staid upper
ropean society into a scandalized whirlwind w
ageous stunts . . . of sending a man spinning w
nparalleled beauty and the temptation of taming
remembered all too well their last meeting two years
Renygat, his Parisian restaurant. He recalled Elise l
up at him as she unfastened his pants, her fingertips br
against a cock that teamed with hot, raw lust, her li
and puffy from his earlier angry possession of her mout
eyes shining like fire-infused sapphires, the taste
lingering on his tongue, addictive and sweet.

*You want to forget your past, Lucien? I'm going to ma
feel so good, you're going to forget everything that happened
your father. That's a promise.*

His body tightened at the memory. He'd believed
If anyone could make him forget for one glorious, nir
moment, it was Elise. It had cost him to send her away
night, but he'd done it. She was a master of manipula
She knew precisely how to slip the most formidable foe

shining mahogany bar facing one another, their hands curled around brandy crystal snifters. He noticed the woman backing away slightly from the man, as if repelled by his hovering. Distantly, he registered that she wore a midnight blue evening gown that clung to full, firm breasts and taut curves. The dress plunged in the back, revealing a profile glimpse of white, flawless skin that shone luminous in the soft lighting. The vision of Mario Vincente's hand splayed across that expanse of bare skin inexplicably ratcheted up Lucien's irritation to anger. The extremely talented chef Lucien had hired from a top-rated restaurant in Las Vegas was a bit of a diva. Mario didn't notice Lucien until he was just feet away. When he did, his brown eyes went wide.

"Lucien!" The brandy-filled glass sagged in Mario's hand. Lucien's gaze flicked rapidly to the singular bottle sitting on the counter—Dudognon Héritage cognac, an item from his private stock in his office. Lucien tossed the polo mallet he'd been carrying on the mahogany bar, the sound of it ringing in the air like a remonstrance.

"I hadn't realized I'd provided you with Fusion's security code. Or permission to access my office and private bar. Explain yourself, Mario," Lucien said, his tone crisp, but neutral now that he understood the nature of the intrusion on his property. True, he was irritated at Mario's infraction, and he would make sure his employee knew it. He just hadn't yet decided if he'd terminate the idiot. He'd never had a fond spot for Mario, but chefs as talented as him were hard to come by, after all.

"I . . . I don't know what to say," Mario said, fumbling.

Lucien noticed the woman's bare, lithesome arm dip, the liquor in her glass sloshing into the curved bowl. For the

first time, he gave the other occupant of the room a curso Mario blinked
glance. He did a double take.

"*Merde.*"

"*Lucien.*"

"What are you doing here, Elise?"

Surely he was seeing things—a face from his past . . .
beautiful face he'd most definitely rather not appear at th
juncture of his life. What the hell was Elise Martin doing i
his restaurant in Chicago, thousands of miles from thei
country of origin, leagues from the gilded cage of thei
common past? Was this some sort of cosmic joke?

"I might ask the same of you," Elise replied rapidly, dar
blue eyes flashing. Understanding made her features flatten
"Lucien . . . *you're* Lucien *Lenault*. You *own* this place?"

"*What*? You two know one another?" Mario asked.

Lucien threw Elise a repressive glance. Her lush lips
snapped closed, and she gave him a defiant glare. She'd
caught his warning for silence in regard to their association,
all right, but that didn't guarantee anything. Knowing Elise,
she hadn't decided yet whether she'd keep quiet or not. A
flicker of anxiety went through him. He had to get her out
of Fusion at all costs . . . out of his life here in Chicago.
Elise Martin would cause havoc anywhere she set a perfectly
pedicured, elegant toe. She'd compromise the foothold he'd
gained by buying a restaurant within Noble Enterprises.

She'd ruin everything he'd already gained on his mission
in regard to billionaire entrepreneur Ian Noble.

"I . . . I'm sorry. Surely one glass wouldn't hurt," Mario
was sputtering. Lucien dragged his gaze off Elise's face. "I
know it's your personal stock, but . . ."

"You're fired," Lucien interrupted succinctly.

"Lucien, yo

He whi

cond he

"How long

r her, and her a
oss her beautiful f
"It's been close to tw
e said, referring to his s
Paris. He had to hand
motion that'd flickered across
ristocrat by the time she spoke. L
ried to decode the enigma of Elise wa
bsession. Who *was* she? Uncontrollable,
resh, golden ray of sunshine that beckone
s elusiveness?

"Lucien, you can't fire Mario," Elise said softly,
mile shaping lips that could probably tempt a man
murder.

"I'm not firing him because of how I feel about you,
said levelly. The vision of Mario's hand on her white ski
flashed into his mind's eye. *Liar.* "I'm firing him because he
stole the restaurant's security code, came onto my private
property and stole from my personal stash."

Her elegant neck convulsed at his concise reply. She'd cut
her long, glorious mane of blonde hair since he'd last seen
her two years ago. She wore it short, the gleaming waves
combed behind her ears. He'd have thought the shearing of
those curls and tresses might have symbolized the taming of
Elise's infamous wild spirit, but he'd have thought wrong.
Elise's rebellion came from her eyes.

Anger stiffene
that her typical c
fire Mario, just
"I can do wh
familiar defia
one she'd w
he'd told h
strong an
"But
"The
into it
prese
doin
E

her hip pocket and make him beg like a hungry dog. And to add to that risk, after that night at Renygat, Elise knew too much.

She still did, damn it.

"I want both of you to get out of here. You're lucky I don't call the police," Lucien stated, starting to turn again. He paused when he noticed Mario move jerkily toward him from the corner of his eye. Apparently, the chef had regained some of his typical hauteur in the intervening seconds.

"Don't be a fool. You have to open Fusion tomorrow. You need me. What will you do for a chef?"

"I'll manage. I've been in this business long enough to know how to deal with employees who steal."

"Are you calling me a thief? An *employee*?" Clearly, Mario couldn't decide which label was more insulting: criminal or paid worker. His color faded beneath his olive-toned skin.

Lucien paused, gauging, taking in the glassiness of Mario's eyes. Apparently, Mario had imbibed his fair share before he'd brought Elise here to ply her with Lucien's brandy. Did he plan to make love to her on the leather couch in his private office, as well? The thought sent his anger to a low boil. He supposed Mario might be attractive enough to some women, but he was in his forties, and far too old to be seducing Elise. No matter that Elise had probably taken four times as many lovers as him, Mario was still a rutting cradle robber, as far as Lucien was concerned.

"I hadn't yet called you a thief, but that's precisely what you are. Among other things."

"You *cannot* fire him!" Elise blurted out. Lucien glanced sideways at her, startled by the panic in her voice, but unwilling to look away from Mario when the other man's hands were fisted into balls. Why was she so desperate over Mario? He'd definitely gotten the impression she was cool about the chef's seduction.

"Stay out of this. It's none of your business," Lucien muttered.

"It *is* my business. If you fire Mario, what am I supposed to do?" Elise exclaimed, setting her snifter on the bar.

"What are you talking about?" Lucien bit out, but Mario wasn't interested in their tense, private exchange.

"You've always been a smug French bastard, thinking you could lord it over me," Mario bellowed. He grabbed Elise's upper arm. "Well you can't fire me because I quit! Come, Elise. Let's get out of this devil's hole."

Elise kept her feet planted and jerked when Mario yanked on her. "Nobody tells me what to do," she exclaimed. Lucien clamped his fist around the other man's forearm and squeezed. Tight. Mario yelped in pain.

"Let go of her," Lucien warned. He saw the flash of aggression in Mario's expression and resisted rolling his eyes in exasperation. He really wasn't up for this tonight. "Are you *sure* you want to start something?" he asked mildly. "Do you think it's wise?"

"*Don't*, Mario," Elise warned.

For a brief second, Mario hesitated, but then the alcohol he'd consumed must have roared in his veins, giving him courage. He released Elise and lunged, fist cocked. Lucien blocked Mario's punch and sunk his fist beneath his ribs.

One, two, done. Almost too easy, Lucien thought grimly as air whooshed out of Mario's lungs followed by a guttural groan of pain.

Lucien shot a "this is all your fault" glare at Elise and

then put his hands on the shoulders of the now hunched over Mario. He grabbed his jacket off the bar stool and urged the gasping, moaning man toward the front door of the restaurant with a hold on his shirt collar.

When he returned a few minutes later alone, Elise still stood next to the bar, her chin up, her carriage every bit as proud and erect as her aristocratic ancestors. Her gaze on him was wary. He walked toward her, unsure if he wanted to shove her into the back of a cab like he just had Mario, shake her for her foolishness, or turn her over his knee and punish her ass for the infraction of peering into his private world.

*By Beth Kery*

Wicked Burn
Daring Time
Sweet Restraint
Paradise Rules
Release
Explosive
Because You Are Mine

*One Night of Passion series*
*Addicted To You
*Bound To You (e-novella)
Captured By You (e-novella)
Exposed To You

*previously published under the pseudonym Bethany Kane

Beth Kery is the *New York Times* ebook bestselling author of *Because You Are Mine*. Beth lives in Chicago where she juggles the demands of her career, her love of the city and the arts and a busy family life. Her writing today reflects her passion for all of the above. She is a bestselling author of over thirty books and novellas, and has also written under the pen name Bethany Kane. You can read more about Beth, her books and upcoming projects at www.bethkery.com, discover her on Facebook at www.facebook.com/beth.kery, or follow her on Twitter @ bethkery

Praise for Beth Kery:

'One of the sexiest, most erotic love stories that I have read in a long time' *Affair de Coeur*

'A sleek, sexy thrill ride' Jo Davis

'One of the best erotic romances I've ever read' *All About Romance*

'Nearly singed my eyebrows' *Dear Author*

'Fabulous, sizzling hot . . . You'll be addicted' Julie James, *USA Today* bestselling author

'Action and sex and plenty of spins and twists' *Genre Go Round Round*

'Intoxicating and exhilarating' *Fresh Fiction*

'The heat between Kery's main characters is molten' *RT Book Reviews* shining mahogany bar facing one another, their hands curled around brandy crystal snifters. He noticed the woman backing away slightly from the man, as if repelled by his hovering. Distantly, he registered that she wore a midnight blue evening gown that clung to full, firm breasts and taut curves. The dress plunged in the back, revealing a profile glimpse of white, flawless skin that shone luminous in the soft lighting. The vision of Mario Vincente's hand splayed across that expanse of bare skin inexplicably ratcheted up Lucien's irritation to anger. The extremely talented chef Lucien had hired from a top-rated restaurant in Las Vegas was a bit of a diva. Mario didn't notice Lucien until he was just feet away. When he did, his brown eyes went wide.

"Lucien!" The brandy-filled glass sagged in Mario's hand. Lucien's gaze flicked rapidly to the singular bottle sitting on the counter—Dudognon Héritage cognac, an item from his private stock in his office. Lucien tossed the polo mallet he'd been carrying on the mahogany bar, the sound of it ringing in the air like a remonstrance.

"I hadn't realized I'd provided you with Fusion's security code. Or permission to access my office and private bar. Explain yourself, Mario," Lucien said, his tone crisp, but neutral now that he understood the nature of the intrusion on his property. True, he was irritated at Mario's infraction, and he would make sure his employee knew it. He just hadn't yet decided if he'd terminate the idiot. He'd never had a fond spot for Mario, but chefs as talented as him were hard to come by, after all.

"I . . . I don't know what to say," Mario said, fumbling.

Lucien noticed the woman's bare, lithesome arm dip, the liquor in her glass sloshing into the curved bowl. For the first time, he gave the other occupant of the room a cursory glance. He did a double take.

"*Merde.*"

"*Lucien.*"

"What are you doing here, Elise?"

Surely he was seeing things—a face from his past . . . a beautiful face he'd most definitely rather not appear at this juncture of his life. What the hell was Elise Martin doing in his restaurant in Chicago, thousands of miles from their country of origin, leagues from the gilded cage of their common past? Was this some sort of cosmic joke?

"I might ask the same of you," Elise replied rapidly, dark blue eyes flashing. Understanding made her features flatten. "Lucien . . . *you're* Lucien *Lenault.* You *own* this place?"

"*What?* You two know one another?" Mario asked.

Lucien threw Elise a repressive glance. Her lush lips snapped closed, and she gave him a defiant glare. She'd caught his warning for silence in regard to their association, all right, but that didn't guarantee anything. Knowing Elise, she hadn't decided yet whether she'd keep quiet or not. A flicker of anxiety went through him. He had to get her out of Fusion at all costs . . . out of his life here in Chicago. Elise Martin would cause havoc anywhere she set a perfectly pedicured, elegant toe. She'd compromise the foothold he'd gained by buying a restaurant within Noble Enterprises.

She'd ruin everything he'd already gained on his mission in regard to billionaire entrepreneur Ian Noble.

"I . . . I'm sorry. Surely one glass wouldn't hurt," Mario was sputtering. Lucien dragged his gaze off Elise's face. "I know it's your personal stock, but . . ."

"You're fired," Lucien interrupted succinctly.

Mario blinked. Lucien started to walk away.

"Lucien, you can't do that!"

He whipped around at the sound of Elise's voice. For a second he just stared at her.

"How long has it been?" he asked her, his quiet question for her, and her alone. He saw a strange mixture of emotions cross her beautiful face—discomfort, confusion . . . anger.

"It's been close to two years since that night at Renygat," she said, referring to his successful nightclub and restaurant in Paris. He had to hand it to her. Despite the riot of emotion that'd flickered across her face, she was all cool aristocrat by the time she spoke. Damn her. Any man who tried to decode the enigma of Elise was doomed to a lifetime obsession. Who *was* she? Uncontrollable, bad-girl heiress or fresh, golden ray of sunshine that beckoned . . . taunted in its elusiveness?

"Lucien, you can't fire Mario," Elise said softly, a witch's smile shaping lips that could probably tempt a man to do murder.

"I'm not firing him because of how I feel about you," he said levelly. The vision of Mario's hand on her white skin flashed into his mind's eye. *Liar.* "I'm firing him because he stole the restaurant's security code, came onto my private property and stole from my personal stash."

Her elegant neck convulsed at his concise reply. She'd cut her long, glorious mane of blonde hair since he'd last seen her two years ago. She wore it short, the gleaming waves combed behind her ears. He'd have thought the shearing of those curls and tresses might have symbolized the taming of Elise's infamous wild spirit, but he'd have thought wrong. Elise's rebellion came from her eyes.

Anger stiffened her features. She must have forgotten that her typical charms didn't work on Lucien. "You can't fire Mario, just because you don't like me!"

"I can do whatever I please. This is my place." He saw the familiar defiant expression tighten her features, the same one she'd wore when she'd been a fourteen-year-old girl and he'd told her that a stallion in his father's stables was too strong and dangerous for her to control.

"But—"

"There's no *but* about it," Lucien said, forcing his tone into its usual calm cadence and volume. He would *not* let the presence of Elise set him off balance. She had a habit of doing just that—of whipping the usually staid upper crust of European society into a scandalized whirlwind with her outrageous stunts . . . of sending a man spinning with her unparalleled beauty and the temptation of taming her. He remembered all too well their last meeting two years ago at Renygat, his Parisian restaurant. He recalled Elise looking up at him as she unfastened his pants, her fingertips brushing against a cock that teamed with hot, raw lust, her lips red and puffy from his earlier angry possession of her mouth, her eyes shining like fire-infused sapphires, the taste of her lingering on his tongue, addictive and sweet.

*You want to forget your past, Lucien? I'm going to make you feel so good, you're going to forget everything that happened with your father. That's a promise.*

His body tightened at the memory. He'd believed her. If anyone could make him forget for one glorious, nirvanic moment, it was Elise. It had cost him to send her away that night, but he'd done it. She was a master of manipulation. She knew precisely how to slip the most formidable foe into